THE PRICE of SIN

Creator: Thwaites, Suzy, Ballina, Author.

Title: Price of Sin

ISBN: 978-0-6457241-0-3

Subjects: Novel. Sex industry, child institutions, bikie gangs, corrupt police.

Cover design: Luke Harris

Text design: Kevin McDonald

THE PRICE *of* SIN

A JOURNEY OF TRUTH

Police corruption, Biker thugs,
accusations of murder, sexual abuse.

SUZY THWAITES

From the author

I owe thanks to Nat for suggesting I write this book and to author extraordinaire Susanna Freymark for guiding me, giving me confidence and showing me in real time how to move forward with the planning of this book. Another person I give my most sincere thanks to is Kevin McDonald. His patience in deciphering all my ramblings has been a work of literary art. Kevin, you are a treasure and I am forever grateful to you. Thank you. Most of all I give thanks and love to Kaye who tolerated the thousands of hours I spent writing, cursing, crying and questioning my ability to put it all down on paper as I wrote some of these chapters.

Thank you, I love you.

PS: Something I have to mention. I swear a lot throughout the manuscript but at those times I was dealing with different situations with people who only understand verbal confrontations. I had to present a tough, no-nonsense exterior as a woman owner-operator or I would have been a victim. In my everyday life away from the sex industry I do not swear and NEVER swear in public ever. I would hate readers to think I have a 24/7 foul mouth because this is not who I am. I am a very respectful person, cuss only when upset or angry and sometimes at home behind closed doors.

DEDICATED IN
Loving Memory of My Mother.

RUBY HANNAFORD

Without whose love and fierce protection of all her children
We would not have survived.

LOVE IS ETERNAL

We Love and Miss you Mum.

Acknowledgement of Country.

I acknowledge the Bunjalung people, the Traditional Custodians of the land on which I reside. I pay my respects to their Elders past, present and future. I extend that respect to all Aboriginal and Torres Strait Islander peoples who reside here today. I also Pay respect to my own People, the Kamilaroi people from the country where I was born in Northern NSW.

Always was and Always will be.

Contents

CHAPTER 1

Mr Jelly Beans

EVERY day an old man sitting outside his campervan on a canvas chair offered me a jelly bean from the large packet on his lap. He had been in the park for months. He looked old and kind of lonely sitting in his chair. I always said, "No thanks".

But one day I said yes. It was hot, I had my bathers and towel in my favourite bag, and I was going for a swim. My skin was still cool from the pool water as I skipped past the man on my way home. He called me over. I sat on a chair next to him as he asked me all sorts of questions.

"How old are you?"

"What school do you go to?"

"Do you have any pets?"

"Are you ever naughty?"

He invited me into his van. He wanted to give me a packet of jelly beans to take home. I knew I'd be the envy of my brothers if I came home with some lollies.

The next 10 minutes were a nightmare.

He lifted me and threw me on the bed. With one hand on my mouth, he ripped my shorts off. I was terrified. His trousers were on the floor. He was a strong man. I was a little kid.

"Fucken' hold still or I'll choke you."

I couldn't scream. The man pressed his hand onto my face tight. His big fingers covered my tears. I felt pain in the place where I peed. His leg banged against my knee. With his free hand he was trying to put his dick in my pee-pee hole.

I struggled, pushing and turning trying to get away from him, and from this van with his packets of jelly beans. Then all this hot wetness poured all over me and down into my pee-pee hole. He let go. I sobbed, lying on the bed, not understanding what had happened.

The man threw a wet facecloth at me.

"Clean yourself up!"

I wiped the tears from my face first. Then I tried to wipe my private parts.

"Get your pants on and get out!"

I couldn't stop crying.

"Say anything to anyone and I'll find you and you'll disappear," he said.

He popped a red jelly bean in his mouth.

"Disappear," he repeated.

I picked up my swimming bag and raced out of the van. Past the bridge. Past the spindly trees in the park. There was wetness in my panties, and it was running down my legs. What was this stuff? Did I pee myself? No matter how fast how I ran, I couldn't escape the man and his jelly beans. And I couldn't stop crying.

At home, breathless, I ran straight into the bedroom I shared with my little sister, Aileen. I was 11 years old. She was eight. Aileen came in clutching one of her dolls. She asked if I was all right. I couldn't answer. The words were there in my head, but they couldn't reach my mouth.

Mum came home from work. I was still in my room. It was hard to breathe. It was like the man was still pushing into my face. I thought I was going to die. And all that hot stinky stuff was still there on my thighs. I started to cry. Mum sat on my bed and hugged me tightly. I told her every detail of what the man had done.

"I'm scared," I told her, I clung to her. "He said if I tell anyone I'll disappear I had no understanding of what disappear even meant back then.

Mum went straight into the kitchen, picked up the phone and called the police. They arrived in minutes. The police wrote down everything I told them. One policeman asked me if the man put his penis in my vagina.

"Did he have sex with you?" he asked as if he was asking me if I was going to school tomorrow. What did I know about sex?

Through my tears, I said the man tried to put his dick in the place where I peed.

"He really hurt me," I said.

The policeman asked my mother for my panties. They were in the bathroom. She collected them and handed them to the officer. He put them in a plastic bag and told Mum to take me to the doctor. The police had called Doctor Anderson already and explained everything.

While Dr Anderson examined me Mum held my hand. She didn't say much. I was scared and shame eked into my body through my skin. Dr Anderson treated me kindly, as did the police.

The man was arrested. The whole town knew what had happened to me. Everywhere I went I felt the eyes of people staring at me. Whispering behind their hands, "That's the girl".

My panties were sent to Sydney for forensic testing. It was months before the results came back. My shame grew, following me everywhere I went. The doctor's report was finally completed. The report stated I had not been vaginally penetrated. I had been badly bruised on the outside with fingerprint marks on my legs but not penetrated. That was the conclusion.

The court found the Jelly bean Man not guilty of raping me. He walked away P; scot-free. Money talks, criminals walk. From that day I became defiant. I was going to fight back.

Months later he was charged again for attacking another girl, only this time he injured the girl internally.

I became an angry little girl who lashed out. That girl became a woman who fought for something better. A woman who would never be a victim again.

OVER the following weeks I realised the voices of children were worth nothing. This was a small country town in which adults ruled, mostly with an iron fist. Parents who physically abused their children were never going to be held accountable. All kids were liars looking for attention and no one in authority even cared. The father was in charge end of the story.

Besides, on reflection many years later, I realised that there were only two police officers stationed in Narrabri, a town of 4000 people. These officers rarely acted against the town folk because they themselves had to live there. And the town had the services of a judge only couple of times a month, so what hope did we have? None.

I never recovered emotionally from the sexual attack from the old man in the park.

I became a defiant, obnoxious, little fighting machine. I was THAT girl in my small-minded, finger-pointing, closed-minded community. I felt like I was being gossiped about every day I left my home to go to school and knew from the nasty, snide remarks from some of my school friends that this was the case. I detested being in that town. I hated my life living in a home with a drunken, violent father. It hurt my heart that I was forbidden to associate with my indigenous school friends who lived right next door to our home and just up the road.

I knew I was going to run away from this life and I started to plan my escape. Saving every penny I could beg, borrow or steal was a start.

I had always questioned everything. After Mr Jelly Bean, I woke up every day feeling like I was carrying around a block of concrete on my shoulders. At 11 years old! I was sick of having fingers pointed at me for being THAT girl.

I lost my best friend Lyn who lived three houses away from my parents' house. Her father moved away after Lyn's mother took her own life. The resulting town gossip also scarred my way of thinking to the point it made me even more determined to get away from this bastard of a town. I didn't really understand what happened. All I knew was I lost my best friend and I was alone.

I SUFFERED terrible beatings from my father for my defiant attitude. I thought maybe I was an uncontrollable child. But I believed that if I did not fight back, I would end up having no say over anything anyone wanted to do to me. I had lived with nearly three years of shame and finger-pointing. Then one night my father came home drunk and I knew I had to run.

My sister Aileen and brothers Jack, Larry and Michael were sitting at our kitchen table eating dinner when Dad stumbled in drunk. The rule in our house was no one was allowed to speak or even smile at the dinner table. Dad sat down and Mum jumped up to get his dinner from the oven. She put it down on the table. We could all smell the alcohol on his breath.

We were all quiet as church mice, looking at each other wondering who he would smack when our little white cat jumped up onto the kitchen table. My father grabbed the cat, wrung its neck and threw it across the kitchen floor. Our cat was dead, my whole being stopped still and my little sister screamed. My mother sat silent and we all cried too scared to speak.

My father stood up walked across the kitchen and picked up the cat, went out to the back door and threw our dead pet cat up the backyard. This event affected every one of us right throughout our entire lives. I knew I had to get away from this life. I was sick of living every waking moment terrified of what would come next.

I planned my escape over the next month. I ran around town doing odd jobs and tried to collect as much money as I could knowing I would have to buy food to survive. What would I know I was just a kid. A country girl who knew nothing of the outside world. What I did know though was I trusted no one.

I did not tell my little sister Aileen I was going to run away because she would have wanted me to take her with me and I couldn't. She was too little. Besides that, she would have told Mum and that would have lined me up for yet another vicious beating from Dad. I loved my sister and brothers and my Mum, but I hated my father.

I had nightmares over watching my father kill our cat. It was like experiencing the Mr Jelly bean attack all over again; only this time there was death. Our house was like living with a block of concrete above our heads, waiting for it to fall and kill us too.

Aileen cried all the time. I tried to be strong and most of the time I was, but there were times I broke down and sobbed. There was a cloud of pure evil hanging over our family; I could not understand why a person would kill an innocent animal. Worst of all we were too scared of my father to talk about what he did to anyone outside of the family.

My father was a town identity who played football for the town as did his brother Kevin. Dad was a good-looking, popular man. Respected by his peers, worked hard and played hard. Small town folks had a silent agreement I am convinced of, no one questioned his and any other men in the town's drinking habits or the way he treated my mother and us kids behind closed doors.

All I lived for was to escape this life of physical and mental abuse from my father and the retribution of the town for accusing a wealthy businessman of a sexual attack against me.

I planned my every move and saved every penny I could get my hands on. My money was well hidden so none of my family could find it.

I also was deeply sad knowing I could not take my little sister with me. I loved and adored her and no matter what I wanted I just could not take her with me. I could not even tell her I was going to run away to the city, which was a 12-hour journey by car. I didn't even know if I would make it, so how could I take her? I cried often because I really loved my mother also. I was tired of fighting an unwinnable fight against a bigoted town.

Runaway I did in the middle of the night under cover of darkness. I dug up my savings and gathered up the little suitcase I had hidden away up in the backyard shed and sneaked out of my family home. I had to make it to the main highway that would take me to Sydney, the big smoke as we country people called it. I was terrified internally, worried sick that my father would find me missing before I could hitchhike a lift to the city.

I made it to the outskirts of town and stood waiting for a car or truck to take me to the city. Every car that went past scared the shit out of me because I thought it would be my father and I would be again bashed to within an inch of my life. I was scared but excited to be leaving a life I hated to the very core of my being.

Two lots of people picked me up, but it was not without stress. I was a little kid with a little suitcase running away from home and having to lie to the people who stopped to pick me up about why I was alone in the middle of nowhere was frightening. I was so scared they would take me to the nearest police station in one of the towns we passed through. It was terrifying.

This tough little, big-mouthed, obnoxious, rebel, little girl at times was reduced to a whimpering puppy, frightened near out of her skin. I had no idea of where I was going, no home or family or even friends in the city I could go to. What on earth was I thinking? All I knew was I had to get away from a life I was unable to tolerate any longer.

I told the people who picked me up was I was going home to my family after a holiday with relatives in the country. I told them I lived near Kings Cross and just need to be dropped off near there. I think the only reason they believed me was because I had my own money and paid for my own food and drink on the way. And my bravado facade I displayed to them.

CHAPTER 2

Surviving Kings Cross

I WAS was turning 15 next year when I arrived in Sydney, the city of dreams. I had convinced myself this was my time.

I was dropped off in Macleay Street in Kings Cross with my little suitcase in tow. I couldn't believe my eyes. I had never seen so many people in my life. The adrenaline was surging through my veins. I was so excited and unnerved all at the same time. I had nowhere to go, knew no one, and was dragging everything I owned in a little bag. I had to sit down and think about what I had done. I was really conflicted and scared.

This side of my persona made me feel too vulnerable. I trusted no one as my trust of others had been violated. I knew city people were very different to country people and from what I had drilled into me growing up, city people often took advantage of others, so I had to be careful.

I was a little kid wandering the streets of the most infamous city in Australia. I was so glad I had been smart enough to save, scrounge and hide every bit of money I could get my hands on before running away. I would have starved otherwise.

I found a little café at the corner of Macleay Street and Darlinghurst Road. It was tiny and run by an Italian family who cooked cheap meals. The place was so popular people had to wait for others to leave before getting a seat. The food was cheap, home-cooked and the mother, father and son who ran the place were lovely.

The mother sensed I was a runaway and she let me leave my little suitcase out the back while I went to find friends to stay with. This was my story to her. She didn't question me; she just said to come back when I was ready. As I walked up Darlinghurst Road, I felt like a kid lost in a dream, my eyes glazed at so many amazing places, people and what I realised were nightclubs. Places to dance the night away.

I found a place called Surf City and I tried desperately to get into that dance club but security wouldn't admit me without someone to take me in. I was very frustrated and tried to convince several men to take me in. They took one look at me and told me to piss off. The music was driving me crazy. I was so excited to be in the city but was getting nowhere.

I didn't want to pick up with any stranger. That thought scared me more than being alone with nowhere to sleep or live. I just wanted to get into Surf City to dance and be happy for the first time in many years. I had never seen so many people in one place in my entire life and I felt like a moth being drawn to a flame.

AT THE Cross there were clubs where men could go into to watch women dance. Later I was to learn they were called strip clubs. Outside each club was a spruiker yelling and trying to convince men to go inside. As I walked past one club trying to get someone to take me into Surf City, the guy on the door grabbed my arm.

I swung around and looked at him and he said to me, "Geesh, hunny you must be making a fortune tonight." I had no idea of what he was talking about. He said, "I have seen you walk by with at least six Johns tonight." Johns? How did he know their names and surely every one of those guys I tried to get to take me into Surf City didn't have the same name.

I said, "Look, mate, all I want to do is go into Surf City and dance, I didn't ask the name of every guy I walked past you with." He stared at me for a few moments and asked my name, I told him it's Suzy. He introduced himself as Pete and said, "Look, Suzy, I will be finished my shift here in about two hours, so come back if you can't find someone to get you into the club and I will take you in, okay?"

As I walked away, I told myself to be careful girl or this might be another jelly bean episode. I wasn't scared because I knew I would never allow myself to be put into that situation again.

Two hours later I went back to the outside of the club where Pete worked and saw that he was waiting for me. He asked me to go have coffee with him across the road before he took me to the club. We sat in the coffee club and chatted and I looked him in the face and said, "Pete, if you touch me, I will fight back and cause you so many problems you will regret this night forever."

He laughed at me and said, "Suzy, you are the wrong sex, I am homosexual." I said, "Please explain, Pete, I am a country girl. I do not understand what you are saying." Pete said straight out, "Suzy, you are safe as I only have sex with men, not females." This blew my little mind. I could feel my face go bright red with embarrassment. Men having sex with men!

I couldn't even comprehend this thought that alone understand it. The only sexual knowledge I had was my own terrifying experience with Mr Jelly Bean. I ended up telling Pete what had happened in my life and that I had run away from home. I also told him how old I was. He had suspected I was a runaway after my dumb answers about me making a fortune from the guys I was trying to get to take me into the club.

We finished our coffee and went to Surf City. The security on the door of the club let us straight in as Pete was very well-known identity Kings Cross. There were several of Pete's friends inside and I was introduced as his little sister. I felt safe for the first time in many years.

I learned very quickly that all Pete's friends were homosexual, both male and female. I had the best night ever and when the club closed, we all went back over to the coffee shop to wind down (a saying of popularity from Pete and friends). I was exhausted but felt very contented and again relieved to be with people that made me feel safe. Pete lived close by and asked where my suitcase was.

The little café was open even though it was 6am. They opened at 6am and closed at 10pm every day seven days a week. It was decided I would go and stay with Pete as he did not want me running the streets. He said it wasn't a safe place for very young girls or boys. This was a far cry from the life I had left behind. I just felt safe.

Pete's little flat was a two-bedroom small place tucked away in the back streets of the Cross. It was spotlessly clean and very arty. I loved his paintings and all his little treasures. His second bedroom was a storage area, but he was going to fix it up for me to live in and have my own room. I couldn't believe how lucky I was to have found and been found by Pete. He was such an honourable, good man.

CHAPTER 3

Locked up and learning so much

PETE set the rules to live by. The main one was to stay the fuck out of any trouble and away from any police interaction as I had no identification to prove I was his sister. Also, I was never allowed to take any drugs from anyone. "What are drugs?" I asked. I received a very detailed explanation of every drug and its effects and consequences. Usually death from overdoses.

My undeveloped, uneducated little brain was soaking all this up like a sponge. I was in awe of this man who rescued me from living on the streets and who knows what else might have happened to me had I not found him. Pete became my mentor and my protector and over time I learned to love him dearly and respected him.

I missed my little sister and my mother. Aileen must have cried her eyes out when she woke up, and found my parents had realised I had run away from home. I also know my mother would have been frantic with worry. I knew they would report me as a missing child and there would be a police bulletin about me sent to every police station in NSW.

I was smart enough to know I had to call home before this became a major search for me. I had no intention of ever going back there, but I just wanted my mother and sister to know I was alive and safe. I called home in the morning knowing my father was at work and my mother was getting ready to go to her job. My mother broke down in tears and begged me to come home. She wanted to know where I was and I lied saying I was in Queensland. This way they would not be looking for me in Sydney.

I assured her I was safe and I needed her to tell Aileen I would call again to talk to her and my mum when I knew Dad wasn't going to be at home. I also knew my mother would report to the police that I had called and that I was missing, but refused to come home.

It would be noted that I was a runaway, alive but whereabouts unknown.

I was happy living with Pete and doing my own thing although there were times, I did take risks such as not paying train fares as I learned my way around Sydney. I wanted to get a job but was too scared as I had no ID and I hated having to rely on Pete to support me financially. I needed to be self-sufficient but didn't know how.

Eventually I was caught riding the trains with no ticket, picked up by police and taken to a place called Bidura, which housed runaway kids and kids who had committed crimes. Again, I was subjected to having my private parts examined. What the fuck is wrong with these adults? They all seemed obsessed with my vagina.

The officers were cruel and nasty. We all were treated like slaves, even the littlest of kids. My parents had been contacted and wanted me home. I was not going home and told the people in charge. If they tried to send me home, I would run again even before I left the city. The courts had made me a ward of the state.

In the five weeks I was in that hellhole at Bidura I became very close to a little girl who reminded me of me. She was scared and had been sexually molested at home. I had a plan and I was going to take her with me. I knew how to get out of this place by watching the officers come and go.

On February 14, 1966, I grabbed my little friend's hand and we ran like the wind, out the big steel-grated front door when an officer opened it to receive a delivery for the home. We reached the front fence and I climbed up over it trying to help my little mate.

She got to the top but I was down and running, she was screaming for me. An officer had grabbed her. I looked back at her terrified little tear-filled eyes and I wanted to turn around and try to get her. My heart was beating out of my chest. I had no hope, so I kept running, tears running down my face.

As I looked back at her little face, the memory of her fear burned into my heart and soul forever. I never forgot her and worried for her, cried for her often over the following months and years. I remembered that day as this was the day Australia changed our money over from pounds, shillings and pence, to dollars and cents.

I ran like the wind and got myself out of the suburb, knowing the place would have the police out looking for me. It took me more than an hour to get back to Pete's flat and I was shaken to the core. Pete was happy but angry I had taken risks but secretly relieved to have his little sister home.

I knew I had to be very careful now and take no more risks because the police were now aware that I wasn't in Queensland and that I was somewhere in Sydney. My future was at risk and it was my own fault, for having too much pride to ask Pete for money to pay for bus and train fares. I knew he would have given me anything, but I was too proud to ask. He worked such long hours.

I WAS back with Pete only a few months and got caught again by the authorities. I was sent straight into Parramatta Girls' Home. This place had a very bad reputation. Justified, I soon realised.

There would be no escaping from this place. The walls were way too high and the place was a jail, not a girls' home. Again, I was subjected to being vaginally examined, and again I was so embarrassed and felt humiliated. I was taken to a clothing store and outfitted with what looked to me like a uniform and sneakers.

The officers were gruff and spoke to us like we were shit under their feet. I was the youngest girl in the place. The first morning I was just about pulled out of the bed in a cell of four girls by an officer. We had breakfast in the main dining room for all the women. About 20 girls were sitting on chairs all around the wall of a huge room.

There was a commotion when the big steel door flew open, a huge man stormed in and started screaming at us. Everybody stood up. The girl standing next to me whispered to me, "Suzy, do not speak. Not one word, OK?" I was a little kid in a big kids' prison. All these women were seasoned female warriors. I had not yet learned how to fight this fight.

I could feel my heart beating faster as he screamed at us all. Then he seemed to rush over and strike that blow that shocked me to my very core of existence.

He knocked a fellow female inmate to the floor, screaming at her, she never uttered a word and there was not one tear from her eyes. He ordered another officer to lock her up in solitary confinement. He pulled her up off the floor and practically threw her towards the door.

She was a big girl who towered over my height and was as strong as an ox. Those women were used to this abuse and physical attacks, but to me it was as bad as the home I had run away from. Luckily, I knew I wouldn't be staying in this hellhole for too long because I was too young.

Years later, that senior male officer was charged with physically abusing the women in Parramatta Girls home and other institutions he was in charge of.

I felt scared to death. I was only in this place because I was considered an escape artist after running from Bidura and they were taking no chances. This place was escape-proof, I transferred away only a week later into what they called an age-appropriate place.

I WAS taken from Parramatta to a well-known home for wayward girls on the outskirts of Sydney. When I reached the Complex, I knew there defiantly was no way I was going to be able to get away from this place. The wire fences were ten feet tall with three lots of barbed wire at the top, and security beyond the understanding of my young brain.

Three other girls arrived at the same time and we all stood in a locked room waiting to be processed by officers. We were told we would meet the governor of this institution.

The law made us all wards of the state and we were told we were there because we had been exposed to moral danger. This happened because we refused to be sent home to our parents or the authorities considered us in danger.

The four of us were escorted into the governor's office. The woman in charge was a well-dressed, attractive female with a kind face. I was not fooled. Standing by her side was a tall, blond-haired, tough-looking male officer. He was second in charge and I guessed he would not be one to be messing with.

I will not give the governor her correct name. Let's just call her Miss Redhead. Then there was an officer in charge of our dormitory. She had a red birthmark across one side of her face and she was a nasty piece of work. We were told in no uncertain words that any bad behaviour would be punished accordingly. We would be shipped off to a worse place located in the middle of nowhere called Hay.

We were taken down to our dormitory after being given two sets of institution-supplied clothes and two pairs of shoes. There were 15 girls in each dormitory and there were four dormitories, each with an officer in charge.

I had been there for around three months and had tolerated being humiliated and verbally abused. After watching other girls suffer the same, I attached myself to five other girls who had been there quite some time.

All six of us used a pin to scratch names into our arms, you know like a tattoo. If it wasn't deep enough it healed quickly without leaving a scar. We got caught and were dragged into Miss Redhead's office. Also in the office was the male second in charge. We were in deep shit.

We stood there shaking in our shoes as we were being sent down to solitary confinement one at a time.

The remaining five of us were forced to scrub a large area of concrete in the assembly area of the institution with soap and toothbrushes. We were given countless toothbrushes as they wore out quickly. Scrubbing concrete out in the sun darn near killed us from heat stroke. This was our punishment.

When it was my turn to go into solitary and I was taken up to the office where Pat, one of my co-offenders, was standing. We looked at each other and started to smirk at each other. The male second in charge pushed her against the wall and screamed at us both.

As he pushed her, he poked her chest and looking at me, said, "You both will do a second stint for being a smart ass." He then marched her back down to isolation. Miss Redhead looked at me and said, "Give me one good reason I do not double your time down there, Suzy?"

I looked her straight in the eyes and said, "Because I believe you are a fair, decent human being and you know we do not deserve this abusive treatment. None of us deserves to be punished in this manner. Yes, we deserve the loss of privileges for our behaviour, but this is child abuse."

Mr Second-In-Charge walked into the office and asked if I would be locked up when Pat came out of solitary. Miss Redhead replied, "No, I have decided that this girl did not step out of line and will receive only one 24-hour stint in lockdown."

I stood there in that office like a robot with no display of emotion, secretly relieved. Meals in lockdown solitary confinement were buttered bread and a glass of milk for all three meals. We all scrubbed concrete and spent our designated time in solitary confinement as required, and never marked our bodies ever again.

I WAS to learn first-hand, that the gossip about certain officers sexually taking advantage of the girls who were incarcerated was spot on. I became the play toy of a certain female high-ranking official.

On the outside of this institution was a cottage, a privilege cottage, that housed four girls who had earned the right to live the last months of their confinement in relative freedom from the restrictive daily life of being behind barbed-wire fences.

Miss Redhead also lived in this cottage. Her private quarters were separated from the girls' bedrooms by only a wall. I had heard gossip about her, but took little notice, although there were many times, she was exceptionally nice to me.

I soon learned she always had a favourite inmate she spoiled. Later in my life, I realised we were being groomed by her to participate in her secret obsession with young girls. As one girl left for home and another one took her place in the cottage.

I wanted out and a spot in the cottage, but I didn't realise there were strings attached. Why would I? I had had no sexual experience even in all my travels of being a runaway. I had a male homosexual protector, Pete, who always had my back. Besides that, I had an intense fear and hatred of men after Mr Jelly Bean. I knew I loved the company of females; I just didn't know why.

The only males who had been near my vagina were Mr Jelly Bean, Dr Anderson and the two disgusting doctors attached to the Bidura remand home and Parramatta Girls Home.

After the horrible punishment of isolation and scrubbing concrete out in the sun for days on end I decided to follow Miss Redhead's advice and work hard to get into the privileged cottage.

I had close to eight weeks to go before I was due to be released and as I had refused once again to go home to my parents and live in that shitty, gossip-overrun town, it was decided I would be released into the care of my Aunty Enid and Uncle Bob who lived in San Souci in Sydney.

They were related to my mother and, although I had met them only once before, any place was better than the home I hated.

I had made it into the privileged cottage by working my guts out and being a lackey to the officers in charge of my dormitory. Whatever needed doing I volunteered. Whatever it took was my motivation to get out from behind the ten feet barbed wire fencing.

Packing up my few treasured little belongings to move into the outside cottage was very exciting to this almost 16-year-old country girl.

I HAD settled into the privilege cottage well and was relishing my well-earned part freedom. Miss Redhead was just so kind to me and she gave me lots of little treats unbeknown to anyone else in the centre. Several times, over two weeks I was invited into her living quarters, which were beautifully furnished and smelled so nice to me.

I did jobs for her like cleaning her place and helping her make little cakes which I got to eat with her and drink soft drinks. I liked her but I knew my place. Late one night there was a knock on my bedroom door, even though 9.30pm was lights out. I had been laying in my bed planning what I was going to do when I got out of there. I jumped out of bed thinking it was one of the other girls. Opening my door, I stared at Miss Redhead. I thought, "Shit, what have I done?"

She said, "Suzy I need your help. I have flooded my bathroom and I cannot clean this up on my own. Please come with me."

I grabbed my dressing gown and followed her through the corridor down to the locked door leading into her private quarters. Down her hallway, into her bathroom. Sure enough, it was flooded with water everywhere, and the water was seeping into her hallway.

Thankfully the floors were all tiled and using so many towels we managed to mop up all the water. I was soaked and so was she. I could not understand how this could happen. Then again what did I know I was just a kid, not a plumber.

Miss Redhead pulled open a hallway door and took two large bath towels out, handing me one. She said, "Suzy, get out of your wet clothes and wrap yourself up." She made us both a hot cup of tea and I sat on her lounge, I was freezing feeling very uncomfortable being naked under my towel. She also was naked under her towel. She got up off her lounge chair and walked over to me. She gently grabbed my arms and pulled me up saying, "Here let me help you get dry."

She turned me around and pulled my towel from around my body, starting to softly wipe down my exposed naked back. I could feel my face turn red. I wasn't scared. I was just feeling overwhelmed. I had two choices, accept what was going to happen or put up a fight. My experience with authorities had proved that no one believes what kids say anyway.

Miss Redhead started to caress and kiss my naked back, her hands silky soft. Expertly exploring the outlines of my young naked body, she too was now naked having dropped her towel. She turned me around to face her and smiled at me, her words as gentle as her touch.

Her eyes were like stars in the night sky, as bright as the universe. She held my face in her hands and her lips touched mine, her tongue sending electric shocks throughout my entire being. I had been freezing moments ago; my entire body was now on fire.

Was I in love? I had always admired her presence and respected her authority and her kindness towards me since being placed in this institution, but now I was questioning my very existence. What did I know about love? Nothing. A physical and mental change was happening on a level I had never experienced.

All I knew at this moment was I did not want her to stop touching me, caressing me, kissing me, sucking me. I was enthralled with her very presence. The way she touched me with such gentle loving kindness was like magic. I had put up with years of physical and mental torture from adults. This was like finding a rainbow at the end of a storm, a gold coin in a pile of black dirt.

I wanted to be taught by her to give back what I was being given, but she was having none of it. All she wanted was to drink the very essence of me from top to toe. When she parted my legs and started kissing and licking me, exploring my now exposed untouched sensuality I thought I had died and gone to heaven.

That night I learned all about female orgasms. I had had my very first and wanted more. I now knew that the gossip about her liking young girls that were rife throughout this place was true and I just didn't care. I was being loved and treated with kindness for the first time in my life and I did not want it to end.

Yes, I became her love toy for the next seven weeks and even though deep down I knew it was wrong, I threw my Catholic upbringing out the door with the rubbish where it belonged. I also knew I had to train my brain to accept that this situation was not going to last.

I was being released soon and this would be the end of my amazing experience with this very beautiful sexual teacher. How strange calling a female predator a beautiful sexual teacher.

CHAPTER 4

Freedom at last

UNCLE BOB and Aunty Enid had started coming to visit me. They seemed nice and treated me okay, but laid down the house rules to me about what was expected of me when I was released into their care. Fair enough, I thought, I had grown up a lot since coming into this place.

I certainly knew now why I liked kissing the few girls I had kissed back growing up in that shitty little country town. I had never had any interest in having a boyfriend. The last boyfriend I had carried my books to school for me. I played boys' games and kicked a football rather than play with dolls.

I had it in my head from the word go that there was no way I was getting married and having kids. No way I would ever allow a man to abuse my kids as my father got away with abusing us. I had this ingrained mistrust of the male authority. They were the abusers and I was always going to fight back.

I was no longer that little 11-year-old who had been humiliated, embarrassed and shunned by the whole town. The girl that dared accuse a wealthy businessman of rape; the girl no one believed anyway. No, I was no longer a pushover, I was a fighter who was never going to stop fighting for my rights.

Uncle Bob and Aunty Enid arrived at the home to pick me up. I had said goodbye to my friends and as I sat in the waiting room my mind wandered to my last night with Miss Redhead, I felt sad knowing I would never see her again. She had made my stay in that place into a memory I would never forget.

There were the formalities of signing papers and getting what little possessions I had accumulated into their car and finally I was able to walk out of there a free human being. I was feeling quite overwhelmed and so much had happened that my brain seemed to be wanting to race non-stop. It took us more than two hours in the traffic to get to Aunty Enid's house and I was tired, feeling frustrated and hot, as their car did not have air-conditioning.

Uncle Bob parked his car in his garage and we grabbed my belongings and went into their house. Aunty Enid showed me my bedroom. It was a single bedroom and all very nice and neat. I looked around the room then sat on my bed. I put away the few things I owned into the drawers and wardrobe and went into the kitchen where they were both waiting for me.

Aunty Enid had made sandwiches and poured me fruit juice, for which I thanked her. They informed me that I had tomorrow off to relax and then the next day they were taking me to the local school where they had booked me in to start school. Oh great, I thought NOT! But I had no choice as it was part of the agreement they had made.

At dinner that night they told me that on school holidays if I wanted to visit my parents they would take me, my answer was no. I wanted to talk to my mother and little sister on the phone but no I did not want to ever visit that town ever again. I hated my father and was worried about my little sister Aileen but could never go there again.

Uncle Bob called my mother that night and I spoke to her and my little sister, we all cried. I loved them so much but couldn't go see them. Maybe Mum could bring my sister and brothers to visit me? I did not foresee this happening, as my father would never allow my mother to be away from home, the bloody control freak he was.

Contented with talking to my mother and little sister I was prepared to give this situation a try, that is try to be a normal 15-and-a-half-year-old teenage girl. But nothing in my life had been normal for as long as I could remember. Up until this point in my life, it had consisted of trying to stand up for myself, every waking moment.

I WAS taken to my new school, booked in and after a meeting with the school principal arrangements were made for me to start the Monday of the following week. I remember the look on the principal's face when he was told I had just been released from a girls' reform school. It was as if he looked straight through me, or was I being paranoid?

My uniforms came from the school's second-hand uniform shop. I was okay with this because I did not want to cause my Aunty Enid any financial hardship. I was just grateful to be out of the girls' home. Sure, I missed Miss Redhead and her adoring physical attention, but I loved my freedom more.

For the first week Aunty Enid drove me to school. Maybe she thought I would get lost. I soon learned how to get there and get back to where I was living; it was only a 20-minute walk anyway. I was not impressed with my new school; I did not like being questioned.

I was getting sick of having to make up excuses as to why I was not living with my parents and it did not take me long to work out who the school bullies were. I ignored them picking on the shy kids who were too scared to say anything until one day. I had had a gutful. Bullies work in packs, but take the leader down and the others will scatter.

I sat watching this smart-arse boy pushing a little girl around. When he grabbed her lunch box and tipped her food out on the ground, I lost my cool. I ran at him screaming and punched him so hard he fell on the ground near her food. His bully mates backed away as I yelled and called them yellow-belly black snakes.

Of course, there were many swearing words in between as I kicked him fairly in the guts. How dare these bastards pick on a little kid half their size? How dare they pick on any kid for that matter, let alone a little girl scared to death of them? I had watched long enough. The schoolyard teachers ran over to break up the fight. Before they got to us, I warned the bullyboy that if he or any of his coward mates come near her or anyone else, I would put a softball bat across his head.

We were all marched up to the office, including the little girl who was in tears and more scared now than she was when they were picking on her. The headmaster lined us all up and one by one we were taken into his office to explain to him what had taken place. He had gotten the crux of the story and then called me in to speak to him.

I spoke quietly about what had happened, addressing him with a look in my eye that gave no excuses for my retaliation. What I said was, "You people are here to teach us and not to ignore bullies in your schoolyard." I also said that if I ever saw those boys picking on another of my school friends, I would take the same action to protect them and myself.

Of course, I was suspended from school for two weeks, and Auntie Enid and Uncle Bob were called up to the school to pick me up. They were also warned that any further violence from me would force him to call the police and have me charged with assault. "Here we go again," were my thoughts. "Fuck it, I am not staying here."

I went back to school two weeks later and all was okay. I had gained a reputation of don't mess with me or else. This suited me fine because I knew I would again punch any bullyboys or girls I saw picking on the shy kids. I also knew the consequences, but I just didn't give a shit. I had just about had enough of all authorities and their control over my life.

CHAPTER 5

Does it ever stop? I am so tired

DEEP in my soul I knew I was going to run again; it was only a matter of time. There was a longing, a feeling of pent-up anger and hurt that I could not put down. I was a lost soul and I had no idea of how to fix myself or deal with my sadness. The only thing I did know was I was never going to give up fighting and I would never stand still and watch other kids being abused in any shape or form.

Going back to that school was very difficult for me, the teachers watched me like a hawk. Rightly so because no one knew more than me that if anyone I saw was being bullied, I would react this time with even more vengeance. It would not have taken very much for my inner timebomb to be set off

I knew I was never going to stop fighting for justice for myself and anyone around me. Especially kids like myself and all the younger ones who lived every day in fear of being picked on for reasons beyond any child's understanding. It felt this load on my shoulders was getting heavier every day.

I wanted to talk to Aunty Enid about how I was feeling but I didn't trust or know her well enough to even try explaining what was going on in my head.

The mentality of those years was all adults believed that children should be seen and not heard. We had no voices, even if some of us tried to defend ourselves verbally we were seen and treated as problem children.

Either that or we were called liars and or attention seekers. Punishment for children or teenagers of lower- to middle-class families was either physical and or total grounding. Not a lot has changed over the decades but at least as time dragged by adults who really cared about kids started to advocate on our behalf.

Days turned into weeks, and I tried to make the best of a difficult situation as far as school went. The saving grace was because of my attitude and bad reputation as being a fighter, no one was game to pick on the smaller or more vulnerable kids in the playground. This made me happy but also sad in another way because I knew I was not going to hang around for much longer.

I could not let Pete know I was out of the reform school because I had no money. I needed money to be able to phone him, but Aunt Enid's phone had a call lock and I didn't know the code. I was never a thief, so taking money from Aunt Enid's purse, which she often left lying around, was not an option.

Any money I ever had, I gained by working small jobs wherever I could. I just had to bide my time and wait for the chance to run again. I knew it would be soon.

CHAPTER 6

Still running

IFELT I was caught up in a never-ending dryer, going round and round with no stopping for even a breath. As planned, I took off from Aunty Enid and Uncle Bob's home. All I had to my name was a small bag of clothes and a few dollars. Of course, I was headed straight back to Pete's house in Kings Cross.

I was 15 and a half and felt like an old lady with the weight of the world on my shoulders. The last four years were swimming around in my young brain; four years of living hell. It was like a fight I couldn't stop. I just knew I had to keep fighting for my rights for justice against authorities that believed every kid was a liar.

Back with Pete and all his friends I felt safe. I knew he had my back and would never allow me to wander into a situation I could not get out of. Pete looked tough. He was physically very fit and muscled with many tattoos. He kept me safe. There were many more numerous situations that happened to me as opposed to these turbulent times living in King's Cross, however I have chosen to stay silent about them and the people involved. One day, perhaps I will disclose them in the future.

For the next six months I lived very well, I was happy and I often called my mother just to let her know I was okay. She and my sister always cried. Aileen was growing up but was still begging me to come and get her.

I just couldn't because I knew she would get the same treatment I had, if caught by the authorities.

I promised her I would get her once I turned 18. She was longing for that day, as she was now my father's new punching bag. God, I hated him. I wished the authorities would stop him but knew country town mentality would change nothing. I hated him and the town I was born in. I hated their small-town finger-pointing gossip.

I was heartbroken knowing Aileen was so unhappy and there was nothing I could do about it until I was of age. Knowing my father was abusing her and my three brothers was very difficult to live with. But I knew I had to be super careful about protecting my freedom.

I was again on the police radar as a runaway teenager. I became very street smart, tuned into who was trustworthy and who wasn't, and I certainly knew what my rights were as far as the law goes. I detested being on the run. Life wasn't easy but knowing I was loved and protected within the community I was living in gave me inner contentment.

I cherished these days with Pete. I was a ward of the state of NSW. This meant the Children's Services Department could do as they pleased with me. Including locking me up wherever they liked when they caught me.

I HAD THE best 16th birthday any kid could ever want. Pete and all his friends held a party to end all parties. I did feel cared for and loved. I knew my sister and mother loved me but I could not live with the violence in my family.

I had been free for almost six months after running from Aunt Enid and Uncle Bob's home and I got careless thinking I had no one to fear. I was dead wrong, I found myself in the wrong place at the wrong time and again I was back in custody. I was concerned about where they were going to lock me up this time.

I faced the Children's Court, not for any crimes they thought I might have committed. In the eyes of the law at that time I was still a minor and as such still exposed to moral danger. Also on my record was a notation that I was a runner, so they had to be very sure I was placed in an institution I could not escape.

It was a convent in Sydney with walls made of ancient stone blocks two and three storeys high. I was astounded as I was taken into this enormous building.

My thoughts were how the fuck am I going to get out of this one? I wasn't, but the saving grace was I had been sentenced to stay there only until I turned 18.

This was only 18 months away. I thought, "No problem, girl, you can do this." I just had to learn to keep my flapping trap shut, be patient and bide my time. This was a place full of nuns and girls. "What could go wrong?" I thought to myself. The inner workings of the convent consisted of four groups of girl inmates. In charge of each group was a head nun, next down the line was a sub-manager who wore a part type of habit, a short veil, but mid-length uniform, stockings and court shoes. After her, was a dormitory woman in charge of our day-to-day routine.

I was assigned to my group of 15 girls. Our nun in charge was Mother Rose. Next was a woman whom I guessed was in her late 50s. She wore the short veil and uniform and slept at the very top of our dormitory. Her name was Francine.

The woman in charge of our daily chores was Max. For obvious reasons this was not her real name.

She takes the Oscar as being one of the most evil disgusting human beings I have ever met in my entire life. There were four groups in this convent. Then another small group of five much older women who seemed to have physical and mental health problems. I was to later learn they were permanent residents and had been in that place for many years.

I felt very sad for these women as some of the girls were nasty to them on a daily basis. I had to keep my mouth shut because the option of the institution in outback Hay was not an attractive thought.

I never did find out how long these women had been in the convent. I asked each of them over the time, but they had no idea. They all just had the same answer ... "a long time".

OUR MAIN sleeping area was a huge, long room with seven beds down one side and eight down the other. At the top of the room were a large single bed, a wardrobe and a dressing table. This was Francine's private space even though it was open to the whole room.

At the bottom of the room was Max's single bed also of good quality and the same furniture as Francine's. There was a doorway that led into a communal block of showers for us girls but there was also a private bathroom used only by Max and Francine. Up the far end of the bathroom were three enclosed toilets for our use.

I settled in and packed my convent-issued clothes into my little single wardrobe. Every girl had one beside her bed. We then all filed into the communal lounge room. At least we had a TV, but we could only watch programs Francine decided as being suitable.

Lights out were 9.30pm. We had only five minutes to brush our teeth and get our PJs on. Francine said goodnight to us all and we were expected to reply, and then get into our beds. I learned that Francine got out of bed at 5.30am. Any of the other girls also could get up at that time to go with Francine to Mass.

This happened six days a week. On Sunday the girls in all the dormitories were taken down into the largest Catholic Church I had ever seen in my life.

My dormitory's daily routine shocked me to the very core of my being. I was horrified, terribly, deeply embarrassed. Every morning we had to go into the bathroom and hand wash our panties. We then had to line up behind each other and one by one had to show the crutch to Max so she could determine if we had washed our panties properly.

I cannot even find the words to explain how I felt. What made this situation even more horrific is that this woman who was third in charge of us seemed to take great joy in loudly telling some girls to get back into the bathroom and wash their crutch out again as it was filthy and their panties stank.

I have never felt so embarrassed and horrified at anything in my life. After Mr Jelly Bean I thought I had experienced the worst from a human being. He was child's play compared to this pure evil bitch and there was nothing I could do about it. This was convent routine. WHY? I still to this day shake my head at the memories.

This was an everyday occurrence and so was her filthy verbal and mental abuse of most of the girls in my dormitory. I waited and waited for my turn to come for her barrage of embarrassment, but for some reason it never came.

I have to say I struggled daily to keep my mouth shut. I wanted to smash her face in but knew if I did, I would be shipped out to Hay a place known for a reputation as hell on earth. I had to stay quiet because I was counting down the months to my release into the real world.

I tried very hard to support these girls emotionally; I kept their spirits up with hugs and kind words. It's very difficult when you are hurting inside yourself. I cried at times with them.

Gossip again reared its ugly head; Max had a thing for young girls only it was not just gossip. She was a viper of the worst kind and I continually questioned why the hierarchy here was not aware of her behaviour. Were they dumb and blind? She was a full-time resident here. My only conclusion was these people were not trained officers in the government service. They were nuns and wannabe dictators ruling the roost over vulnerable young girls who were too scared to complain.

I had only six months to go before my time was up and I was having a difficult time. We went to school in the morning and in the afternoon, we were sent into the laundry to work to make the convent money.

THIS WAS a commercial laundry on the grounds of a convent. The work was very difficult and exhausting for children. Many of these girls were little kids. I worked in the ironing room, which was separate but part of the huge factory floor. The floor had massive commercial washing machines and two huge roller-ironing barrels the sheets and pillowcases were put through.

The drying machines were big enough to hold a human being. My section of the room was a wooden bench that had built-in ironing boards. On top of these benches were steel pipes that ran from one end of the room to the other. Connected to the pipes were rubber hoses that fed into a small heavy iron.

At least 30 of us from different dorms were assigned to the ironing.

Another nun was in charge and she was a tyrant. Little Mother Slave Driver, I called her. "Children could not be trusted", was her statement to us every day, without fail.

The convent handled all the linen from a very upmarket hotel. We also had to iron all the chefs' hats and waitresses' blouses all from the same hotel. On top of that were priests' vestments and altar boy smocks from across Sydney.

Talk about child abuse! This place made third-world countries look like a walk in the park. This slaver driver of a nun would inspect every item we ironed and God help us if she found one crease that shouldn't be there. She would scream and rant at the girl and then crumple the item up and throw it on the floor.

We were expected to work like dogs and were punished if we didn't meet our quota for each day. I detested this sorry excuse of a woman. It was a toss-up between her and Max who was the worst.

I soon learned Maxie was worse. I had had a difficult day in the laundry and had gone back up to my dormitory to get ready for dinner. I was tired and hot I asked Max if I could have a shower before dinner.

She agreed, on one condition. That I put rollers in her hair before I went to bed later. I agreed. After dinner, I followed through with my agreement and she sat on her chair at the end of her bed handing me the rollers. She was being very nice for a change.

No one in the dorm could hear what was being said because they were all in our lounge room with Francine. She said she was going to have a bath and needed me to help her as she had a bad back. I knew what she was, but I also knew I still had four months left to be set free.

I cringed and nodded, thinking "How the fuck do I get out of this?" I hated this woman with a passion. I walked down into the lounge room and told Francine I would be helping Max when she called for help to get into her bath. The other girls looked at me, some sniggering.

I felt sick inside. Max called out to me and I walked down to her bathroom. She had run her bubble bath and I looked at her very unattractive body with disgust. She handed me her sponge on a string and told me to wash her back. I did what I was told I felt I wanted to vomit.

She then stood up and proceeded to masturbate, asking me to come closer. She took my hand and forced me to take over rubbing her vagina. I was absolutely beside myself with anger, embarrassment and repulsion. I had to keep my cool here or I was going to be well and truly done like an over cooked dinner.

I calmly told her, "Maxie, I am sorry I have no experience in what you want me to do." Luckily for me Francine walked to the door of the bathroom and called my name. Thank God I was dressed. I threw the sponge in Max's bath and answered, "Yes, Francine I am coming now."

I felt my face was red from being ashamed and embarrassed, but Francine said nothing. How could these people not know about this child abuser? This woman had been getting away with this behaviour for years. This situation was so fucked up. More to the point how was I going to avoid her for the next near four months?

The one thing that was keeping me sane and somewhat calm was the memory of Miss Redhead and my experience with her. At least that was a loving sensual experience unlike this pig of a woman's behaviour.

I believe the convent hierarchy either knew about her behaviour or refused to believe any of the children who complained. In their eyes this was God's house and everything they did was according to God's word. The children were all liars and as this was an institution not controlled by the government, they answered to no one.

What I also knew was that one day I would report or at least write down everything that happened to me and other young girls at the hands of the very people being paid to protect us and look after us. There had to become a time in the future when these people were going to be held accountable.

CHAPTER 7

My final meltdown

I HAD been conflicted, angry and tired, and my stress levels were near out of control. I had managed to avoid another bathroom incident with Max and was being singled out by her for punishment over my decision to avoid her sexual attention.

Add to the mix the screaming banshee Little Mother Slave Driver in the laundry and I was near exploding. One day I had been to school in the morning and couldn't concentrate on what the nun who was our teacher was trying to explain. Once again, I was in her bad books too. We went for lunch and then down into the laundry to do our designated jobs.

Every girl was expected to iron at least 20 priests' vestments; 10-15 altar boys' gowns, 15-20 hotel waitresses' blouses and the same amount, of chefs' hats. This fucking place was a hotbed of forced child labour. Punishment for not meeting our quota depended on the mood Mother Slave Driver was in.

I was ironing like there was no tomorrow, trying to ignore Mother Slave Driver and her spiteful screaming at us all. She suddenly stormed around to my ironing board and was yelling in my face. She threw what I had been ironing on the floor then rushed back to her steam press while still yelling.

I stood there at my ironing board in complete shock. I had had a gutful of this slave-driving, child-abusing hellhole. I had had enough of them screaming bullshit. I screamed at her as I ran towards her, telling her that I was going to kill her as I ran around the long table to get her. She took off like a deer spooked by headlights in the middle of the night but still in flight from fear.

The whole place was in an uproar as other nuns working in the laundry ran toward me to stop me from getting to Mother Slave Driver.

I had lost my shit. It was me being the banshee now with threats that I meant from the depths of my soul. Tears of anger rolled down my face and I could not stop screaming that I was coming for her and she had better not ever turn her back on me.

I had no hope of getting to her that day. I was not a big kid and these nuns were taller and stronger than me by a long shot. I was thrown into a locked room close to Mother Superior's office and left there until I had calmed down. I had to wait for the arrival of Mother Superior whom we had rarely seen.

This was serious and as I pulled myself together, I tried to prepare myself for a trip to Hay. It is a really bad institution for wayward troublesome girls. Everyone was terrified of being sent to Mother Superior but when I was called into her office, she was very kind to me and spoke quietly to me.

Unlike the abuse I had become accustomed to since being in this place she calmly asked what had taken place and why I had lost my temper. I spoke to Mother Superior in a very, quite subdued voice. I told her straight out and also that I did not care if she sent me to Hay. I would be turning 18 soon and I had lived in her convent of hell long enough.

I spoke to very quietly and in a non-threatening way. I said that when I did turn 18 and was released from wherever I was, I was not going to keep my mouth shut. This convent was a prison for children being forced into child slave labour, harbouring hidden female sex abusers and nuns who mentally and verbally abused children daily.

Mother Superior told me she would investigate my accusations, and in the meantime, I would be deprived of some of my privileges as punishment. I left her office guided by another nun back to my dormitory. Francine greeted me wanting to know what had happened. I told her I did not want to discuss anything with anyone. Thanks, but no thanks.

I was made stand down at the foot of my bed as part of my punishment until my future was organised. I was not permitted to watch TV or mix with the other girls in my dormitory. I was also not permitted to talk to anyone unless it was the nun in charge of my group, Francine or Max.

I didn't give a shit really, as I had had a gutful of this child labour camp called a convent. However, I was concerned about being sent away to an institution with a reputation of being a hell on earth.

We went down to dinner. I was made to stand up at my table to eat my meal. I believe this was to stop me from speaking to the other girls. I didn't care as I believed I would be shipped out of the shitty hellhole in the next day or so.

I waited and I waited. Each day I had to stand up at meal times, stand at the foot of my bed unable to watch TV with the rest of the girls and was pulled out of bed to stand at the foot of my bed 30 minutes before anyone else woke up.

This treatment went on for a week and I was getting nervous. Max ignored me, thank goodness, and the other girls treated me like a hero for standing up to Mother Slave Driver. I whispered to them someone had to stand up and be counted and it was me. I also said that when I am taken from this place and the shit starts again stand up and fight back. Stop being a bunch of pussies If you want changes you have to fight for them. Regardless of the consequences.

Finally, I was called back to Mother Superior's office and as I was escorted there I thought, "Oh well, Hay here I come."

The nun who escorted me to the office knocked on the door and Mother Superior opened it and asked me to come in and take a seat. She sat behind her desk and looked straight into my eyes. She said, "Suzy, you still have three months left on your internment here." I looked at her waiting for the crunch.

The crunch that came was way off to what I was expecting, and a far cry from probably what I deserved. I listened intently at what was being said. I felt like I had been struck in my face by a bolt of lightning. I was speechless, did I hear right? Was this yet another game, being played out by people who lived their lives playing games with the vulnerable?

I had spent nearly 18 months in this God-forsaken place, tolerated being humiliated and embarrassed daily. Been a hair's breadth away from being used once again as another sex toy of a so-called pillar of society yet here I was being told I was to be released.

I sat in my chair across from that nun unable to speak. I was in utter shock. Mother Superior had organised all the legal paperwork for me to be released into a girls-only halfway house. They also had organised several job interviews for me once I had settled into my living accommodation.

I could not comprehend what was being said to me. Everything I had learned about being held accountable for my actions was being thrown out the door. "This was a mistake and I am being played," was my thought. I kept my mouth shut.

If I had I been in a government-run and -controlled institution, I know that after trying to assault an officer I would have been shipped out to Hay. This was Catholic and they were in control of what went down here. They were a law unto themselves; answerable to no one.

They needed to get rid of me before I became a bigger problem. I was astounded at what was happening. My departure was going to be the very next morning. I had lost control and tried to assault a nun. Max would have been next.

I thanked the universe that I was being moved away from this physically, emotionally and mentally destructive environment. I was being released back into society as a free young lady.

The icing on the cake was I also had accommodation to call my own. I didn't care what it looked like as long as I did not have to share a room with anyone else. I was also looking forward to being able to go back and see Pete. I missed him terribly and had been able to speak to him only on the phone since coming into the convent. He had been refused permission to visit me as he was not from blood family.

CHAPTER 8

Freedom at long last

THOSE younger years of my life toughened me up mentally; they gave me the fighting spirit and determination to never give in. I learned very early how to play an adult game in a child's world. I had to survive.

After my early release from the Catholic convent, I was settling into my lovely new accommodation and learning the ropes at a job I liked.

My job was as an usherette in the Palace Theatre in Pitt Street in the city, only a short bus ride from Chippendale where I was living in a female-only accommodation house.

My eyes started to wander. I was lonely, a nagging feeling like a toothache. I wasn't seeking sex – the sex that I knew from being groomed by Miss Redhead – I was just lonely.

A lot had changed in Kings Cross during my incarceration behind convent walls. The drug scene was rife. Big-time criminals had moved in and taken over. They were probably there all the time but I chose to be oblivious to it all back then. My main objective was to just survive, I learned that if one was involved in any shady activities, one was not safe, and there was the VERY high potential of one could just disappear.

Pete was planning to move away from the city with his new partner as he had had a gutful of the standover merchants, blatant drug dealers and the police corruption that was apparent all over Sydney.

On many occasions I listened to the ladies of the night complain about having to pay each of four Vice Squad cops $10 a night.

Then they complained more because the 21st Squad came on duty at midnight. This squad was formed as a flying squad for trouble shooting in any areas "requiring attention" throughout New South Wales. The girls had to disappear or face getting caught and fined. I started to spend less time in the Cross because I did not take drugs and had no intention of getting involved.

I was happy with my little life. I had offers of dates from patrons and staff where I worked but I had said no to everyone. However, I was attracted to two customers who came to the theatre. One was a young guy who gave off the air of being a bad boy. The other was a mature-age man who was very elegantly dressed and had the manners of a gentleman. I was very wary of both.

Another regular customer at the theatre kept asking me to go out with him. In truth, I found him attractive physically, but again I was very wary as I guessed he was in his mid-20s.

He rode a Harley motorcycle, but was not affiliated with a club. He was just a social rider. I had a great six months being his so-called girlfriend. What a disaster! We were out riding in the Royal National Park near Sutherland one Sunday and we collided head-on with a car.

He died and I ended up in hospital with a compound fracture of my right leg. I almost lost my leg. I was in a hospital bed with a steel cage around my leg. Steel rods protruded through my leg, with half the lower muscle missing.

What a nightmare, worst of all was his wife about whom I knew nothing came to visit me. I was just overwhelmed with sadness for her and his two children. We cried together. She did not deserve this. After she told me I was not the first affair my sympathy for him was nil. She was such a decent, lovely woman. I felt like a home wrecker. I wasn't. I had been conned again.

It took two skin grafts, another operation and a year of intense rehabilitation to recover physically from this encounter. Mentally it has never left my mind; I wore skin-coloured bandages from ankle to knee for years after. I then started wearing long pants. I still today dress in the same manner, ankle-length skirts and pants to hide the scars.

My trust of the opposite sex was severely damaged and I found myself questioning every act of kindness to me by men. I didn't hate men; I just didn't trust them.

My Catholic religion ruled homosexuality was a sin against God. I was not a lesbian. I just liked women. I felt safe in their company and the sex was amazing. I did not want to be involved in a relationship with a woman. In my world, a girl was supposed to get married and have children. That was expected of every good Catholic girl, but then again in the eyes of my parents and the law I was not a good girl.

By the time I had healed, I started to try to mend my relationship with my family. My mother came to Sydney to see me in hospital and my father told her not to bother coming home. She came anyway. After her visit and undergoing rehabilitation for my leg I started to hitchhike back to my family on weekend visits.

I desperately missed my little sister and mother, but knew I would never again live in that town. I had and still have such a close bond with my darling sister Aileen. I could not imagine my life without her.

CHAPTER 9

Fake marriage, then a real one

I HAD been hitchhiking back home to Narrabri for months. Not just to see my mother but my little sister who was my world. Aileen lived with me in the Cross for a while, but had gotten herself involved in a very toxic relationship. I was so worried about her and rightly so. he was a woman basher.

She moved back home to live with her new boyfriend and we still had contact by phone and when I came to visit Mum. We were country girls and Aileen was not happy living in Sydney; the pace was way too fast. We did have lots of sister time and danced our feet off every weekend clubbing.

I got a lift on one of these trips back home by a man 21 years older than me. I believe now that I was drawn to him because I had a father's fixation. I never had a real father; the one I had grown up to detest was an abuser and a drunk.

At least this man Kevin was single man, how could I go wrong? I thought.

Kevin and I ended up living and working in a small country pub, just out of Kingaroy in Queensland much to the disgust of my mother. He was too old for me she continually nagged me. We got married hippy style in our backyard. What I didn't know was this marriage was a farce, not legal in the eyes of the law.

I started to get very sick and didn't know why, I was young, fit, worked hard and ate well. I got so ill I ended up going to the doctor. I was pregnant.

My God, what did I know about having babies? It was 1972 and I was only 21. To make matters even more complicated I was told because I had rare blood and the baby's life was in danger. The medical fraternity called them blue babies back then and not too many of those babies survived.

I lived my life for the next seven months in hospital, sick as a dog. According to the doctor I was a month overdue and if I had not gone into labour soon, he was going to induce the birth. I had no idea what he was even talking about that alone understood what he was planning to do.

I spent five days in labour walking around the hospital near insane from the pain, smoking my head off. The nurses were too scared of me to stop me from smoking. I guess also being a small country hospital they felt sorry for me.

My doctor had a drug flown in from Brisbane. I never knew what it was, but two doses at 10.30am and my child was born at 10.45 am.

My son was born looking like a skinny little snake. He was transferred into a humidicrib and had tubes coming out of him everywhere.

My husband arrived drunk and was thrown out of the hospital. I was cleaned up and put into a ward and a minister arrived the next morning because my son was not expected to live. My son was baptised and I never left his side even though I was ordered back to bed.

He was born four pounds in weight and 21 inches long with red hair. The tiniest little skinny thing I had ever seen. His skin was peeling off in droves. Like me, he was a fighter and against all odds he survived.

I was unable to breastfeed him because he needed a special formula and he was also born with six toes. This was put down to morning sickness drugs I had taken that first month. I was glad I took them for only a month. Six weeks later I took my Greg home weighing six pounds.

While I was in the hospital all those months my husband had secured a job in a little town called Proston and we had a home organised by his boss for us to move into.

I was like a fish out of water, having a new baby who was so tiny. Although we had everything materially that we needed, Greg needed so much more care. He was a sick little baby and it took me months to get him settled and his feeding needs met.

I also knew I had to go and register his birth at the local courthouse so I would receive his birth certificate. I kept asking Kevin where our marriage certificate was and he kept evading the subject. In the end, I lied to Kevin saying I needed to get Greg's special formula. I planned to go to the courthouse and apply for a copy of our marriage certificate.

I needed that certificate to register Greg's birth. At the courthouse there was no copy because the marriage was a big fat lie. Kevin and his friends dreamed up the whole thing so I would stay with him. His friend's wife designed a so-called certificate to make it all look legitimate. In the eyes of the law my son Greg was illegitimate.

Regardless, he was sick and he needed me. I had to watch him every waking moment in case he vomited and the fluid went into his lungs. He had had multiple blood transfusions to disperse the antibodies in his blood but he was having problems keeping his milk formula down.

KEVIN was coming home late at night drunk or half drunk and at times bringing a mate home expecting me to cook for them both. I was looking at a clone of my father and I was one very unhappy young girl. I had made my bed but knew it was only a matter of time before I walked away.

This came sooner rather than later after he bashed me black and blue in one of his drunken moods. I was not prepared to listen to my screaming child scared of his father hitting me.

Kevin used to come home nearly every night drunk from the hotel and claimed the dinner I had cooked was spoiled. One night I had had a gutful of him so I wrapped his dinner in silver foil and grabbed his pillow and a blanket, walked down to the pub and marched into the public bar.

I put the plate of food on the bar and dropped the pillow and blanket at his feet. I told him, "You spend so much time here you may as well eat and sleep here." Of course, his mates laughed. He was furious at the embarrassment. I just didn't care anymore I had had enough; I was leaving this one too.

I waited until he went to work, rang Aileen, who drove up from Narrabri to get my son and me. Getting away from him was a logistical nightmare, but we did it.

On the way to my parents' home, we faced roaring floodwaters. We were stranded in a motel in Moree just an hour away from home with a sick baby. What a nightmare.

I had no idea of how I was going to cope in the future. Social Security offered me $46 a fortnight. Were they kidding? It cost almost that much for Greg's special formula.

After a visit from an officer from their office to Mum's home, I was accused of living with a man in the house. I told them to stick their money up their arses and made a formal complaint to their Sydney office.

A month later they said I had been accepted for that money, but I told them again to stick their money where the sun didn't shine. I got a job with my mother in the RSL Club's kitchen. My beautiful sister Aileen looked after Greg while I worked.

Gregory was 13 months old and already walking but was struggling to keep his balance due to his six toes. We had three appointments at the Children's Hospital in Brisbane. Luckily hitchhiking with a baby was easy.

I MET Robbie, a truck driver, while hitching to Brisbane. He was 16 years older than me, single and had never married. He was married to his job. Our friendship and relationship evolved over six months. He was a decent, hard-working man who adored my son and me.

Robbie supported me in every way and sat with me while my son was in theatre having his extra toes removed. Greg healed quickly and had perfect coordination now for his balance.

I was very honest with Robbie right down to the fact that I liked being with women. When he asked me to marry him.

He loved me so much he even agreed to let me seek women's company when I needed it.

We married in our home at Loganholme in Brisbane and all my family attended, even my father. Robbie loved my son like he was his own and treated me like a queen. I loved him dearly, but part of me was missing something.

I had a good man and the best husband. What more could I want? My son and I travelled in the big truck with him a couple of times a month and life was good, I had had several little affairs with women while I was married to Robbie.

One woman, Ashia, fell in love with me and wanted me to leave Robbie and she would leave her husband. I stayed and she left her husband. I refused to accept that I was a lesbian. She was a lovely woman with two daughters, but I just could not and did not want to leave my husband or even entertain the fact I was a homosexual.

I had close to 10 years of marriage to Robbie, he was a very good husband and I did love him. To be honest I also used him as an excuse to run from my suppressed feelings of being a lesbian. He was the outer protection of my hungry heart and physical longing for female company.

We had an understanding and I respected his love and protection, while I was not in love with him, I loved him anyway. He was a faithful, hardworking decent man, a man any woman would be proud to call her husband. My family also loved him and respected him. My only regret was I hurt him deeply when I left him. He forgave me for which I remain thankful.

During our time together, illness took me into a direction that would affect the rest of my life.

CHAPTER 10

Forced into a new life

ROBBIE ended up in hospital in Dubbo very, very, sick with adult measles and our truck had to be left on the side of the road. The company we were subcontracting for had to come to retrieve the trailer load of their goods. They did and I had to organise for our prime mover to be loaded onto the back trailer of another truck to be taken home to Brisbane.

The other little truck we owned with its driver was not making enough money to pay our bills, road tax, fuel tax, income tax and running costs. The list of bills was endless, so I had to get a job. Having been out of the workforce for years no one wanted to hire a woman with a child and no recent work experience.

Hell, I was a 23-year-old woman struggling to survive with a sick husband in debt up to our necks. I had applied for so many jobs and kept hitting a brick wall at every turn. So I took a job in a little massage place in Boundary Street, West End. My first step into the sex industry. Robbie wasn't happy about this and it caused many, many arguments. But bills had to be paid. I handed all my money to my lawyer every couple of days so he could pay and deal with all our creditors.

While it was not against the law to give a massage, it was against the law to provide a sexual service of any kind with that massage. I was appalled, angry and downright offended on that first raid I was involved in. The Queensland Vice squad sent an agent into the premises, that paid for a massage service but also asked for and received a hand relief. The cop paid in cash they had marked in advance, left the premises and straight away he and four other cops came racing up the stairs yelling and barging through our rooms.

My door flew open and I stared at two of the cops. I was fully dressed so knew I had broken no laws. The cops were yelling abuse at us all and demanding identification from everyone. The lady who had provided the sexual service to the cop was arrested and charged under the Prostitution Act.

She had charged the cop for the extra service. They took the marked dollars off her. It meant the cop got a free sexual service. I learned quickly that that was how they played the game. The worst part was we could do nothing about it.

It was disgusting and we were treated terribly, both verbally and roughly as they pushed the girls around the room, emptying handbags all over the floor, throwing any paperwork from the office desk on the floor and taking money from the cash drawer.

I REMEMBER my first day in this new job. I was 23, slim with long blonde hair. I was considered attractive. To be honest I was scared, not for my physical safety but for my ability to provide a professional sexual service to a stranger for whom I felt nothing but repulsion.

I gave the impression of a tough, take-no-shit-from-anyone and stand-alone fighter. In truth, walking into this tiny room to face my first client who was naked lying on a massage table was terrifying. The worst part was I knew nothing about how to provide the service he expected. I didn't have the guts to ask more experienced staff members.

I pretended to the boss I knew what I was doing when in fact I knew nothing. There was an art to providing such a service and I knew very little. The first 20 minutes were to be used to give the male client a massage; the last 10 minutes were supposed to provide a 'happy ending' if the clients asked for it and paid in advance.

While I massaged my first customer's body, I chatted about nothing in particular. When I asked him to turn over onto his back, I saw his erection. My face blushed, I could feel the heat in my cheeks. In a low voice, he asked for hand relief. I cleared my throat and quoted the price. He reached across to the side table for his wallet. His penis still erect, and he handed me the money. I tucked the notes into my little work purse and hid the purse in the back pocket of my jeans. I knew other staff wore sexy, revealing underwear on the job but I was not that blasé yet. This was my first job. The man paid me extra money to be topless.

I took off my white shirt and black bra. I felt exposed as I stood over the man while I jerked him off. As I massaged his penis with oil, I kept trying to think about what this money was going to be used for. We were in debt and I was standing in a low-lit room holding a stranger's erect penis.

I felt disgusted with myself. I don't know why because when younger I had done much worse to survive and had been taken sexual advantage of by people in authority. I could feel in my hands the man's excitement. His penis grew harder by the second. I wanted it to end and end it did. All up his chest and over his face. Vomit rose into my mouth.

No one had prepared me for this. How was I to know I was supposed to have a bunch of tissues in my free hand to catch this release of semen. "Sorry," I blubbered as I rushed out of the room, bare-breasted across reception out to the back toilet where I spewed my guts up. I was sick to the very bottom of my being.

I was embarrassed and disgusted with myself. Tears rolled down my face. "What the fuck have I got myself into this time?" was my only thought.

I pulled myself together and went back into my workroom to apologise to the client. The man was a decent guy and assured me it was okay. He even gave me a $50 tip.

He was my first client and he knew it. The other girls thought it was hilarious.

I quickly learned the art of giving a male client hand relief and the importance of having tissues on the job.

Money was money and I had to find a lot of it to stop creditors from putting us into bankruptcy. I chose to do this job and knew I darn well had to control my revulsion and learn the art of disassociation to be able to continue working in the industry.

CHAPTER 11

Police raids get violent

URING the next 12 months, I noticed a change in operations in this industry; supple at first. I knew the detective in charge of the Vice Squad, along with the rest of his crew due to all the raids on that business. I felt something had to change because what was happening was disgusting and immoral in my eyes.

But there was nothing we could do about anything. Every day I walked into that place I was at risk of being caught and getting a criminal record. It was scary shit. What was happening annoyed and disgusted me. One of the worst moral offences against women was being played out right before my eyes. There was nothing I could do about it. In fact, the women in the industry were being exploited by the very authorities employed to protect us.

The day I decided I was going to stay in this industry was on a day we had been raided. The brutality towards us was incomprehensible. The little parlour was destroyed and all our money was taken as so-called evidence. They would have all gone off to the pub and got pissed. No one was caught breaking the law. There were too many of us as witnesses for them to lie that one of us was caught with our pants down. They were very angry.

I decided that my family deserved a better life financially and all the women in this industry had to learn to fight back. I had no idea of how I was going to make a difference, but I was. Fuck these corrupt bastard coppers.

The owner of the business had gone into hiding and DeeDee – not her real name – was left in charge to run the business and control staff rosters. DeeDee, an Englishwoman in her 40s, was a very good businesswoman. She was genuine, honest and caring. She had respect not just for the struggling young working girls but also for the clients who came to the business.

We played dumb every time the cops came searching for the owner. We had no choice as we needed our jobs. Dee was a very attractive, sexy woman. Five feet seven inches tall, with a sexy English accent, with dark brown hair and a peaches and cream complexion. Her looks and personality captivated the cop in charge and a personal relationship developed.

What a story: a high-ranking Vice Squad detective having a secret affair with the manager of a rub-and-tug illegal prostitution business. How did I know? I allowed them to meet for their little interludes in my high-rise unit not far from the business.

He would just turn up unexpectedly at any time of the day or night when she was on shift. He never gave us a hard time. We just worked around him while she talked to him in the little kitchen.

Over many months the cops became very cordial due to 'arrangements' between the managers and owners and police. It made it easier for everyone concerned. These cops were supposed to be out chasing SP bookies and illegal brothel operators, but every weekend they were on our premises drinking grog and getting free sexual services from staff.

I had learned earlier in my life that asking no questions kept you safe –physically and financially. I kept my eyes and ears open and watched how everything associated with the sex industry worked, from the bookwork down to who was who in the police and who the male owners were.

I HAD taken this unit so I did not have to drive home to Loganholme where I lived with my husband. I also needed to protect him and my family from prying eyes of the police.

He was away for a week at a time once he came home from the Dubbo hospital. I was working up to 16 hours a day trying to get us out of our financial mess. My best friend lived and worked in a catering and events business in the Valley, so I had a full-time babysitter.

I was determined we were not going to lose our trucks or business regardless of Robbie's anger at me working. He wasn't aware of what I was doing really. It was a closed subject when he was home. I took time off from work, went home to him and played the role as his wife.

Because of the laws in Queensland, any man who was connected to a woman working in a massage parlour or an illegal brothel could be charged with living off immoral or illegal earnings. I made a point of keeping my own private life well away from the eyes of the law, I did not trust the police.

THINGS were changing in the industry. Everything seemed to be operating smoothly over the next 12 months until one of the big-time female owners went missing. She owned four or five large beautifully set-up premises around Brisbane. Police descended on every one of her business premises, questioning everyone trying to find her or at least information on what had happened to her.

She supposedly disappeared wearing many thousands of dollars' worth of jewellery and taking many, many thousands of dollars in cash. This made no sense to anyone in the industry. Something was off.

Gossip was rife such as her husband put her into the foundations of one of his building projects or she ran away with a wealthy client because she had had a gutful of marriage,

The bottom line was her body was never found, and the industry was starting to become very dangerous for workers and female owners. A female owner with a place in Mt Gravatt had her place go up in flames, and her daughter's little place at the Gabba was broken into and wrecked.

The male owners had started to flex their muscles, and the women in the industry were scared. We were all scared not just the female owners, this included the women who worked for them. The little business I worked for in West End looked like it wasn't going to survive because Dee Dee had, had enough and her family had to be put first and foremost. I knew I had to make a few very serious decisions about my own future.

I DECIDED to go out on my own. I rented a little house in a suburb away from mainstream Brisbane, staying away from the three major male players who had taken control of the city. All I wanted was to look after my family's finances and give my child a better life than I had. I had paid off all our debts and decided I would take this industry as far as I could.

The decision to stay in the industry wasn't easy. I agonised over it for weeks, but I conceded and came to the decision that I was no longer going to tolerate anyone taking anything from me ever again. If my husband did not like it or agree, then he too could pack his shit and fuck off. I did love and respect him, but I was tired of the financial struggle of paying everyone else and us ending up with nothing.

What I did do was to play it safe. I put everything in an assumed name – Jeannette Mac – which would make it difficult for the police or anyone else to track me down. People in the industry knew the place was mine but knowing it and proving it were two different things. I had security cameras installed and as this property was on a dead-end street the cameras recorded any cars or people coming down. One on the steel front door sent images to a monitor on my front reception desk.

This gave us the edge in case of police raids so I could warn any staff who may have been in an uncompromising position in the workrooms. One could not be charged with an offence if one was doing a massage being fully clothed or even scantily clothed. Each room was fitted with a separate alarm to warn the ladies that cops were at the front door and to get their clothes on urgently if needed. There was also an alarm in case the lady was put into a potential confrontation with a client

There wear three workrooms, each decorated differently: a black-and-white room, a beach room and a Marilyn Monroe room. We may not have had an opulent example of a brothel compared to the other male-owned and operated Brisbane premises but my place was warm and welcoming.

Overall, the little Ellen Street house was beautifully set up, spotlessly clean with top-quality linen and towels needed for the clients. I had a laundry downstairs so washing and drying could be done as it was needed and the main attraction was the security set-up for the safety of staff. The business may not have been the Hilton but it certainly was a pleasure for the clients to relax.

The business was new and the nearest massage-brothel business was at least 20 minutes' drive away. It was far enough away not to cause any retaliation from any of the male owners in town.

My business attracted a different type of lady. They were not the dolly bird type whose appearance portrayed them to be untouchable and demanded money for every slight touch. They were the more down-to-earth, natural, caring type of ladies and I liked that persona. Clients also like them and felt more comfortable.

AT THIS time a very smart, well-informed politician was saying everyone involved in the industry should be paying tax. Subsequently a Taxation Department team was set up to investigate who was or wasn't paying tax.

The guy put in charge of trying to set up a taxation agreement between owners and workers was a very decent man. He assured us the Taxation Department did not care about how we earned our money as long as we declared it and paid tax. I thought this was fair enough. This happens in all legitimate employment jobs so why not in this one. Tax is tax regardless of the nature of the job.

He kept files on us all and I become quite fond of him. I did not have a problem as I was declaring my earnings after expenses in my real name. He visited me several times over the coming months at my home and workplace trying to sort out what my monthly tax payments potentially would be. He was doing this project with all Queensland illegal brothel owners and operators. I do not doubt for one moment it was a very stressful time for him. Trying to organise owners that have spent their entire lives avoiding police and taxation would have been a nightmare.

Intimidation from some male owners towards him would have given him many sleepless nights. He arrived at my Brisbane home one after-noon unexpectedly. He had parked his car on the next street and he did not want to be seen collaborating with the so-called enemy.

I believe he knew we were all being set up for a fall by not just the Taxation Department but by the police. He indicated his car had been broken into and all his files stolen. I believe this did not happen and he was hell-bent on protecting us.

I knew this day was coming because this police force could not be trusted. A couple of months later he called me on a public phone telling me he had retired from the Taxation Department after more than 20 years and told me to stay safe.

SEVERAL inner-city places had been raided and my receptionist called me to say an officer from the Crime and Corruption Commission, an investigation team set up by the Queensland Government, had called to request an interview.

I was on high alert and became super observant. I decided I would double my security and not talk to anyone on the phone about work-related issues. I was also extra observant about being followed.

I drove across the other side of the city to call the CJC. Something just told me this was not the run-of-the-mill inquiry from a police department. This was a red flag for what was coming for everyone involved in the sex industry. I rang the number and asked to speak to the detective who left his card at my Ellen St business. I told the switchboard who I was and they put me through.

The first thing that cop said to me was, "Oh, you are calling from a public phone box." How right I was to be very careful. There were so many new IT inventions coming onto the market and I knew the police had access to them years before the general public became aware of them let alone be able to purchase them.

The detective requested I attend the Coronation Street building for an interview. I asked if there was a warrant waiting for me, and he said no. I declined to attend and, as they had no idea who I really was or what I looked like, I knew it was time to close my business as difficult as it was going to be.

Self-preservation kicked in and as soon as I got off the phone with that cop, I knew I was going to have to sit down and put into place a very careful plan of exit from my premises and business in Ellen Street. I had no choice; it was close down or face a potential jail sentence. Having all the security dismantled and the contents of the house removed was done over two nights during the early hours so as not to invite any unnecessary attention from the police, we worked right up to the last bed being removed.

All furniture and contents went into storage. Within a week I had vacated and shut down everything. I was very sad and annoyed that I had to close my illegal brothel, but knew it was in my best interest. It's not as if I hadn't recouped all my financial outlay in setting up the place. I had more than covered my financial outlay. It was still going to be difficult for me to walk away. Jeannette Mac disappeared into the woodwork.

I paid any outstanding bills in cash, had the phones and electricity accounts closed. This ensured when police investigated my operation it would be near impossible for them to trace me. I had to come up with a new plan to support my family.

CHAPTER 12

Trouble follows me to the Sunshine Coast

I DECIDED to move to the Sunshine Coast to establish another business venture. I figured it was far enough away from what was happening in Brisbane and if I was very careful, I would be okay.

I moved into a house not far from one of the main streets in Maroochydore and found a tiny office in Cotton Tree to run an outcall escort service only. This became another saga of playing cat-and-mouse games with the police. I felt confident that the police would find it more difficult to prove a prostitution crime from the operation of an escort agency. They could easily raid a brothel, catching ladies in the act of an offence.

The Nambour police station was in control of the whole of the Sunshine Coast and a certain senior sergeant Detective Bassil hated sex workers, massage therapists and anyone else that even remotely presented as a potential sex worker.

As there was no service being conducted from my small little office tucked away behind a doctor's surgery, he was finding it difficult to get any evidence against staff or me. He raided my office several times over a couple of months and got nothing. This infuriated him.

For the long hours I was planning on being open for business I needed at least to have comfortable surroundings. We needed coffee and to be able to eat when meal times came around and nap before calls came in. Overall, my little office was very comfortable.

WE DID not take bookings from private numbers. I considered anyone calling from a private number was either someone with something to hide or a police officer. I tried to take no chances on either a police bust, or a lady being attacked.

We were very careful on any outcalls we took over the phone as we knew police were recording our calls. We made sure that all conversations were non-committal on taking bookings. Adding to my caution, I had scouts drive around any motels or holiday units at least 40 minutes before a booking was confirmed. I treated every booking as a police set-up.

When we found the police were setting us up, our ladies just did not show up for the booking, then we shut down the office for the night. We went home knowing the Brisbane cops would leave town the next morning. This runaround game we played with police went on for months and months. I decided to rent a unit on the top floor of a security building in Bradman Avenue so I could monitor any unexpected arrivals.

Detective Bassil, not his full name, detested me and in one of our confrontations he threatened to set me up with drugs and "jail my ass". Uniform officers were pulling me up and threatening to book me for made-up driving offences, costing me time and money, and points on my driver's licence. I drove a new car and being booked for unsafe tires was bloody intimidation. Once I was pulled over for non-working taillights. The cop came right up close to my face and said, "I will not tolerate whores in my district."

I had my lawyer sit with me for three days in case Detective Bassil turned up and fulfilled his threats. In the end, I called a Member of Parliament in Brisbane to inform him of what was happening on the Sunshine Coast. I had had enough of the threats and intimidation.

This politician was on the police corruption bandwagon, so I knew he would listen to my complaints. The only trouble with making a stand of this nature was the person making the complaint was usually harassed even more, set up and either jailed or run out of business.

About a week later a police inspector based in Brisbane called and asked for an appointment to speak to me. I agreed but said he had to come to me.

"I will not put my safety at risk, you people have not yet found the missing madam that disappeared in Brisbane," I told him. I did not intend to be the next missing person involved in this business. I told him I wanted my own witness on hand during the interview so I wouldn't be the next Simone Vogel.

I also pointed out to him that the last time there was a so-called police corruption inquiry a witness under police protection died from a drug overdose in a house at Chermside, in Brisbane.

A day and time were arranged and I went out and bought myself a miniature voice-recording machine. I did not trust these people as far as I could throw them. The day of reckoning had arrived and at 10.30am two high-ranking officers not in uniform arrived.

After checking they were who they said they were I invited them in and sat them at my dining room table. My first words to them were, "Before we go any further, I am advising you that I will be recording all of our conversations." I still have the recording.

I told them this was because of the abuse and threats from Detective Bassil in Nambour. "The tape recording is my proof of what will be discussed today. If you have no issues, I will start by asking both your names, the date and time and I will state my own."

I placed the small tape recorder on my dining room table and pushed the record button. I stated my name and address where this recording was taking place. I repeated my complaint against the officer who threatened to set me up with drugs. Both officers stated their names, police rank and gave their police badge numbers also the Brisbane Police Command Headquarters as their address.

I also repeated the name of the Member of Parliament I reported the local detective to. I stated in no uncertain terms that I did not deal in drugs, stolen property or guns. I was merely a mother trying to support her kids and make a living.

Detective Bassil had charged me with using a false name, which was not an offence as long as that false name was not being used with intent to defraud. "Your detective was angry and had unfairly treated me with illegal threats, he was not happy that these charges had been dismissed in court," I told them.

The judge dismissed the charges because he could see for himself, that I was only using that false name to protect my two children from being bullied at school should my correct name have been put on the front page of the local newspaper.

"In my opinion, your detective in charge has overstepped his authority and if this continues, I will take my case to every newspaper in the country and *Current Affair*," I told them. "I pay my taxes and I have rights. He has made this personal and I refuse to live in fear of his vendetta against me."

The two officers listened to my complaint patiently and did not interrupt me as I spoke. They were both pleasant, although they did point out to me that if anyone breaking the law were caught, they would be charged for whatever the offence was. I agreed to this, but stated there is a big difference between being found guilty or pleading guilty if staff or I commit an offence, and then being charged with a trumped-up criminal offence by a police inspector who hates my very existence.

The officers and I concluded the interview after being in my unit for about two hours. They left after promising to investigate and call me to discuss their findings.

Within a month all harassment stopped and Detective Bassil was promoted back to an outlying suburb in Brisbane. This was just as well because the politician I contacted died suddenly during an operation in hospital.

There was fallout for me. Telecom, as Telstra was named back then, demanded a $1000 deposit to keep my phone lines connected. I had a good credit rating, always paid my bills with them in cash and could not understand why I was being singled out. According to the telecommunication laws, anyone using their phone lines to commit an offence could have their phone lines cut off.

I had no criminal offences recorded against me even though I was running an illegal escort agency and the only time I had been charged up to date was thrown out of court. I paid the $1000 bond to Telecom and shut my mouth. I really could not afford to lose my phones.

IT WAS time to expand, so I rented a little two-bedroom house in Maroochydore and set it up as a working house. It was in the same street as the police station so it was back to playing the same game as in Brisbane.

It was the middle of the 1980s and I had purchased a little home in Yandina for my husband and children, well away from what was happening in Maroochydore. In the eyes of the community and police I was living in a high-rise unit on Bradman Avenue, so I felt I had everything under control. I had opened a hairdressing-beauty salon in Mooloolaba, which was making money. Every afternoon I drove out to Yandina and took care of the kids.

I bathed them and cooked their dinner, put them into their pyjamas and bed then drove back to work or to my unit. My husband was working locally, driving a concrete delivery truck. I came back every morning to get the kids breakfast and get them to school. This arrangement was perfect for me and the kids were happy. If anything was to happen with the police my husband had his income and could not be charged with living off illegal earnings. And we appeared to be separated as husband and wife.

THE MASSAGE and escort service businesses were rolling along fine, with little police interference. However, one night I was sitting in my unit after returning from Yandina. I was tired, feeling physically worn out and not very well. I just had a feeling something was not right. My phone then rang off the hook. There had been a raid on my workhouse. Girls were stressed and crying, two of them had been arrested.

There had been a full-on police ambush and the ladies had been arrested and were at the Maroochydore police station, expecting to be released on self-bail shortly. The house was a mess although my phones had not been ripped out of the wall as it was as they had been on all other raids from police.

The cop in charge of the raid called, asking me to come down to the station for a chat. My first thought was to call my lawyer but on reflection, I decided to go with one of my drivers on my own because I was assured, I would not be arrested. Also, there would be a witness to me walking into the police station if I disappeared.

I made sure my driver took photos on his phone of me entering the police station. Call it paranoia but I was taking no chances. I was ushered into an interview room and a cop called Harry – not his real name –introduced himself as the Vice Squad inspector in charge.

The resident uniform police officers treated him like he was a god. I was determined not to allow these cops to walk all over me. He was treating me with respect and we chatted idly for about 15 minutes. He then told me, "Suzy, we have three ways of doing this and you can choose which way we will proceed.

"One: I can arrest you and all of your staff and tomorrow's news will be massive, naming you all and the fines will be massive.

"Two: I can go back out and close your business right now and advise Telecom of illegal activities being conducted via their phone lines and within days you will have no business.

"Three: We can come to an arrangement now which I have the authority to approve on the spot that once every six to seven weeks I will phone you and you can make arrangements with one lady to be charged with prostitution in any name she chooses. She will get a fine and you pay it. We the police will be seen as doing our jobs and you as the business owner can still operate unhindered."

He told me, "Listen, Suzy, you have had a bloody good run here. Yes, you have cost us money by the antics you have pulled in evading my operatives in trying to get convictions but it's time now to play the game as it will be a winner's game for all of us. It's your choice. Suzy, I will get you a coffee and when I come back, I expect your answer."

Five minutes later Harry came back to me with a coffee.

The choices were non-existent really. What choice did I have? I agreed to Harry's terms and after another 20 minutes of conversation, I was shown to the front door where my driver was parked outside to take me home.

Instead of going home I went down the street to my little workhouse where all my deeply upset staff were waiting. After assuring the two ladies that they walked back down to the workhouse after being released that names were being changed on their charges. Also their relief was that I would be paying their fines, everyone settled down.

I told them about Harry's arrangement and every six to seven weeks one lady would be arrested under an alias. No more verbal abuse, no more missing money, and no more cat-and-mouse games. We virtually now had the green light to operate, without fear of any police raids.

Everyone was happy with the arrangements; no more fear of their names being splattered all over the front page of the local newspaper. No more embarrassment of being caught naked or having sex with a client in their workroom and relieved that no more money would be going missing. The sex industry in Queensland as we all knew it had already changed but we up on the Sunshine Coast were now going to be falling in line with the rest of the state.

We were free of harassment from the Brisbane owners too. However, I had a very scary run-in with a man setting up at Noosa. He had set up a gym and was dealing in steroids and God only knows what else. I didn't want to know and neither did I care. After several calls and threats from him I told him straight that if he came near me, I would blow his fucking head off.

I WAS not scared of him or any of his thugs. Two days later local cops raided me, looking for a gun. They virtually took apart every place I had looking for this non-existent gun. I was fuming and rang Harry to complain about police harassment, which he had promised me would not happen. After many hours, Harry called me back and told me that the cops had a tip-off I had a gun.

"Harry, I told you when I first met you, I did not deal drugs, stolen property or guns." I then told him of my run-in with "Mr Strongman" from Noosa. I have no idea what happened after that but I had no more threats or calls from Mr Strongman. I believe Harry intervened which made me very happy. I am not and never have been a violent person, but have and always will stand up for myself regardless of who the person is. Besides that, there was no way I would have had a gun police could easily find.

I ALWAYS knew that doing a deal with the cops would have a downside. That downside ended up being visiting cops using my premises as their go-to place for free sex, grog, food and party play time.

Also, several local detectives believed they had the right to visit for coffee anytime they felt like it. Some ladies did not mind, as they liked the particular cops involved and they did favours for each other. Favours I did not want to know about. In hindsight, I should have taken more notice.

The business thrived for several years and as the police arrangements were acceptable. No more raids happened, money didn't go missing or there weren't any stand-over antics by other industry owners. I remember a couple of interstate detectives visiting and we all partied both at my work premises and on the beach late at night in a drunken free-for-all. I was there and no I was not naked like everyone else.

SOME strange little things were happening over a period of about three months. Remember I am very suspicious and am always watching my back and trusting very few people. Several times I felt I was being followed. I wrote down the car's their number plate and gave it to a cop called David, but nothing came of it. I put it down to my paranoia.

I had a Telecom guy I had become friends with. Over the years he would help me when anything went wrong with my phone connections. I had him on board for more than three years but was very, very careful that no one knew who he was.

There were many times he helped after raids when police ripped the phones out of the walls to try to stop my business from running. He was a decent, honourable man who asked for nothing and would accept nothing from me. He just had a soft spot for women who were trying to make a better life for themselves and their children. He also hated the way we were treated by the police. He was a widow and had no children. None of my staff knew of his existence. I was very fond of him; it was more like he was a father figure to me.

As far as I was concerned everything was running smoothly. The cops were happy, we were happy and every couple of months we copped our bust and I paid the fines. Local cops ignored the little brothel on the same street down the road. Everything was honky dory, yet something was not right or was it my paranoia once again?

My sense of needing to watch my back seemed to come to the fore on and off all the time. The Brisbane Vice Squad came to town every six or seven weeks after calling me to advise me I needed to get a staff member organised to sign on the dotted line. We were treated with respect and sat around my office drinking coffee while the paperwork was done.

They did their job and drove back to Brisbane after submitting the paperwork to the police station in Maroochydore. A week or two later the fine would come to my workhouse and I would pay it with a smile. Little did I know all the police visits my work premises were being filmed by the investigating sleuths attached to the inquiry into police corruption.

I detested being obligated to comply with this arrangement, but the cops were in charge of our very existence and there was nothing I could do about it. Different cops sent to do the job took great pleasure in exercising their authority over us all. Snide remarks, nasty comments towards myself and the lady who was signing for the coming fine were par for the course.

But something didn't add up. I became very aware of my surroundings, watching and noting mentally situations that were not normal in carrying out my everyday chores.

I looked for unusual activity around my workhouse and Maroochydore unit carpark. I checked always on cars that I felt were following me.

I wrote down number plates of cars I thought maybe following me and had my lawyer check who owned the cars. Most times these checks went nowhere, however there were times when my suspicion was dead on the money; they were unmarked cop cars.

LATE one Friday night I received a distressing call from the workhouse from a lady telling me that the cops had raided our premises. They ripped phones out of the wall, had taken all the money from the night's takings, dragged a girl around the lounge room by her hair. They had taken all the paperwork from my office desk, arrested two ladies and virtually made a mess of the house. The ladies were traumatised. How could this happen when there was a deal in place with the police?

I was furious. I got into my car and drove down to the house. The place was a total mess, with girls crying, phones destroyed and everything in the house a shambles. As it was very late at night there was not a lot I could do. However, I called Harry in Brisbane, who did not answer his phone. I rang the local cop I was used to dealing with and went off my brain at him. I will call him David, so an hour later David and his offsider drove their unmarked cop car into my premises and parked out back. As it was so very late instead of me calling and pulling my Telecom guy out of bed to come to fix my phones, I walked over to the public phone box outside my little workhouse and made an official complaint to Telecom.

Ripping phones out of the wall is an act of vandalism. I told Telecom this was a business and the reconnection and repair were urgent. I was assured by the faults department team member who answered my call that my lines would be fixed and working by 10am later on in the day.

I then walked back into the house to vent my anger and frustration to David and his offsider. I yelled and screamed like a banshee reminding the two cops that we had an arrangement and this bullshit raid was not part of it. I wondered what was coming next.

The ladies and I were attempting to clean up the mess the other cops had made. We all sat around drinking coffee and dissecting the event. Not one person in authority connected to the police had a clue why this had happened. This was one of the times I was so glad I didn't pick up the phone and call my friend in to fix my phones in the workhouse.

Little did I know the whole episode that night was being filmed by the CJC team of investigators gathering evidence for the Government's Police Corruption Inquiry. They even had the film of David and his offsider arriving and parking out the back of my premises at that hour of the night and entering the back door of my premises.

Harry rang me at 7am and assured me he knew nothing about this raid and did not sanction it. He warned me that I needed to be very, very careful as things were happening in Brisbane. Harry told me that in the next couple of days there would be a major public announcement. He also told me to keep my mouth shut if I was approached by any police investigators.

I closed my little workhouse for the night, feeling defeated. I was angry and very concerned over my future. It was like living in a reoccurring nightmare, always seemingly waiting for the next axe to fall. I drove back to my unit and sat quietly. I needed a clear head for my plans after what had happened last night on my work premises.

More to the point I needed to evaluate Harry's warnings about what may be coming for everyone in the sex industry. I did not fear for my safety, but I did fear for my family. I knew again I had to accumulate every dollar as quickly as I could. Moving operations and moving house was going to cost thousands. I surmised that I might have only six to eight weeks before I would have to shut up shop.

This opening and shutting my business ventures and moving from place to place was very exhausting. Besides I was the most contented I had been in many years and did not want to leave the Sunshine Coast. How could I rip my family away from here again?

Later in the morning my phones were reconnected and we all jumped in to make the workplace operational. We all agreed that whatever the future held we would work until we couldn't. The mood in the house was very unsettled.

We had to keep a close watch on what outside motel bookings we took and how we were going to handle a future potential police raid. We agreed that any lady going on an outside booking would drive herself but a driver would follow her to make sure she was safe and that there were no cops hanging around waiting to arrest her.

I think we all realised our police protection arrangement was coming to an end. None of us had any idea of what was just around the corner.

CHAPTER 13

Corruption inquiry shakes up Queensland

THE SHIT sure did hit the fan. There was going to be an official investigation into corruption in the Queensland police force. The name of the inquiry was going to be called the Fitzgerald Inquiry, headed by Tony Fitzgerald QC.

After cleaning up the workhouse left in a mess by the raiding cops I called Harry and local detectives. This resulted in nothing except that we were all walking on egg shells extremely worried about what was happening in Brisbane with the announcement of the inquiry.

The inquiry's reach stretched to my business pretty quickly. Fitzgerald Inquiry investigators contacted the owner of my building told him if he did not remove me from the house, he would be charged with assisting to run an illegal brothel.

Not in my wildest dreams did I think the owner of my little workhouse would be so freaked out. He planned to demolish the whole fucking building.

He was a well-known local businessman who did not want a scandal of any kind attached to his name. He told me he was pulling the bulldozers in and going to demolish the house. I had one month to vacate.

I knew I had to be very careful about everything I did and who I spoke to on the phone as I knew my phones were more than likely being tapped.

All contact with any cops was non-existent. However, I did keep in mind Harry's warning about talking to any investigators.

In the next few weeks, I worked the business nearly 24/7 accumulating every dollar I could knowing I was going to need the money. In fact, we worked right up to the night before the bulldozers were due to arrive the next day at 8am. The scene was hilarious. We were trying to get all the furniture out of the house and on a truck as they were preparing to pull it down with two bulldozers. The local newspaper reporter was taking pictures and doing a story on the brothel being demolished.

I smiled sadly as we drove away that morning, knowing the Sunshine Coast era was over. I needed to be serious about my future. I had so much to organise my head was spinning. I also had to come to arrangements with my husband about my children. I spent the next week paying all outstanding accounts and packing up my belongings.

I decided to move back to Brisbane. I was driving back and forth daily looking for a house to live in. I knew the coming Fitzgerald Inquiry was no joke. Corrupt police were not going to be able to get out of their web of filth this time around.

My Brisbane lawyer told me that the inquiry investigators were leaving no stones unturned. At the end of the day everyone involved would face the inquiry and more than likely be jailed as a result of the police corruption arrangements. What did the future hold for me and my family?

My argument would be that I was forced to do as I was told or the cops would have set me up on trumped-up charges and I would have been jailed anyway. I had no choice. It was play the game, or end up losing everything I had worked for all those years. I needed to go back to my trusty law book and research.

Official corruption charges were very serious and jail was a given for everyone involved in running or owning illegal brothels in Queensland. It didn't seem fair to me. I was a nobody, a mother just trying to live her life and give her family a better life. I was worried but knew I just did not have time to sit and feel sorry for myself.

I had to get my shit together and move forward. I had a plan and had read up on the laws that were in place and I figured I had a way around what was on the horizon. I have never been a quitter and I wasn't going start being one now. I had work to do and plans to implement.

IT WAS back to Brisbane AGAIN. I took a two-storey house in Brisbane near West End and set up the upstairs to live in and the downstairs flat for a lady to work out of. I left my husband living in our house in Yandina. By this time, I had entered into a lesbian relationship with a woman who worked for a security firm. I took my daughter Sandy to live with me as my son wanted to stay with my husband. Sandy was born in 1977 and was five years younger than Greg and had been a far easier birth.

By now all hell had broken out with the Police Corruption Inquiry. The first high-ranking cop to roll over was Queensland assistant police commissioner Graeme Parker, who proceeded to name the who was who in the zoo within the police ranks and criminal fraternity.

I also bought the house I had moved into and now had another mortgage to worry about. Moving into the house was not difficult, but it was tiring. I had to get everything set up as fast as I could and I needed to get my daughter enrolled in the local school.

The whole of Queensland – police and criminals – were shitting their pants including me, although at the time I thought I would be okay because I knew I did not pay the police any cash, unlike other big-time owners. Little did I know that my arrangements with Harry were still officially an act of corruption in Australia.

I knew my business and I would be named in the inquiry. The future was looking bleak however David, one of the detectives on the Sunshine Coast that Harry controlled, called me and asked me to come and speak to him. I told him I felt I was being followed but would try to organise something.

The next day I got on the back of a motorbike, wearing a full-face helmet, and my friend and I travelled up to Mapleton to meet David. I arrived up there pretty sure I had not been followed and we talked. I told him I would not lie for him under any circumstances and for him not to call me ever again because my phones were tapped and I was being followed.

I was convinced my phones were being monitored and my home bugged. It was so bad I never used the phone or talk about business at home. I would go for a walk around the block to talk. Even with my partner the only conversations at home were school, her security work or anything of a general nature.

This situation was extremely stressful. Our calls were taped, and our movements monitored to make sure we were not in collusion with anybody under investigation. My nerves were shot to pieces, and I was starting to feel the physical effects of the stress.

EARLY one morning I noticed a car that didn't belong in the street. I knew it was probably attached to the CJC or the Fitzgerald Inquiry investigators. The next morning that same car was back across the road and I told my partner it was the one from the day before.

She took a pen and paper marched over and confronted the driver. She made sure he saw her write down his front and back numberplates, screamed abuse at him, and came back into the house.

When he drove away, she phoned Woolloongabba police station, gave them the registration number and told the cops he was stalking us.

In the meantime, yet another car appeared in the street. I walked out and wrote down that car's numberplate. Within a few moments, the cop at the Woolloongabba station came back on the phone and asked if she was going through a divorce. She said no and he said the plate belonged to a private investigator. I knew then I was definitely being followed. My paranoia was justified. Then came the story of yet another cop rolling over. It was Harry. I was astounded.

Harry was incriminating every illegal brothel owner, SP bookie and all other corrupt police officers involved in the so-called police joke. That also included the Police Commissioner for Queensland Terry Lewis.

My mind was racing. Two major high-ranking police officers had rolled over and named every corrupt player from the very bottom of the food chain right up to the top.

Then a Member of Parliament was charged with corruption. Fucking hell this sure was getting serious.

Everybody involved would be forced to co-operate in the coming months with the Fitzgerald Inquiry investigators or go to jail. I was so emotionally drained and worried about how I was going to raise the funds for my legal defence. I was sick.

It seemed that nearly every time I ate anything or even looked like having a drink of alcohol, I would end up hugging the toilet vomiting my heart out and in shocking pain. This went on for weeks and weeks and I ended up in the Mater Hospital.

I HAD gallstones. They were treated and I went home, but they persisted. They decided to operate. After leaving the hospital after a consultation I was approached outside the hospital in the street by two investigators attached to the inquiry asking me to have a chat with them as they could help me. They flashed their IDs as if this would impress me. I told them to fuck off.

I again reminded them of a witness in a previous inquiry. She was under police protection, but died of a drug overdose. No way was I going to put my life in their hands, besides that I am not a dog, a police informant. I went home angry, sick and worried about having my gall bladder removed in a week.

After the operation no more horrific pain and after months of not being able to keep food down, I was back on track. But my stress levels were up and down and staying calm was very difficult.

The only income I had was rental income from the flat under my house and it barely paid our living expenses. Thank God my partner had a good job with a security company that paid the mortgage on the house we were living in and my estranged husband had his own income that paid for the mortgage on the Sunshine Coast. I felt like a little bird unable to fly because my wings were cut off.

The male brothel owners in and around Brisbane were being constantly raided and shut down. No matter how they reopened or under what guise, the police raids were relentless. Every owner of every illegal premises was being named and shamed by the inquiry and that included all females, myself included.

I had heard gossip that a couple of females had rolled over and one had gone into witness protection. This protection hadn't helped the woman who had died of an overdose. It was being mooted that another female owner had gone missing and was a victim of the people who were corrupt.

No matter who said what or promised what I was saying nothing to anyone about anything.

CHAPTER 14

The Fitzgerald Inquiry starts

THE POLICE inquiry had started and every day the court was packed as one by one criminals were ordered to appear before Tony Fitzgerald to answer questions about their activities. The inquiry prosecutor's questioning was brutal, no holds barred.

The newspapers every day were filled with the names of who's who in the criminal world. These court appearances generated so much public interest not just in Queensland but Australia wide. The owners of all Queensland brothels – male and female – were all served with subpoenas to appear.

I was very concerned not just for my safety but for that of my daughter going to school just up the road from where I lived. I was worried about my son and husband living back on the Sunshine Coast.

I was worried about being caught working from the flat under my house even though it was not illegal for one lady to work by herself on her own. The lady I had working was a mature English lady who lived out near Gatton and she stayed each week then went home to her husband.

The inquiry seemed to go on forever and each day more and more police corruption was being exposed. It was a feeding frenzy for the media. No one had ever thought anything would ever come to light because the corruption went to the very top of the food chain.

About a week before it was my time to appear before the inquiry I was contacted by the team from ABC TV and asked if I would be interested in taking part in a program on police corruption. I know I should have said no but after all the bullshit floating around the public arena, I felt I had to set the record straight. I went anyway but I wore a wig and dressed differently from normal and was very careful about what I said. I made no reference to what was going on in the court or to any particular person.

THE MORNING came for me to appear and again I wore a wig and got into court hours before the media showed up. I was a nervous wreck. I ran into several ladies who used to work for me. They apologised for signing statements. I replied it was not an issue as long as they had told the truth. I felt sorry for them and guilty that they had been dragged into this.

It was my fault for doing the deal with the cops in the first place. The staff members and the two cops from the Sunshine Coast were there and over the next few days, we all were put up on the stand. One after the other they all spilled their guts. The media had a field day. My stress levels were so high. I developed a rash all over one foot between trying to avoid the media taking pictures and filming for the night's TV news. It was a nightmare.

I spent all of one day on the stand. At one stage after vigorous questions from the leading investigator, I spat the dummy and yelled, "So I am going to be punished for the uncontrollable sexual urges of the police, am I? They said, 'jump'. I said, 'How high sir'. Sure enough, my words were printed in the Brisbane newspaper on the front page.

They had evidence of me going up the coast on the motorbike, had statements of the police party on the beach of visiting police we entertained and probably a lot more that would be presented at my own up-and-coming criminal court trial. The media lapped it all up.

On one hand, I was relieved all these corrupt police were being exposed but on the other hand I was fearful for the physical safety of my family. No way I was going to out corrupt cops as I had a family to support.

What kept coming into my mind was the death of a whistle blower in police protection. Also on my mind was the missing madam in the 1970s whose body, even until today, had never been found.

I stated under oath I never at any time paid the police cash. They cost me cash and sure enough, my words appeared in print in the newspapers the next day. Halfway through my questioning, they called a recess because they found out I had appeared on the ABC program on police corruption.

After looking at the film they decided I had broken no contempt of court laws. It was back on the stand. I went home each day from court exhausted mentally and physically. This was only the beginning because I knew that David and myself were going to be charged with official corruption.

The inquiry seemed to drag on forever but my days there were over and I knew I had to find a lot of money for my coming legal fees. I needed a lawyer and a barrister to represent me and the way the trials already in court were going the people being found guilty were facing a very long time behind bars.

ONE BY one my ex-staff members stood up in court and told the truth. I was angry and disgusted at their exposure. They were on the stand because David had been pressuring each of them for free sex and they felt they had to comply because they worked for me. They needed their jobs and they did not need him or his cop mates harassing them outside of work.

This is the problem with police on the take. Give them an inch and they will take a mile. They believed they were untouchable and they were at that time. They knew there was nothing we could do about it. Who were we going to call, the police? This was the way we were forced to live and operate, or we would have been put out of business and jailed.

Several times over the next few months my lawyer advised me to name corrupt police and go into witness protection. Each time I told him to tell them to fuck off I have a daughter to protect.

My lawyer told me to put my house up as collateral for the coming legal fees as they were climbing. Each time I declined and dropped a thousand here and there into his account as I earned it. I was determined to pay all amounts of money owing and at least pay up to 12 months' mortgage early before I went to jail. I worked my guts out to get the money to pay my legal fees, and in the end, I sold more than $40,000 worth of jewellery for $10,000 to pay the balance to the lawyer.

I was prepared to fight my charges. I believed I did not commit any criminal offence. I complied with what was demanded of me and my business by corrupt police. I had convinced myself I was innocent of official corruption.

How naïve was I? Totally yes! Anyway, my criminal trial was coming up as was a politician being held at the same time. I was so grateful he was getting all the headlines and my case was delegated to page two. The third day into my trial my partner took me to lunch. Unbeknown to me she had been talking to my lawyer who had been in negotiation with the prosecutor. She told me about their proposed, potential deal for me over lunch.

CHAPTER 15

My deal and prison time

MY CHARGES were owning and operating a bawdy house, a brothel in today's terms, and three charges of official corruption. However, if I stopped fighting them and pleaded guilty to the bawdy house charge and two charges of official corruption, they would drop the other corruption charge and would guarantee I would spend only six months in prison.

The alternative was all charges would stand and I would likely to be found guilty of all charges and the sentence would be up to 10 years with a minimum of five years. To add insult to injury, my trial probably would go on another couple of weeks with legal fees far beyond what I had saved to pay my lawyers. The bill would be so high I would lose my house and my family would be destitute.

I remember sitting at the restaurant table with my partner with tears running down my face. I felt destroyed inside. I had been given the afternoon off after negotiations between my lawyer and the prosecution to think about the deal. What was there to think about? Once again, I had little or no choice. My mind was racing, trying to figure out how I was going to find a way out of all this mess.

What choice was left for me? Fucking none. I did think about it and I was angry. I felt defeated, however if I were going to comply it would be on my terms. I needed more money, so I said I would take the deal on one condition. I needed six weeks to earn the extra money to pay up seven months on my mortgage, cash to support my daughter and to pay the bills on hand. Later that afternoon I called my lawyer and stated my terms.

He called me back around 5pm and said they accepted my terms, but gave me only five weeks before sentencing, not six weeks. How fucking generous. Thanks, Mr Prosecutor. I took only that night off to rest my mind and gather my physical strength, I knew I was going to have to work my arse off to earn all the funds I needed.

The next morning, I did not have to appear in court to plead guilty to my agreed charges. My lawyer did it for me and the prosecutor set the date five weeks later for sentencing. All negotiations had been done, so I knew what my future held for me over the coming months. In the next five weeks, I worked day and night to get the money I needed and prepared my daughter for my being away.

I felt relieved that it was all going to be over soon, my crimes came from having no option but to co-operate with corrupt police. I had no choice, cooperate or jail is no choice.

I was even cheeky enough to phone Boggo Road Women's Prison and tell them I was coming and get a list of what I was permitted to bring in with me. The officer who took my call thought I was playing silly buggers, but I assured her I was coming and I even gave her my name.

The bottom line was I owed my legal team nothing and I had all the funds I needed to keep my household running. My bag was packed to take into court on the day I was being sentenced and I had cash to pay for the little things at the jail's fortnightly buy-up.

My day of reckoning, October 3, 1990, had come and I headed off to court to be sentenced, luckily for me again the politician Don Lane was facing a sentence for corruption and the front-page headline the next day was about him. I made page two.

I was 39 when I received a three-year jail sentence – one year for the bawdy house offence to be served concurrently with the two years for the official corruption charge – with a six-month parole if I behaved. The powers-that-be kept their end of the deal, so I was content with the outcome, and I would be okay because I knew how to play their game.

I spent the afternoon in the cells under the courthouse and waited to be transferred to the women's prison at Boggo Road. What a day what a year. I was bloody exhausted both physically and mentally. Roll on the prison. I sat in my cell on the hard bench and looked around me wondering if this is the type of cell I will be in when I get into the women's prison.

My cell down under the courthouse consisted of two benches, a toilet and a hand basin, and it was very cold. I could hear people screaming obscenities at the officers in charge. It was not a consoling feeling I can assure you. The officers came to collect me about 4pm and loaded me and two other women into the prison van.

I was glad I was taken from the cells to the van without being photographed. It was bad enough knowing that the media would have me featured in their papers the next day. Knowing there were going to be no pictures of me on the front page was a relief. The photographers were too busy trying to film Don Lane. In one way I felt relief that all this public attention was coming to an end. On the other hand, I knew I had to be very careful about getting involved in any prison politics.

CHAPTER 16

My prison time begins

AS THE van pulled into the prison complex I remember my feelings were very surreal. It was like I was in a wide-awake dream. But looking up at the top of the walls and the armed guards in their little towers, and when the huge prison gates closed behind us, made it all so real.

As they opened the van's doors, I did not feel scared for my safety. I just felt overwhelmed by my predicament. I looked up and saw a big perplex bubble with two ladies looking at our arrival, watching us closely. This bubble was attached to the prison officers' mess where these women worked. Working in this section, I was later to learn, was a privilege and held a few little perks such as being able to eat the same food as the officers at mealtimes.

The admission process was thorough, with many, questions relating to our health issues and if needed our medications. The body search was necessary but somewhat confronting. "Please remove all your clothing, ladies," said a female prison officer to the three of us just brought in from court. "Hands up, ladies, feet apart, and please prepare to be bodily searched. If you have anything contraband now is the time to disclose it and hand it over."

The female officer ran her hands under my exposed breasts I was told to bend over and I had to part my bum cheeks. I was asked to cough as seemingly this would dislodge anything that may have been inserted into my vagina.

I couldn't understand why anyone would risk trying to take drugs or contraband into a prison, but people do, and the prison officers have a job to do. Nevertheless, this procedure was confronting and embarrassing to me. Despite being in the business of selling sex in my private life I was a bloody prude.

You just cannot even begin to process the experience of being marched through prison and the sounds of huge steel gates being shut behind you as you were taken from one section of the prison to the other.

The sounds of the steel doors being unlocked and closed behind me made me feel like a caged animal, waiting for my executioner. My reputation had preceded me due to all the publicity and one of the officers had remembered my call to the prison weeks before to ask what I was permitted to bring in. I made light of the fact I was prepared for my incarceration that day.

We were made to shower and were given a set of clothes consisting of jeans, a white t-shirt, prison sox and prison sneakers. Our underwear was permitted after being carefully searched by officers. We could have our shoes but only after our family posted them in and they were searched by screening at head office. The whole admission process took more than an hour and we were then escorted into a section of the prison for remanded, newly convicted or high-risk violent prisoners.

We were going to be assessed for transfer into the mainstream prison sections in the next few days or weeks. My observation was this prison system was finely tuned and every moment of every waking day every prisoner's time was planned and adhered to by officers and prisoners.

THE THREE of us who were sentenced that day were marched to our designated cells. I ended up in a cell by myself. My mind was in overdrive as I looked around me. Was this going to be my home for the next six months? So many questions with no answers as yet.

It was very overwhelming emotionally but at the same time, but I was relieved the consistent stress of trying to deal with the court was finely over and my obligation to repay society for my unlawful behaviour was about to start. About 30 minutes later the prison officer came back and banged on my door and telling me to step back from the door as she opened it. The other two ladies and I were taken to the prisoners' recreation room for our nightly meal.

The room had enough tables and chairs to seat up to 20 women who were here in the remand section/high security. This section also housed women that were violent and could not be put in other sections of the prison. For example, there was one section holding women who were pregnant or had given birth to their babies in jail.

My block also contained women who had to be protected for one reason or another. Further up the block was another general section for low-security prisoners and then there was the section containing two rows of mobile home-type units. These units were designated for women on the verge of being released on parole or prisoners waiting to be transferred over to the outside halfway house to serve the last few months of their sentence.

I was carefully trying to assess every other woman within my section. All these different personalities confined to one large room were bound to create a clash of opinions and behaviour. Often anger between prisoners causes retaliation between unstable women, which in the past has caused death in this prison. By the time I went back to my cell that first night I knew who was who in my zoo.

That night I reflected on not just that day's events but the previous 12 months of upheaval. I do not ever remember questioning my choices and decision to be involved in the sex industry. I drifted off into unsettled sleep.

There was a routine we all had to adhere to every night and again every morning. The morning routine was simple, officers woke us up by banging on the doors, and we were given 20 to 30 minutes to get up, showered, dressed and make our beds.

The next few days other prisoners asked me all sorts of questions. Was it all true what they have jailed you for? Who were the corrupt cops? They asked me if I knew various corrupt cops. Some of these women told stories of shocking abusive treatment by some of these corrupt police. So many vulnerable women were taken advantage of by some members of the police force during those years of their 'dictatorship'. Women from all walks of life, non-sex workers, shoplifters; mainly women who were guilty of what they had been charged with. However, several had been set up for non-compliance with police demands.

There was nothing anyone could do to get away from these corrupt cops. If you chose to fight them the only winners were the defence lawyers and in my opinion some of them were suspect.

I WAS very careful with my answers because I didn't know if any of my fellow prisoners had flapping traps and would pass on any information to officers. I kept my mouth shut, which landed me in prison, darned if I was going to open it now.

They asked me if I was going to open another place when I was released and if they could come to work for me if and when I did. Some were just curious to know what it was like working in a brothel or working as an escort. What could I say? Life is great working as a prostitute or owning a brothel? I always told them you had to make choices according to your circumstances. You had to think very carefully about the long-term effects, both physically and mentally, before stepping into the darker side of life.

It adds stress to your life being involved in the sex industry. Having to have sex or complying with devious sexual requests by clients regardless of being financially compensated has adverse effects on women in the industry.

THE FOLLOWING week all new prisoners were interviewed by a couple of senior officers and assessed on previous criminal records, behaviour patterns and a mental health check. We were also seen by a visiting doctor. These results were then scripted for any medications required and sent to the clinical nurse on staff. The routine prescribed drug dispensed to prisoners was done at the special window of what the prisoners called the legal drug shop. The women had to line up and be called by name to the shatterproof, glass-enclosed secure room. The nurse then handed out what medication was prescribed for that prisoner and she had to take her medication with a glass of water in front of the nurse. This was supervised by a prison officer who checked the prisoner's mouth to make sure she had swallowed her medication.

All the new intake prisoners were interviewed separately and questioned on our work experience and any job qualifications in the outside. We were then assigned to the section of the prison where we would be spending our sentence after being assessed as low, high or medium risks.

These assessments determined our jobs in the prison. I was assessed as low risk, non-violent and a reasonably compliant prisoner. I was astounded to be told I would be moved up to what was considered a very privileged section of the prison. I was going to be sleeping in my caravan-type donga, much like the miners stay in while working in the mines.

I was assigned a job in the officers' mess to help cook, serve and clean up after meal times for the officers. My kitchen experience had come from my mother who was a chef. I worked for her for six months at our hometown RSL club. At least L knew a little about preparing food and serving it properly. I had a key, which I wore on a shoelace around my neck, to come and go out of my living accommodation. None of this made sense to me. The Government had spent many, many thousands of dollars of public money to gather enough evidence against me to put in prison.

Here I was in prison being given privileges way beyond my understanding. Now I did feel like a political prisoner. It's like suddenly realising heads had to roll and mine was one of them.

THE NEXT morning, I moved my possessions up to my little donga. My caravan was very comfortable and gave me privacy. It was a relief to be out of maximum security even if it were just one day.

There was one large donga where we could prepare our food and have tea, coffee and just hang out if we had spare time. There was also a shower and toilet block we could use. We were all held responsible for cleaning

The other five women there with me were trusted inmates who were either waiting for transfer to a halfway house or waiting for parole.

Several of them had been in prison for many years on various serious charges including murder.

Our mornings started with a shower, dressing for work and having breakfast together in our kitchen. Then we were escorted to our prospective workplaces. Mine was the officers' mess, which meant I started work early because officers had to have breakfast before they started their day shifts. Four of us worked in the kitchen to prepare food not just for the officers but for all the women in the prison.

The senior female prisoner in the officers' mess kitchen had been working there for quite a few years and was a very good cook. She was in the middle of completing her chef's degree, thanks to the Prison Education Department for prisoners.

She was a lovely woman. I found it difficult to believe she had murdered her partner and attempted to dispose of his body. He was a wealthy Gold Coast businessman. He had been physically abusing her for years and one day she just snapped.

AS USUAL I found myself getting involved when I see injustice towards vulnerable people. I don't know why; I just cannot stop myself. In prison it was no different.

The first instance was on my second day in Boggo Road. There was a delay in getting medical assistance to a long-term prisoner who had cut her wrists and was sitting in the toilet draining her blood into a plastic container and drinking her blood. The sight was horrendous. She had been jailed for the murder of her partner. In prison she stabbed two inmates with a meat fork. One died and the other woman was seriously injured, which was why she was still in maximum security.

Regardless of anyone's crime or mental instability, I have always believed everyone has the right to receive urgent medical assistance. I understand trying to control a violent, unstable person is difficult, but to delay or deny medical assistance is unacceptable.

I voiced my unwanted opinion loudly.

By the time the ambulance arrived we were all in lockdown in our cells and she was screaming obscenities at the prison guards. The woman was sedated and her wounds stitched up and bandaged. She stayed in the locked ward of the Princess Alexandra Hospital overnight and returned the next morning.

The second issue I found myself involved in was the inaction of the prison hierarchy towards a woman who informed intake prison officers that she was on the contraceptive pill for medical reasons. Why would a woman need the pill in a women's prison? The prison governor and board decided that no female prisoner needed to be taking the pill.

In a matter of weeks, this woman started to haemorrhage. It was horrific. We desperately tried to stop her bleeding. We told the officers on a shift of her situation and she needed a doctor but to no avail.

I want you to imagine a woman lying in bed, unable to get dressed because blood was flowing like a river from between her legs. We kept packing her up with prison-issue towels and it seemed as fast as we packed her up, we were having to take the blood-soaked towels to be washed.

We cried with her and I promised her I would get this draconian rule changed either within the prison system or by media exposure.

By day three, this woman, who was in her 40s, was still bleeding heavily and was starting to go downhill. She was as white as a ghost, sleeping all the time and too tired to even get off the bed to go to the toilet.

That was it as far as I was concerned. I marched up to the office and requested to speak to the head officer in charge for this shift. I told her if this woman died from blood loss, I would be the first one giving evidence at a coronial inquest into her death and I would name everyone I requested help from over that three-day period.

This situation was inhumane, illegal and absolutely unacceptable. I was very angry and upset that there was a woman potentially dying from blood loss and the prison authorities were dragging the chain.

My little tantrum got results and within the hour an ambulance arrived to take her to the hospital. Two paramedics wheeled the trolley through the gates to our section of the women's prison. We all gathered and clapped our hands loudly as they came up the walkway, much to the annoyance of the officers.

The paramedics took her vital statistics, hooked up a drip into her arm and gently lifted this ghostly white body onto the sliding board. Not white as in skin of white women but white as in her complexion and then put her onto the ambulance trolley.

The lady was given a medical curette, blood transfusion and a three-day stay in hospital then returned to prison. After she returned from hospital, she was given permission to go on the pill she needed to stop any further health issues. A win for prisoners' rights and welfare was a win anyway, you looked at it.

The third confrontation I had with the prison authorities was over our rights to see our own private doctors should we have any medical issues. This was not workable for Boggo Road women's prisoners. However, I did have a win for the halfway house ladies later. I believed we had the right to go to our own doctors, especially if we could pay for our visits to an outside doctor of our choice.

WHILE I respected every officer in this prison there were a couple I truly disliked and felt were cruel. I understand officers must be tough, physically and mentally, to do their job properly. There is a very big difference between being tough and being downright cruel. Taking pleasure from humiliating and degrading prisoners is abhorrent and acceptable.

Some of these women prisoners had nothing to lose as they were incarcerated for a long term for violent crimes. Altercations with other inmates meant nothing to them except perhaps a day or two in lock-down. Treatment for mental health issues 20-plus years ago was virtually non-existent in the prison system. Uncontrollable, violent behaviour was treated with sedation.

I was shocked at the number of women being treated for depression and mental health issues in prison. I understood this because being locked away in this environment for any great length of time would send any normal human being crazy or cause major depression. The women had to be protected from themselves and the officers had to be able to have some sort of control to be able to protect themselves from physical harm.

I just wanted to do my job, serve my time and go home to my family. I had no intentions of causing any problems. But I have that very annoying habit of not being able to keep my mouth shut if I see or hear things that did not sit right on issues of women's rights. I made mental notes every day.

CHAPTER 17

Stunned by early release

EIGHT weeks into my sentence I was preparing to go to work in the kitchen of the officers' mess. Our day shift officer knocked on my door and told me I was required to attend the governor's office before work.

I thought what now? Had I stepped out of line somewhere? Broken any rules? I couldn't recall doing anything I shouldn't have done. I gulped down my cup of tea and hurried up to the Governor's office.

"Take a seat, Suzy." No one called me Suzy except my mother or someone in authority when I had stepped out of line. This was going to be serious. Here we go again.

How wrong was I. She told me the prison authorities had decided that as I was a low-security prisoner and had a good work ethic on top of my good behaviour.

The board had decided that I would be transferred into a halfway house for female prisoners soon to prepare for integration into the community.

I sat on my chair gobsmacked. Instinctively I asked why?

"Well, Suzy, the judge set your release on parole at six months. You have been here for eight or so weeks and we believe you are ready to move forward to prepare you for release."

I couldn't believe my ears. I felt something was very smelly. Nothing was adding up, I had to think about this and stood up saying I had to get to work as I was needed in the kitchen.

I promised I would drop back in on my break between lunch and dinner and left the office. I wasn't feeling calm in any shape or form. My mind was racing. Were they trying to get rid of me because I knew too much? Were the authorities concerned I would find out other secrets being hidden? Was my flapping trap becoming an issue? Maybe it was my obsessive paranoia kicking in again. Nothing was making sense.

Who the hell goes to prison after being convicted on serious criminal charges only to be told eight weeks of a transfer to a very low-security house. This was unbelievable. I was excited but cautious.

I was being offered part freedom. I didn't know how to feel about the thousands of dollars it cost me for my own legal defence. I had left my 12-year-old daughter without a mother and couldn't have contact with my son or visits from my ex-husband. Nothing made sense.

I dropped back into the office on my back to my section of the prison to speak to the officer in charge. I asked when this was going to happen and when could I call my home to speak to my family. She said my transfer would take place within the week and I needed to give my home address to the office for the officer in charge of the halfway house. If agreed I could stay in my own home on weekends away from the halfway house. Unbelievable.

I phoned my partner at home and told her what was happening. Tears of excitement flowed at both ends of the call. My daughter came to the phone and she broke down in tears too. I told my partner the house would be inspected to make sure it was suitable for my weekend visits.

The following week seemed to fly by. The day before my transfer I said goodbye to my workmates in the officers' mess and the other prisoners I had become acquainted with over the last nine weeks.

I felt a little sad for the ladies being left behind especially for the few suffering from mental health issues. Vulnerable ladies, girls who were unable to stand up for themselves. I hoped another big mouth fighter for women's rights would come in and take back up their cause.

THE DAY of my release I was packed, dressed and ready to go, sitting in a waiting room. An officer in plain clothes came into the room and asked me to check the list on her clipboard and to sign it. I was given a plastic bag of my jewellery. I don't know why I thought I was going to be taken away in a police wagon. The officer escorted me to a sedan was waiting for us to leave the prison complex. An officer called Ronda (not her real name) drove out of Boggo Road Woman's Prison and pulled out into traffic.

She worked permanently at the halfway house and told me what was expected of me; a rundown of the rules and regulations. Nothing new here was my thought in those moments, I know how to play this game, but nevertheless I had no intentions of rocking any boats.

The house was in a suburb called Albion on the northside of Brisbane, we pulled into the driveway. I was surprised at the lovely gardens, trees and outdoor furniture. Another officer greeted us and showed me into her office for my induction into the house. I will call this officer Julie, not her real name, as this must be protected for privacy.

The main two rules were no drugs and no alcohol. Breaking these rules meant instant removal back to Boggo Road Prison. I had no problem with these rules as I did not take drugs and I rarely drank alcohol. The rest of the rules were basic really.

We were responsible for our own room and shared the cleaning and cooking. After I settled in, I went downstairs. Two of my fellow prisoners were in the kitchen making lunch. There were only the two officers and us. Three other ladies were out at work and wouldn't get back here until around 5.30pm. We introduced ourselves and had lunch. Julie and Ronda sat with us and we all chatted idly about nothing.

The property was very secure. It had high fences completely around it, security cameras on all outside doors and an alarm system on the doors should they be opened from the outside at night. There were duress alarms in the girls' lounge and in the office.

I was quite overwhelmed at being half-free. It was both amazing and unnerving.

FIVE permanent prison officers were attached to this property working in shifts. We had a public phone in the corner of the lounge room, away from the main relaxing space and we could call whom we wanted to if we had the funds.

We could call who we wanted, but we had to report to the officer in charge on the shift who wrote down the name of the lady making the call, the date and time of day it was. The called number had to have been recorded earlier.

Our time was supposed to be spent applying for work. The parole department was always looking for jobs for us and often had interviews lined up for us with prospective employers. It was easier for ladies to apply for employment with sympathetic employers. I guess I was lucky really because I remained idle for only a few days. I had an interview lined up for me at a place that looked after abused children and this organisation also supervised the treatment of both children and their parents.

Officer Julie was going to drive me to my interview to the Child Protection Centre on Thursday, just days after I had arrived. At 9.30am Julie and I were sitting outside the office of the manageress in charge of this organisation.

I was nervous but excited at the prospect of having a job and mixing with people in the real world. My name was called, I glanced up at the woman who opened the door and smiled. She was very classy, a well-educated woman. There was no mistake about who was in charge of this organisation. I walked over to her office and she ushered me in and closed the door behind me after telling me to take a seat, she then positioned herself behind her desk in front of me and introduced herself.

"My name is Miss Reynolds. You can call me Sharron when you come into my office but you must address me by my title out in public or within the compounds of this complex. I hope this will be acceptable to you, Suzy."

My interview proceeded with her asking me about my background and my marital status, children I had and past work experience in any fields of employment. "How do I answer these questions?" I remember thinking. I was very honest and upfront with her and I think she was intrigued. I really was honest with her and shared some of my own abusive childhood incidences with her.

I told her I understood how these children felt and the fear and uncertainty of being with adults who were supposed to have loving intentions towards them.

My interview lasted for well over an hour and as we were talking, she busily wrote everything down, making notes and ticking boxes here and there. She said to me, "Suzy, I will finish my paperwork and I will advise your supervisor as soon as possible my decision on your possible employment with us. I do have two other interviews today; however we do expect this to be sorted by tomorrow. Thank you for coming today and I extend my appreciation for your patience."

Sharron opened to door for me and I addressed her as Miss Reynolds, thanking her in a voice loud enough for officer Julie to hear. Driving back to Albion officer Julie asked me how I thought my interview went. I told her I was honest about my background but felt I pulled it off. I told her she would probably get an answer by tomorrow as the organisation needed someone very soon.

Here I was, halfway to freedom and out looking for a real job in the real world. I wasn't pinning my hopes on this job, but the fact I was in the position to be looking for a job was very encouraging.

The prison authorities had inspected my home that week and had interviewed my partner. I knew the officers visiting my home would be happy with what they found.

BY 5.30pm that day I had heard nothing about my job interview and I felt a little disheartened. Who would want to hire a woman who had spent years being a madam in the sex industry, was incarcerated for owning a brothel and even worse was in jail for official corruption?

Seriously very few employers in their right minds would even entertain taking on such a person in their business, would you?

At 9.30am the next morning Lorraine an officer I had not met before, called me into her office. I got the job. I was so excited I near jumped over the desk and hugged her I couldn't believe it.

I would be starting work at 9am on Monday at the centre. I had to get there by myself by train and report to Miss Reynolds' office. The halfway house was going to supply me with a weekly train ticket and I would be expected to take my own lunch to work.

I was just elated at this news, not just because I got the job, but also because it would give me something worthwhile to occupy my mind and physical being. Then officer Lorraine told me that I could call my partner and ask her to pick me up at 5pm to go home for the weekend. I felt like I had won lotto. I was so overwhelmed and excited.

I called my partner and everything was arranged for me to be picked up later that day. Officer Lorraine called me back into her office and told me I was not permitted to leave my home under any circumstances.

My attendance in my home would be checked by security officers attached to the prison department. These checks would be done at any time of the day or night when I least expected it and I was not permitted to have any alcohol and or drugs. Should I break any rules I would be taken from my home on the spot and be taken straight back to Boggo Road.

My partner arrived on time and I climbed into the car for my trip home. I was just so excited to be finely able to relax in my own environment with the people I loved especially my daughter Sandra.

AS WE DROVE across the city to my home at Highgate Hill I looked around at the passing traffic and city lights. You do not really understand or appreciate the world around you until you lose your freedom. The traffic being peak hour was a pain in the butt, however, I still soaked up the sounds and smiled at the frustration of what other drivers must have been feeling. I was just beaming with happiness. As we pulled into my street, I could feel my heart beating faster, my excitement screaming through every fibre of my being.

At home my daughter ran screaming with delight down the back stairs crying tears of joy. We hugged each other tightly and just cried; up the back stairs, we went into my kitchen for a cup of coffee and a long night of conversation.

Sitting around the kitchen table was my partner, my beautiful daughter and Nellie.

At that time in my life, I believe Nellie was 80 years old and she considered me as being the daughter she never had. I will talk about Nellie in detail later. Right now, I was relishing my freedom in my own home, away from jail and the halfway house. Nellie took herself off to bed around 10.30pm and we night owls sat up chatting until the wee hours of the morning.

I remember waking up to a banging on the front door, bang, bang, bang. Who is this? It was 6am. I flew out of bed running to the front door to see a man outside holding a clipboard.

He introduced himself as a parole officer investigator. I opened the door after he showed me his identification proof and invited him in. He asked to be taken out into the kitchen. How strange were my thoughts at the time, but this was normal I found out later, the security check was not just to make sure I was in my home. It was to check that we had not had a drunken party last night. Rules were rules. No drinking or taking drugs while on home release. I was still a prisoner.

I cherished my next two days of freedom with my little family. We played board games, ate great food and reminisced about past events.

I was not looking forward to returning to the halfway house, although I was more than excited to be actually going into the Child Protection Centre to start my new job.

Saying goodbye on that first Sunday to go back into the halfway house was very difficult. My daughter broke down in tears. I cried. I hated leaving her. I felt like a bad mother, unable to console her distressed child.

I was concerned because I felt she was not coping with me not being in the house. Yes, my partner was taking her to her softball games every Saturday, but she was not a happy little girl. The worst part of all this was I could do nothing about changing our situation. We drove into the car park of the halfway house. My little suitcase was filled with the extra personal belongings I wanted with me... extra clothes, photo frames with pictures of my family and my make-up, perfume and extra shoes. With lots of little extras, I felt content.

I handed my suitcase into the office, so the officers could search it for contraband. This was normal procedure; I didn't have an issue with this as I had nothing to hide.

After dinner reality set in. I was going to be trusted to find my way to my new job via train. No supervision, no prison officers, in fact no one breathing down my neck. I was looking forward to the adventure, finding my own way around in a suburb I had only ever driven through.

The next morning, I signed my day release document and officer Lorraine let me out the front security door and gave me directions to the centre. I had already driven the route before I came back the day before, so I knew how to get to the local train station and where to get off the train for the child protection centre.

This was the start of my very exciting day. I was a prisoner incarcerated for crimes against the state, free to ride on a train going to a job only nine weeks after being put into a woman's prison.

It was totally incomprehensible to me. I did enjoy taking my first train ride into the unknown; the sights, the sounds and the new smells. It was all surreal, unlike anything I had ever experienced.

CHAPTER 18

My first real job in years

MISS REYNOLDS welcomed me after I arrived without any trouble finding the centre. She explained what she expected of me and thanked me for dressing appropriately. Not too dressy and not too casual. She talked about disassociating my personal feelings towards the prospective parents that I would come into contact with while working here. Some of these parents had assaulted their children and some were fighting Children's Services to get their children back.

If I had any opinions, they had to be kept to myself.

What came next really sent me into a spin. Miss Reynolds asked me for my driver's license so a copy could be put into her files, then handed my set of car keys for one of the staff cars. She then gave me my jobs for the day. I had to pick up the parents and bring them into the organisation for supervised visits and counselling with their children in care.

Driving a company car five days a week all around the city, and being responsible for parents' and children's safety every day was such an overwhelming privilege. I was having trouble digesting such trust.

My allocated car was a Ford Focus and not a very old car, very nice with a little navigator on the dash and all I had to do was type in each address of each of my pickups. I was feeling very confident on one hand but seriously conflicted over everything on the other hand. I mean really? Think about all this for a moment! Put yourself in my shoes!

I shut my mind, collected my paperwork and headed out to Redcliffe to pick up my first clients. The drive to pick them up went quickly and I pulled up outside a modest home on a very quiet street. However, everything was not normal which is why I was here picking up these people up. At least these people were getting help and their situation was being handled as opposed to nothing being available when I was a child.

The first couple came down to the car and I got out to introduce myself, they gave me their first names only, the male I guessed was in his mid-30s. Casually dressed, clean looking and pleasant to speak to. His wife was a little, fragile-looking and softly spoken brunette. I knew who wore the pants in this family.

They had two small children in care and they had been attending this centre for the last six months on a weekly basis.

I still had two families to pick up and thankfully they were living close by. My second job was only 15 minutes away. The couple came down from their unit and after introductions, they got into my car. The man looked to be to be in his mid-20s and although a little scruffy looking he seemed quite a jovial type of guy, a surf-loving, sun-tanned not unattractive male. The girlfriend, I estimated was still a girl. A giddy, loud laugh, little party animal.

The first couple were ready to be taken back to Redcliffe. Away we went after they settled into the car.

I had the third address for my next pickup and went straight there to collect them, knowing by the time I got back to the centre the second couple would be ready to be taken to their home.

I pulled up outside a very nice brick home in a quiet little cul-de-sac, opened my car door and went up to the house and rang their doorbell.

The man answered the door and grunted when I introduced myself. I told him I would wait in the car. I was not impressed with his attitude. My opinion did not count. I was a prisoner on work release doing a job allocated to me, not a counsellor.

His wife was not unattractive but she seemed mentally preoccupied and was very quiet. She barely spoke a word to the centre. They were being shown their counsellor's office. I quickly organised the second couple to take them home.

I had to ignore their nastiness on the way home. I foresee major arguments between them this evening. I understood why theirs was not a good environment for a child.

I came back to the centre and waited for the third couple to finish their appointment. The woman had been crying, her make-up was washed away by the tears. Her eyes were bloodshot and she looked like an emotional wreck. The husband had a smug look on his face. The journey to their home was in complete silence.

My day was coming to a close and although I felt content with my day's work, I was feeling tired mentally. I felt sad that these couples had lost control of their children temporarily but glad that the children were being kept safe.

After I arrived back at the centre Miss Reynolds called me into her office. She asked how I thought I went. My reply was I had had a great day and believed I did my job well. On the way back to the halfway house I had the sudden realisation that I had a real job out in the real world. What a strange feeling after all these years of living on the edge of a dark lake. This was my life for the next nearly four months leading up to my six-month release on parole.

ONE Friday afternoon just before I was to head back home Miss Reynolds called me into her office and told me that officer Lorraine was on her way over to pick me up and take me back to the halfway house. My mind was racing. This had never happened during the 10 weeks I was working here.

Lorraine arrived and came into the waiting room to collect me. "Come on, Suzy, you have an appointment to attend." As far as I knew I had no appointments booked. She said we would talk in the car.

Officer Lorraine started to explain to me that the prison authorities had granted permission for me to visit my barrister had applied for me to go to his chambers.

She also informed me my parole had been granted and that when I left the halfway house next Friday to go on my weekend home visit I would not be coming back.

I could feel the tears well up in my eyes but I was determined not to allow her to see or feel my reaction, I could barely believe my ears. I was excited but very curious as to why I was going into my Barristers office if my parole release had already been approved. Nothing was making sense. Officer Lorraine went quiet.

Then she said, "Suzy, I am not trying to tell you what to do, but I am advising you to think carefully about any decisions you may make after your meeting with your barrister." Her tone of voice was not threatening but held warnings. I felt intimidated again.

I had just spent five months and seven days incarcerated at her Majesty's pleasure, even though it turned out to be one of privilege for me. I had paid for my crimes against the state. Fucked if I was going to allow any cop or prison officer to ever stand over me again.

I went very quiet for a few moments and then looked over at her, I said to her, "Lorraine, are you threatening me?" "No, Suzy, I am just suggesting that you think carefully before speaking or making any decisions which in the long term may affect your future."

After a short wait at my barrister's chambers, John asked me to come in. I went in by myself. I felt so nervous and confused over why I had been summoned. I had decided to say nothing and plead guilty to nothing.

Two people were in John's office. One was a strikingly attractive blonde woman in her 40s. I will not give you her real name, so let's call her Amanda. The male, Mike, also was dressed in very good quality clothing. They looked a formidable team, but what did they want from me?

After some chit chat Amanda looked me in the eyes and said, "Suzy, our TV station would like to do a story on your life and experience, which has resulted in the loss of your freedom from the fallout of the Fitzgerald Inquiry into Police Corruption. We would like to put together a type of documentary, which includes your personal experience of being in prison, the people you came into contact with and how all this upheaval has influenced your life.

"We can promise you we will give you complete control over what we present and we are prepared to sign you up on a contract with a financial amount that we are sure you will be happy with, and we will pay your contract fees in advance. We are also prepared to pay all legal fees involved to your legal representative before we leave this office."

I was silent. Amanda spoke again. "The money we pay you will give you a new start in life, Suzy."

I was stunned. I couldn't believe what I was hearing. I was a nobody in the game of the big-time players in the sex industry. What I was, though, I was the first female illegal brothel owner jailed from the fallout of a police corruption inquiry and certain people believed I was a political prisoner, a scapegoat who had suffered the consequences of a political agenda.

No wonder I made people nervous. I then knew why officer Lorraine had warned me. I was listening and observing all three people in this posh large office. I was no victim, not then and not now and fucked if I was going to allow anyone to portray me as one.

The contract fees would be $65,000 paid in cash into my bank account plus all legal fees and all expenses daily while the documentary was being filmed. I looked at these people sitting in front of me and spoke with a firm but soft voice. I told them I had had the opportunity to avoid a jail sentence by naming corrupt police and being put into witness protection. I chose not to. My silence had sent me to prison and I accepted my punishment.

"To be involved in what you people are asking of me would once again probably put my family in danger," I told them. "This would also put a target on my back for the rest of my life as being a snitch, a dog. No amount of money you offer me now or in the future would be enough to compensate me for not being able to sleep peacefully at night.

"I do not want you to think I am scared or that I am living in fear of certain people. This is not the case I am a very proud woman and I value my integrity. Most of all though I love my family and their safety is paramount above all else. I want to be able to go out in public, enjoy shopping with my kids and take them anywhere they need to go without looking over my shoulder for the rest of my life. Thank you both for coming here today, I do appreciate your more than generous offer, but I have to decline this offer. I am sorry."

I saw the disappointment in their faces. My barrister John just smiled at me. I stood up and shook their hands one by one. I told John I would call him the next day after I had finished work.

Officer Lorraine was waiting for me. She couldn't help herself and asked what happened. I asked her how she knew what was going on. She said all she knew was that I would be speaking to two people from the media. My barrister had applied to the Prisons Department for permission for me to attend his office to speak to two members of the media. Perhaps the department was afraid I would reveal things I had seen while in Boggo Road. The only thing I told Lorraine was that I had been asked to participate in a documentary about my life and that I had rejected their offer. The less they knew the better.

It was Thursday night and as we drove into the car park at the halfway house. I knew I was going home the next day, back here Sunday afternoon then after next week I would be sleeping in my own bed every night into the future.

The next day I knew it was going to be a great day. I felt happy that my time in the halfway house was coming to an end very soon. It's not like being here was difficult because it wasn't. It was a walk in the park. That weekend at home was fantastic and we were all excited that this time next week I would be home permanently. My daughter Sandy was ecstatic and we sat down and planned our next weekend like two kids being allowed to get up to mischief. I was very pleased I did not drink any alcohol that night.

At 10pm officers knocked on the front door to check I was following the rules. I took great pleasure in telling them their visit here would be the last one as next weekend I was out on parole. They already knew it anyway but perhaps they thought I might lapse and have a drink tonight. No way would I step over any lines this close to freedom.

The week flew by. We had a little get together in the staff room at my work on my last day – cakes, soft drinks, followed by speeches. I thanked all the staff at the centre especially Miss Reynolds for giving me a chance to work at the centre. It was a privilege and enjoyable to be involved. I felt useful and appreciated for the first time in a very long time.

I cannot begin to even describe how I felt that Friday afternoon after arriving back at the halfway house knowing I was going home permanently in just a short time. I was packed and waiting for my partner to arrive to pick me up for the very last time. Freedom was beckoning and I sure was ready for it and a future away from the control of the immediate staff of the prison system.

At 6pm my partner pulled into the car park and came into the office of the halfway house. All my belongings were waiting in the foyer. I rushed back into the ladies' lounge room, hugged everyone, thanked them for being great company, over the last few months and said my goodbyes to them and the officers. I signed my release sheet and walked out that door for the very last time.

ONE THE way home, very emotional, tears of relief flowed. I cried, unable to stop or control my emotions. I was so relieved to be a free woman at long last these six months past had been a marathon of personal learning on how to build up a wall of emotional and physical armour. I had to battle every day to keep my flapping trap shut over so many issues within a system that should have given more assistance to women prisoners who were broken.

Driving into the carport was an absolute feeling of euphoria, the excitement overwhelming as my daughter ran down the back stairs and into my arms, we both cried. Bloody hell, this crying business had to stop. I was exhausted. I walked inside and Nellie was crying.

The kitchen was decorated with balloons and 'welcome home Mum' signs. Food plates all over the dining room table, a cake with 'I love my Mum' written on it, a bucket with ice and a bottle of Moet champagne.

This was the best homecoming any mum could wish for, and I was defiantly going to get tipsy.

We all had the best night in many, many years. I sat in my kitchen feeling the darkness of the last six months float away from my soul.

I fell into my own bed that night, contented and so very glad my incarceration was finely over. I was free physically but still had an 18-month parole attendance to complete.

On Saturday morning, I marvelled that as of today I could go anywhere I pleased and with whomever I pleased. I was answerable to no one. Seeing my daughter happy made me happy and the smile on my face seemed like it was set in concrete. This treasured weekend was not going to last forever. Monday came and I knew it was decision day.

I dropped Sandy at school. My partner had gone to work at 6am and I headed back home. I sat with Nellie and we chatted about how life had been for her and Sandy while I had been away. My partner had been drinking on and off and this caused issues. I knew I had in the future I would have to address this issue.

Because I still faced 18 months' parole and I could not afford to attract the attention of the police. If I faced any charges whatsoever I would be sent straight back to jail. I had to have a plan, I had no job, no income and there were limited funds in my bank account.

I SPENT the week applying for jobs. What a joke. It was demeaning and embarrassing having to disclose I was a prisoner out on parole. It's perfectly understandable why so many people, men and women end up back in prison. They are defeated before they even start.

There were no re-training programs for released prisoners and people relied on their parole officers to find businesses that would employ ex-prisoners.

At 9.30am on Friday I arrived at the parole office in Woolongabba to keep my first appointment. I waited some 30 minutes then my name was called. I was very surprised. Standing at the door was an officer from Boggo Road Women's Prison. I call her Helena as she is no longer with us.

Helena was a truly beautiful woman, both inside and out. She did care about the women in prison and was a woman of integrity whom I really respected. I felt grateful and thrilled she was going to be my parole officer. We chatted for the next hour. I told her I had been applying for jobs to no avail and was thinking of going back to school to learn a trade. She thought this was a brilliant idea and would help me with whatever I needed to the best of her ability. I really liked this woman and knew she would support me in whatever I chose to do. I had two visits to the parole office over my first month of freedom and because I had a good clean prison record Helena decided that I could go on monthly parole reporting. That suited me just fine.

I still had not decided what I wanted to do. I did not even finish my first year at high school, had no qualifications of any worth and probably would have failed any school exams. Don't get me wrong though. I may not have had very much schooling but I was no dummy. Anything relating to business bookwork, money affairs and people skills I considered myself street smart.

I had decided to go to college to train as a hairdresser. I visited Ross Adams School of Hairdressing at Stones Corner and had an interview, collected the paperwork and went home to do my budget. This training was going to be full-time, five days a week over 12 months.

The course was recognised by the Queensland Apprenticeship Board and certificates would be issued on completion of my exams. I figured that by the time I completed my schooling and gained accreditation my parole would nearly be completed, I would probably buy or set up my own hairdressing salon. On my next visit to my parole officer Helena, I showed her all my paperwork and we discussed all my plans. I had already by this time paid my entrance fees and bought my textbooks.

Helena was thrilled and I knew her report to the parole board would be favourable. She was happy to schedule my parole attendance times around my school.

CHAPTER 19

A new life begins ... I hope

IATTENDED my parole office when required each month and my parole officer Helena told me she and the board were more than impressed with my progress. I also was very settled and was handling my course with ease, even though I was at times frustrated with trying to learn the different ingredients used to add or change the colour of a person's hair.

We had extra income coming in the door thanks to my partner and what she had done by renting the two-bedroom flat under our house. I did not want to know or be involved in that. I just wanted to get my accreditation and buy or open my own hairdressing salon. We all sat for our six-month tests of general knowledge and I breezed through my test in top form.

My cutting skills were getting better as were my general overall skills working with colour and perming of clients' hair. I was nowhere near being a hairdresser capable of winning any competitions, but I was doing okay.

About eight months into my hairdressing course and I saw an ad in the *Courier Mail* for a hairdressing salon at My Gravatt for sale. It was in a small shopping centre smack bang in the heart of several huge churches and a private religious school. The advertised price was $10,000 below its commercial value and there was a 10-year lease.

I called the agent and made an appointment to meet him at the salon on a Saturday morning to meet the owner and look at her set-up. I tried to sort out how this would work as I still had three and a half months still at school before I gained my senior hairdressing certificate. Passing my exams was not going to be an issue.

Saturday morning came and I drove out to Mt Gravatt to check this salon. I wanted to see the owner's proof of earnings and listen to the reasons she was selling. I looked around the small shopping centre and parked my car.

Inside the salon looked nice. To a prospective client walking by it gave the appearance of being affordable not overpriced as most large salons were. I worked out I needed to put $20,000 plus stock to bring it up to what I wanted.

The owner Leanne had a senior hairdresser working there and I asked if that lady would stay if she sold the salon and was told yes. My mind was in overdrive; I wanted this salon but also needed to look at her financials. Leanne showed me her filing system for her clients. She had listed clients' names and what church they were attached to, whether they drank tea or coffee or none at all if their church banned caffeine. Also on each card was a note, reminding the hairdresser, not to use any swear words. If it wasn't so serious it would have been hilarious, but it worked and I was glad Lorraine was so inventive.

It thought that if I bought this business, I would have to learn to shut the fuck up and keep my trap shut. Could I do that? I would have to learn really fast, if I wanted to keep all these regular clients coming here.

IN THE next few days, I went off to school and continued my training. I searched for answers on how I could buy the salon, stay at school to get my accreditation but keep the income rolling into the salon while I was not on the premises. It took three days for Leanne to send me her salon's financial figures.

When I received them, I sat down in earnest to juggle my way around trying to make all this work. It was not going to be easy, and I wondered even then if should I walk away or if should I take the risk. I arranged to go back and have another look at the salon, stay a while and have a more detailed chat about why she was selling her business.

I told Leanne I would give her a definite answer within the week. I also needed to rethink my own finances as if I bought the salon, I would not be debt free. I did not have the income I once had, back when I was involved in the sex industry. I was a broke student relying on meagre income support from what was being paid for by my partner and my beautiful Nellie.

I decided to buy the salon. I went to the bank to borrow the money I was going to be short. I organised for Karen the senior hairdresser to stay on and work full-time and I hired a third-year apprentice to work with her. I would go from school each day over to the salon, do a reconciliation of the day's takings and do any washing and drying that had to be done.

This routine would only have to be for a little over eight weeks and I felt comfortable with this arrangement. Contracts exchanged hands and all monies paid to Leanne were paid, I was nervous because I really did not know the hairdresser being left in charge although she had been working for Leanne for over two years.

Karen had to phone me every morning when she arrived at the salon and again at 5pm every day on closing the salon. I would work in the salon alongside her on a Saturday. The apprentice had Saturday off, saving me money in wages.

The salon was holding its own although not making a lot of profit. Once I graduated and started working in the salon, I knew everything would be fine.

EXAM day had come, a day of intense concentration, stress and worry about being able to remember everything I had been taught technically. Becoming a hairdresser is not just being able to cut and blow dry someone's hair.

I think I was the last one to finish my exam papers and as I walked up to my teacher and handed them over, I could actually feel the waves of relief rush through my body.

Our results would be in the next morning. We all showed up at school early, everyone was excited yet worried. We all passed and I topped my class!

At 40 I was the oldest student in the whole school not just in my class. I had not even completed high school yet here was proof if you want something bad enough and are prepared to commit 100 per cent to whatever it is, you will succeed.

We had a very busy day in the salon the next Saturday and I was thrilled with my takings for the day. I looked at the stock cupboard and thought the shelves were looking bare. In the two or so months I had had the salon I had spent another $1000 on replacement stock and I needed to do a reconciliation of income against stock use.

Coming up also was my last visit to my parole officer; I would be totally free from the control of the parole board. This would be a very good year for me I thought as I drove home from work, very tired but contented, no more school, no more parole restrictions.

I would finally be a free woman.

OVER THE next few months, as I worked in my salon alongside the two girls I had working for me, a shop had become vacant next door to me. I thought the rent was very cheap and there was no relaxation therapist in the centre or even a suntanning bed within 10km. I would look at the financial feasibility. I believed each business would complement the other if I could put this together. I went home from work that day and sat down to do my projections on the possibility of opening another business.

I contacted the owner of the shop and set about going into negotiations on a lease, before I settled on a deal I advertised for an acupuncturist, a genuine massage therapist, and a Reiki healer. I also wanted to find a qualified counsellor who would bring her business into my new project part-time.

Within a week I had found all the people I needed who were happy to pay me a commission on all clients they would see on my premises. I signed a two-year lease and then set about converting the shop into a reception area and three treatment rooms with a special room for anyone using the tanning machine.

The cost of outfitting the salon was minimal, probably about $3000, but the result was very professional and with all the little nick knacks spread around and full-side framed posters of the human body displayed that place looked fantastic. I had also bought the latest model Sun Tanning Machine to put into the salon. This alone would bring in a lot more funds for the business.

My hairdressing salon and my new health centre were both doing okay. They were holding their own but having two businesses involved so much bookwork I was beginning to wish I had not taken on so much so soon. I also had little doubts creeping into my head about our massage therapist.

Tori had genuine qualifications, which I had investigated before I allowed her to be a part of my business, but something was nagging at me. I thought something was just not right. Maybe it was the way she started to dress to come to work. Maybe it was the amount of make-up she started to wear. Maybe it was the fact that 80 per cent of her clients were male. Something was not right.

I didn't want my new business to be involved in the illegal sex industry I had paid my dues. I had worked too hard over the past 18 months and spent way too much money to have it all blow up in my face.

I organised a private meeting with Tori, the massage therapist, away from the salon on a Sunday. When she showed up, she arrived on a Harley-Davidson Fat Boy motorcycle, dressed in full leathers. This attire was a side of her I had not seen. As she got off her bike, took off her full-face helmet and shook her hair loose, it felt like a rush of adrenaline had surged through my veins.

We chit-chatted about her bike, and how long she had been riding and then I got down to business. I said to her that what we discussed was to be kept between us. "Should I hear anything back I will terminate your contract with my health centre," I said.

I told her I had been involved in the illegal sex industry for many years and was jailed. There was no way I was going to allow anyone to threaten my new business or any potential of being charged with any criminal offence. "You are a sole trader and are contracted to my salon, however, the lease of the salon is in my name as such this makes me responsible for all activities carried out within the walls of my salon," I said.

I also pointed out that providing a massage service was not illegal but providing a sexual service with that massage was a criminal offence. Tori assured me that she was not providing such a service, I knew by instinct she was lying. I pointed out to her the procedure cops would use to procure a criminal charge.

"Tori, you do not know these men. You have no idea if they are businessmen or cops. It's their job to fool you into providing this service."

I also pointed out that she would be arrested and marched out of the shopping centre like a criminal in front of every other tenant and my business would collapse.

I told her to stop or "you will be asked to cease working on my premises. Please understand I know people".

If she wanted to be involved in the industry she could do so as a private worker in premises on her own and operate within the law. After all this she knew that she was not fooling me and admitted she had been providing the extra service.

"Tori, you must stop now or finish up working in my salon. I cannot allow you to endanger my freedom or both my businesses."

Tears rolled down her face as she told me her story and why she had resorted to supplying the extra service. She had come out of a volatile relationship with a female partner and had debts that were crushing her. She still had to pay half the mortgage on a house she was no longer living in and rent on the place where she lived.

I put together a plan that would protect my business, her name and keep her out of trouble. She was to tell the clients she had provided with a sexual service that this service was no longer available on my premises. She would get a local motel that would allow her to book a room (there were several in Mt Gravatt) and she would see clients on Monday and Friday.

I knew that by helping her I would lose money from her bringing business into my salon. But the extra money I was making from the tanning machine would make up for the loss of her money on the two days she would be away from my business.

I left my meeting with Tori after hugging her and assuring her that everything between us was okay and I thanked her for being honest. I felt relief that everything had been sorted before my business had attracted the interest of the Queensland Vice Squad.

I had dodged a bullet, a minefield I would have had no chance of getting out of because of who I was and what I had been involved in in the past. Guilty by association would have been the order of the day for Tori and straight back to jail for me.

The new arrangements were working out fine. Tori was much more relaxed. I had lost minimal funds by her taking her own business away from the centre, this made me feel much more settled. This information was kept away from everyone working in both my businesses.

CHAPTER 20

Holding on by a thread

FOR THE next six months both businesses held their own ground financially. Neither was making huge profits, but it was acceptable. I knew the Vice Squad was occasionally scrutinising us. I had experience of the way police set traps for a business being suspected of carrying on any illegal activities.

Every time they sent a cop to the health centre, I caught them sitting nearby in their obvious unmarked police car. They stood out like neon signs in the middle of the night. I knew Tori was toeing the line and I was not concerned, but I still called next door and warned her a cop was coming in as a client and the others were parked nearby.

Once they sent in a client who looked for like a drug dealer than a cop. He was tall, skinny, untidy, long-haired and smelly with tattoos all up his arms. The giveaway was I saw him get out of a car and the car drove off with three other men in it. They parked up the road keeping the salon in view. This gave me a full view of them from my reception desk.

I rang Tori and told her a suspicious character was on his way in for an appointment he made earlier in the morning. He had booked an hour massage. Tori was confident and unafraid of anyone, least of all a man. She was also a very attractive woman. Men couldn't help themselves in her presence they folded every time.

The booking lasted 45 minutes and the cop stormed out of the salon calling her a slut and a prick teaser. I stood at my salon door laughing. Later she told me the cop had been sweet-talking her during his massage. He insisted on her giving him the full happy ending and even offered her an extra $200 on top of the $80 he had paid for the massage.

She said she consistently told him this salon was not a brothel and that she was not a prostitute. He tried to touch her up and she firmly told him to leave her body alone. After the fourth time of telling him no, she raised her voice and the acupuncturist who was with his client came out and banged on Tori's door asking if she was okay.

Tori opened her door exposing the cop with his erect penis and complained loudly to the acupuncturist that the client was being abusive and demanding a happy ending, which she does not provide. The cop was asked to dress and leave the premises or they would call the police. He demanded a refund of his money. Tori told him she provided the massage service and he was getting no refund.

This day wasn't a good day for the cops besides not obtaining any criminal charges from the Health Centre, they had lost $80 of police funds on a massage. We never got another visit from the Vice Squad.

Tax time was looming and I knew I had to spend time on getting my books on track, so I warned my two hairdressers that I would be taking time off over the next month to get both businesses' paperwork ready for my accountant to prepare my tax returns.

I needed a stress-free environment to get my act together and as my daughter was at school, my partner at work and only Nellie at home I was going to set it all up at home in the peace and quiet of my lounge room.

I had been going through my receipts and purchases for the two months before my graduation from college and while my senior hairdresser and apprentice were running the salon on their own for five days a week. These figures were not adding up.

Over the next three days, I tracked every product that was used in my salon against the daily appointments. I kept checking and re-checking every transaction and outlay, every client payment slips from the cash register and still I came to the same conclusion – someone in my salon had been stealing from me.

I was astounded, furious and very offended, but most of all deeply hurt. I went into work on the fourth day. I needed to do another stock-take and collect the last two weeks' client cash register receipts and copies of the client's daily booking sheets from the appointment book.

I told the girls I would be taking two days off next week; one to finish my bookwork and one to visit my accountant. I still treated both girls with respect, but I really struggled. I was so angry and hurt. I could make no accusations until my accountant confirmed that I had been defrauded of money and products.

While checking the last fortnight's accounts I again uncovered inconsistent transactions and missing products. I saw my accountant Col and gave him all my paperwork. I pointed out what I had found and that I needed him to either conform to my findings or find out where I had miscalculated.

Col asked me that if my fears were true what was I going to do. I just looked up at him with tears in my eyes and said, "Col, I will decide when you have done your job." He said he would have it done by the next Tuesday.

I was conflicted about what to do if my fears were proved true. Legally I could bring in the police, but it could draw attention to my past. I went to work that Saturday morning and was relieved we were so busy I barely had time for a conversation with my senior hairdresser. I could feel her glances and told her my quietness towards her was just tiredness.

When I got home, I badly needed to debrief but poor old Nellie was the only one home. She was in the early stages of dementia and would understand nothing of what I needed to get off my chest.

LET ME tell you about Nellie. My mother was in charge of a small nursing home in a suburb of Melbourne. There were eight residents and my sister Aileen was on the nursing staff. My mother had been working there for two years as a chef. When the home was sold the new owner ordered my mother to serve up any food the residents did not eat for their next meals. My mother was horrified and rang me in tears. This woman also ordered the nursing staff to double some of the residents' medications. Mum was so distressed she was going to resign as were my sister and other staff members but she could not leave Nellie and another resident behind.

At the time I was married to Robbie and he was in and out of Melbourne every week, so we devised a plan to sneak them both out of the home and bring them up to Queensland. I was living up on the Sunshine Coast at the time and had room, so I said I would look after them both. We virtually kidnapped them, but as Nellie and Patrick were not wards of the state, we were not committing a criminal offence.

Mum's plan was to say she was taking them shopping. My sister sneaked their suitcases of clothes and meagre belongings into the boot of Mum's car and after lunch they left the home. Robbie met Mum and helped Nellie and Patrick climb up into the cabin of his big truck and they all set off on their journey to Queensland.

I was to become the daughter Nellie never had. She was 72 when she came to live with me and I loved her dearly. Sadly, Patrick was not a well man and after a short sickness passed away three months later from a lung condition.

I looked after Nellie for 21 years. She had bowel cancer at one stage and after a traumatic operation, the doctor said they couldn't get it all. Nellie lived for another five years. I believe this was because she had no idea, she even had cancer.

Nellie had a son but did not know where he was. The Salvation Army said they would help track him down. About a week later one of their officers rang to say her son had passed away back in 1984. I did not have the heart to tell her. Nellie was 93 when she passed over. I was privileged to be part of her life.

WHEN my partner arrived home that Saturday, I told her what I had found about the missing salon stock and money. I had to find a solution without involving the police. I really could not afford to have my name splattered all over the news again as I would lose clients from my businesses.

We exchanged ideas but seemed to be getting nowhere. I decided that if my accountant agreed with me, I would fire both staff members on

Tuesday afternoon at closing time. I would get my accountant to tally up what I owed them both in wages, pay them after getting them to sign my wage book and take the salon keys off my senior girl.

My accountant called me at lunchtime on Monday saying that my calculations were correct and asked what I was I going to do about this fraud. I told him I was going to sack them and asked him to work out what I owed each girl up until 5pm the next day so I could pay them out.

I woke the next day with a heavy heart. I was also concerned about me being physically up to working the long hours in the salon on my own.

The last client left the salon at 4.15pm and I closed the front door. We cleaned up, made a coffee and the girls sat down in the clients' workstations. I spoke very quietly but firmly. I told them I did not feel angry toward either of the girls. I was disappointed and very offended that they had taken advantage of an opportunity to hold on to a job that would have been guaranteed well into their future.

I calmly told both girls they were fired.

My third-year apprentice broke down in tears sobbing. My senior hairdresser defiantly told me I legally could not fire either of them and she just stood there staring me in the face. I gave them documents the accountant had prepared listing the products used, the appointments and the money taken.

The choice was theirs. I could press charges against them both for fraud and we could fight this out in court or they could walk out that door with all wages paid up to 5pm that day and this would be the end of their employment here.

They took the money, signed the wages book and left.

I sat down and started to call the clients who had booked for the next day to change their appointment times. I knew some clients were loyal to the girls and would probably cancel their appointments after being told neither would be available to do their hair. I was prepared for future loss of earnings but believed my wages bill being now non-existent would outweigh my loss.

I had no sooner arrived home and sat down at my kitchen table when my phone rang. It was the mother of my senior hairdresser. She ranted and raved for at least five minutes. I did not interrupt her I waited patiently for her to shut up, I then calmly but firmly asked her did her daughter show her the document from my accountant, and her answer was no.

I suggested she ask her for the document and we would talk again. I said if I had any trouble from her or any member of her family, I would have the daughter charged with theft.

Thirty minutes later my phone rang again, this time it was the father of my fired apprentice. His told me I was in breach of the requirements pertaining to the employment of the Queensland Apprenticeship Board. "I will be reporting you to them tomorrow and I will be taking legal action against you," he threatened. My reply was, "Go ahead, I will see you in court."

I decided overnight to tell any client who asked why the girls were not at work the truth.

About 4.45pm that day a supervisor from the Queensland Apprenticeship Board rang and said he was following up a complaint from a student's father that I had fired his daughter.

I told him, "Yes, I fired both the apprentice and my senior hairdresser because they had been caught stealing from my business." I asked him if I could fax through the related document prepared by my accountant to him proving this to be a fact. I sent it to him.

He said he would look at the fax and phone me back. Fifteen minutes later the phone rang and I could tell by the tone of his voice I was not going to have any issues with his department. He asked me if I was going to take legal action against her and I said was no.

He was extremely nice to me over the phone and thanked me for being so cordial in how I had handled this issue.

I told him that I would be grateful if he could explain to this girl's father how lucky she was that I was not taking legal action against his daughter. I also told him I was aware of my responsibilities in assisting apprentices but under the circumstances, I could not have an untrustworthy person in my employment.

I worked out how the girls were able to get away with stealing from me. Appointments were written in pencil, so they rubbed out the figures from the book, but still did the work. I had to toughen up. I had my meeting with the three people working in my health centre and they were astounded at what had transpired in my hair salon. I wanted their appointments to be written in biro in future. They agreed

I found and hired a part-time senior hairdresser. She was a married woman with grown-up children. We worked well together and the clients improved. The takings went up and I believed I was back on track.

Then my life changed again. My daughter phoned to say the police had come to the door asking for me. She put the detective on the phone.

I told him to come back I would be home by 5pm as I was at work and could not speak to him on the phone. I headed home thinking what the fuck now?

CHAPTER 21

The cops are back

I WAS worried. I had no idea why the cops would be on my doorstep. Then again, I did have a private sex worker paying rent to my partner for the downstairs flat under my house. I knew the Queensland laws and I was very concerned. Did I need my lawyer to be present or would that infuriate the cops and bring me more issues?

I drove home. My worried daughter met me and said, "Mum, what's happening? Are you going back to jail?" I decided I would do whatever it took to avoid another upheaval in my daughter's life. I could feel my stress levels rise as I waited for the police to come back.

Two detectives arrived half an hour later. I told my daughter to visit her mate in the street but told her not to say a word to anyone. I was still dressed in my salon uniform with my name tag pinned to my shoulder. There was no mistake on who I was. The detective introduced himself and his offsider and showed me his police identification.

He said, "We are here to investigate the fact that you have a prostitute working from your house in a flat downstairs. We need to clarify some information." I felt they were fishing for confirmation of me being involved in the illegal sex industry. I replied, "Look, sir, I work six days a week in my own hairdressing salon. I am sure you have done your homework.

"I also operate a legitimate health centre in the same shopping centre as my hair salon. I am also very sure the Vice Squad has visited my health centre many times, and have ascertained my business there is and always has been a genuine health centre. The woman who is renting the flat under my house comes and goes as she pleases. She pays rent, which is collected by my partner.

"I have nothing to do with what she does in her private life. In fact, I probably have spoken to her only a few times in the last couple of years. You are informing me that she is a prostitute. My understanding of the Queensland laws is that any woman working as a private sex worker works legally, if she is working from the premises she is living in. Correct me if I am wrong!"

The second detective spoke to me in a nasty manner, you know the drill! Good cop! Bad cop. I kept my cool as he accused me of once again running a prostitution racket. My reply was quite firm, "I have nothing to do with what she does and who visits her."

The nasty cop interrupted me and said, "Suzy, we will be investigating you and this operation and if we find any evidence you will face charges. We would request you leave a message for your tenant that we want to interview her. We have been to your flat several times and left our cards but she has not contacted us."

The detective in charge looked at me realising they would get nothing further from me and said quietly to me, "Suzy, if you were charged again with an organisation offence involving this house, we will make a request under the Confiscation of Proceeds of Crime Act for an order to take your house.

I told them that any further interviews would be conducted through my lawyer.

The thought of losing my home terrified me. I had worked my guts out to put and keep a roof over the heads of my family and there was no fucking way I was going to stand still to allow the law to take it all from me.

I called my lawyer John at 7pm and repeated every detail of the conversation, firstly he asked me why I didn't call him straight away. I then explained the real dire situation I had found myself in.

"You have a sex worker operating from a flat under your house. If that woman admits and signs a statement that she is paying you money each week to allow your premises to be used by her for the purpose of prostitution, you will have your home taken from you under the confiscation of assets.

"Regardless, if your partner collects the rent, this property is in your name and as such this makes you complicit in collecting monies illegally gained. You must take action urgently, to protect yourself. Protect your assets, and protect your family."

I was silent, shellshocked and could feel the waves of despair flood every fibre of my very existence.

I called my partner and told her about the cops' visit, their threat and the call with the lawyer. "Come home. We have to get this shit sorted as soon as possible or I will lose the house."

I thought about calling my new hairdresser to ask her to work alone tomorrow but that was out of the question as we had a busy day ahead of us.

Yet another life-changing event was looming and I had to be very careful about any decisions I made because my family's entire future was at stake and probably my own freedom. In my mind I had done everything possible to change my life. I had a legitimate career my daughter would feel proud of. It was like fate saying my old life would always come back to haunt me.

My partner arrived home and we sat talking about my visit from the police, my conversation with my lawyer.

We were all set in our lives. My two businesses were holding their own financially and my daughter was happy at her school. I felt I had no choice but to move. My partner wanted to stand our ground and fight back but I knew deep down I would not win this fight.

After many years in the sex industry, I knew that if the police were gunning for anyone, they would leave no stone unturned. I would lose everything I had worked for and the legal costs would be devastating.

My plan was to sell my house. The funds after the mortgage were to be paid out would give us enough for either a deposit on a house or block of land in NSW. I would sell the hairdressing salon and hopefully sell the health salon. We left the flat downstairs vacant to not attract any more police attention.

Reluctantly my partner agreed with my plan. However, my daughter was devastated and didn't want to leave her friends or her school. I tried desperately to convince her, but she would not listen. I was upset for her, but I really had no choice.

I contacted a couple of local agents to appraise the house and talk about me putting the house on the market. The next week my partner organised our tenant Jeanie to collect her belongings from downstairs and her tenancy was terminated. She was terrified of a police interview and as no one knew her correct name there would be no chance of her being found.

I put the sale of the house into the hands of an agent I had known personally. He had been an agent in the West End area for more than 20 years. I started to look for homes for sale over the border in NSW. I found a company that was doing land-and-home builds at Kingscliff just over the border in NSW. They could also access finance.

We signed a contract on the land, but I needed my house to sell and at least my hairdressing salon. The health centre was operating with three sole traders. I was sure we could work something out if a buyer did not come forward.

I decided to tell my salon and health centre staff about my decision. I didn't disclose the real reason; I just explained that I was tired. I promised I would do the very best to ensure they were all left with their jobs.

I had had three offers on my house and I declined all three. The agent recommended I take the house to auction. On the day of the auction, I took the morning off work thankfully.

I was excited but nervous, I really needed my house to sell so I could get my life organised and get the hell out of Queensland. I sat in my kitchen listening to my agent to the six people who attended. After the auction, the agent came up the back steps and told me the best offer. I told him to tell them to fuck off.

The agent called me at the salon and put another offer to me, once again I said no. I needed a certain a figure or it would put all my building plans in Kingscliff on indefinite hold.

Sunday was a lost day and I used it to recover. I needed all my energy for the coming week to rearrange my finances and weigh up my options.

A few days after the auction my real estate agent called and said he had received another offer on my house. I told him in no uncertain words not to bother if the offer wasn't what I wanted. He told me this offer was worth thinking about.

He came around to the house. The offer was $5000 under what I wanted but it came with a huge deposit and a 12-week settlement. I wanted to dance around Brisbane with balloons and a trumpet. This was a perfect outcome. I was short $5000 but I had 12 weeks to make it up.

I told him the next morning to contact his buyer to tell them I had accepted their offer. He would drop around after I got home from work with the signed contract.

I was a very happy camper. Work was like a breath of fresh air, nothing fazed me at all and my smile showed everyone I came into contact with that I was a happy, girl. I signed the contract that afternoon and called the builder and advised them I had a contract signed on my house and that I would fax it to them as soon as I arrived at work.

I told the builder to get on their bikes to build my house as I needed to move into my new home after 12 weeks.

My daughter had started to become defiant and angry about having to leave her school and friends. I didn't know how to handle all this. I hoped this issue would settle down soon as there was so much for us to do over the next couple of months.

I HAD 12 weeks to accumulate every dollar I could for the big move, also on top of that little extras kept creeping into what I wanted in my new house build. Talk about having champagne tastes on a beer income ... taps, bricks, tiles. I never complained I was so happy knowing I was leaving Queensland and that I had dodged a legal bullet.

Over the next six weeks I drove to Kingscliff every Sunday morning to check on the progress of my new home. Everything was on track. I was beginning to get very worried about my salon and health centre not being sold. They had to go so I put ads in every home-delivered newspaper covering Brisbane and the Gold Coast. Within two weeks, I had a buyer for my hairdressing salon. The amount was pitiful but it was the highest offer out of four. I lost more than $20,000, but I didn't have a choice.

The health centre was another headache. Every prospective buyer either thought it was an illegal operation or once again they wanted the business for nothing.

I decided to have a meeting with the three sole traders who had been with me since opening the centre. I had a solution I hoped would interest them. They listened to my suggestions intently. I asked them to take over the salon lease between them, meaning all three would own the business together.

All I was asking for was the funds I had outlaid to set up the salon. Really, they were going to get the business for nothing. At the end of the day, they said they agreed to take over my lease and pay my establishment costs. I told them I would get my solicitor to organise the transfer.

Time was not on my side. I had only six weeks to finalise everything. My home was already in shambles with boxes of belongings near piled up everywhere.

I also owned another property in Browning Street West End, but it had been rented out to tenants, so I had no issues with paying the mortgage on that property.

For the first time in more than two years I knew a deep, dark cloud was starting to lift from my very soul. I knew it was not going to be easy. I had no job, no immediate prospects of opening a business legal or otherwise in NSW. My new house was just about ready for the builder to meet me on site to hand over the keys after final inspection and approval.

I couldn't believe everything had fallen into place. I drove down to Kingscliff so excited and as I drove into my street I nearly started crying. It wasn't just a new house it was the start of a new beginning. All I had left to do was drive back to Brisbane and finish the move. The removal truck would be on the doorstep the next day at 7am. By 1pm we pulled away from the house.

CHAPTER 22

Yet another new start

I HAD SOLD my house in Brisbane and my salon and sorted out my health centre and sold my hairdressing salon at Mt Gravatt. My partner and I were off to Kingscliff in northern NSW. I was very excited even though I had reservations over the longevity of my relationship.

This was my dream house and we spared no expense. From the street the home very nice, not opulent just very nice. I never ever allowed anyone in the sex business to know where I lived. Call it paranoia but the safety of my family came first.

I really enjoyed living in Kingscliff. I enjoyed the privacy and quietness of being able to shut out the world when I came home. The property was only minutes from the lovely little local shops and 30 minutes from the huge shopping mall at South Tweed Heads. The Kingscliff Bowling Club was moments away and had a great entertainment area overlooking the ocean.

The saying around town was this was God's waiting room, and from the number of elderly people living here, I probably thought perhaps it was. What a beautiful place to wait.

I was 42 when I opened a small one-person hairdressing salon next to a takeaway food shop heading into Kingscliff. It was minutes from home and the shop rent was cheap. Even though there were three other hairdressing salons in town, nobody was catering to people on limited incomes. My little business did very well and my clients were genuine, decent people. They just had a week-to-week existence financially. I kept my prices low and affordable for all these people.

I had signed a 12-month lease. The owner said this was to give me an out if the business did not turn out how I had hoped it would make financially. Sure, it was small but looking after people that would not have been able to afford to have their hairs done was better than having the worry of having to compete with three other salons and a high rent outlay added to wages each week.

The couple who had bought the takeaway food business had ploughed their life savings into buying the business and they lived on the premises. They were very friendly and hardworking dedicated to making their business successful. The food was home cooked and much cheaper than the food shops along the beachfront.

I had been operating my salon for around six months when I had a phone call from my landlord. He wanted to meet me the next morning at the shop. I thought this was strange as I was ahead in my rent and I knew I had done nothing to upset anyone associated with the building or any of my clients.

When I arrived at work the couple from the food shop greeted me and asked if the landlord had arranged to meet me. I told them at 8.30am and they said there meeting was at 9am.

The landlord arrived and was all smiles and good manners. He told me he wouldn't be renewing my lease because he had decided to sell the whole block for future development.

I was gutted. I asked how long did I have? He said if he had a buyer before my lease was up, a condition of sale would be for me to stay until my lease was completed. If I left once, he had a contract of sale I could do so with no penalty.

I thanked him for being up front with me, closed the door behind him and broke down in tears. How the fuck was I ever going to live a sociably acceptable, legal lifestyle when every time I tried, situations like this keep stepping in the way.

I made myself a coffee and pulled myself together as I had a workday ahead of me. My problems were nothing compared to some of the people who came into my salon.

The news was going to destroy the couple in the food shop. They had paid a lot of money for their business and they had definitely not recouped their initial outlay. Even worse they were going to be homeless.

Anne and Terry walked into my salon and waited until I had finished with my client. The wife broke down in near uncontrollable tears; her husband was enraged. He threatened all sorts of legal action against the landlord. Our futures had been designated by fate and there was nothing anyone could do.

I DRAGGED myself around my salon that day trying to come up with a plan. I did not know how I was going to survive this upheaval. There were few shops to rent further up along the beachfront and if vacant the rents were double or triple what I was paying. And a fourth salon would not be financially viable.

My choices were very limited and I knew I had to get back into the illegal sex industry. I knew the industry back to front. A second attempt at running a legitimate, legal business had blown up in my face.

I decided that if the landlord scored a contract, I would walk away and set up an escort service. I would run it from NSW into Queensland. I had all the contacts and staff I could call on so it was all systems go. I could operate in NSW without breaking any laws. The following weeks were very difficult, telling my clients I was going to have to close the salon bought tears from most of my female clients and even some of the men.

They had become part of my life. I would listen to their problems and help if I could. Sometimes it was helping them get local community services access to food vouchers and I drove a few ladies to Tweed Heads to get their groceries. Some of these women had no one.

About seven weeks later, the landlord told me contracts had been signed with an eight-week settlement agreement with the new owner. I thanked him and congratulated him on the sale. I told him I would take up his offer to vacate with no penalty and asked that he advise me of a takeover date at least two weeks before the handover.

He also told me he wouldn't change me rent for the month before I left. With this extra income I decided that for my last two days of being open I wouldn't charge my regular clients for any service. All haircuts, perms and colours would be free. I still had lots of stock so I would use it on my clients.

During that week I decorated the salon with goodbye banners and hung balloons and streamers. I organised with Anne and Terry for plates of sandwiches and hot finger food to be bought in on and off over the two days, they were grateful for the extra money.

The two days were a hoot; sad with lots of tears but we all had a great time. Every time I completed a service for each of my clients, they gave me a hug and most had tears in their eyes; me too. These two days made me very happy inside, deep within my heart, but with sadness that I struggled to put down.

CHAPTER 23

Still in the illegal escort game

IKNEW I still had to operate illegally as an escort service in Queensland until I could sort out how to set up a legal business in NSW. I still had a mortgage and needed an income while I set about trying to find premises to operate a legal brothel.

I started operating a visiting service only, from phones connected to a unit I owned in West End. I had this unit rented, but I had to get my agent to kick the tenants out because on inspection they had six other people living in the unit with them. The smell and damage they had caused to my kitchen and bathroom was horrific. I was lucky insurance paid to fix the damage.

The unit was vacant, so I connected a phone line and the calls were being diverted to my work mobile. This was very intricate and secretive but difficult for the police to gain evidence.

The police in Queensland were out to get illegal brothel operators and massage parlours pretending to be genuine therapists, so I knew I would have at least six to nine months before I would have any more issues with them. They seemed to be leaving the escort business alone.

I had to pretend to every caller that I would be coming to see them. There were two ladies working for me so I gave general descriptions that were close to them. I would take the booking and client details; check they were who they said they were and their address. Only then would I call the lady and give her the client's details. She would arrive at her booking and go into the bathroom and send me a text saying she was okay and had his money. She would ring me from her car once she had finished her booking. This way of operating was not going to be forever.

Neither lady would ever disclose who was behind the agency. They were not just sex workers they were friends and very loyal friends at that. We remain friends still to this day 23 years later.

As soon as I had a more legal, permanent situation I would shut this service down.

I planned to sell that unit once I had stability with a legal operation this side of the border. Working in this manner also allowed me to feel safe from a police raid. They could not come into NSW without the authority of the local police commander.

I SCOURED all of Tweed Heads before checking the Chinderah industrial estate. I approached a man called Sandy Scott who owned a huge property at 17 Morton St. I spent many weeks with Sandy setting out what I wanted to do. I didn't have all the funds to get these premises off the ground on my own so Sandy suggested I take on him and his friend Victor Elliot as partners.

While I wasn't happy to take on one partner let alone two, after many weeks of discussion and planning I decided I would agree, only if it was done legally and through an accountant and lawyers. Our company was set up with the three of us as joint owners and with me as the owner-manager of the day-to-day running of the business.

Sandy was in his 50s and gave the appearance he would verbally rip you up and spit you out. Which I was soon to learn he did on a daily basis to anyone who he believed had done or said something to deserve it.

In my opinion Sandy had no filters emotionally or verbally. Looking and listening to him speak made you step back and weigh up your reply. He really was an unhappy man and seemed to be constantly angry.

He lived in a beautiful waterfront home just off Kennedy Drive in South Tweed Heads. His son Daniel, his Asian wife and child lived in the house with him. There was no mistaking who was in charge of everything that happened in this house. Sandy ruled the roost with an iron fist. His son and daughter-in-law did not dare disobey. The situation concerned me. The atmosphere was like a timebomb ready to go off at any moment.

Victor was a handsome man, very well educated and extremely well-spoken. He was the type of man any woman would take a second glance at. He had a well-respected job at the local hospital and owned several properties. His business interests bought in a huge income on top of the well-paid wages he received working for NSW Health. He was not short of a quid and was a smooth operator.

Sandy and Victor were total opposites. You had to ask how could this friendship work. Yet they had been friends for more than 20 years and had been involved in many other business ventures. Their friendship and business ventures worked well because Victor was the architect, pedantic planner, and Sandy was the brawn, the tradesman, workhorse, organiser of people.

WE SUBMITTED our plans to Tweed Council. After a few adjustments to the building and after submitting a business projection plan it was approved. This was no mean feat and many of the councillors were not happy with having a brothel in their shire. However, the law was the law, and the brothel was being put in an industrial estate. Basically unless the council wanted to find themselves in court, they had no option but to pass the plans for approval.

Vic also owned 19 Morton Street, next door, and with my prompting to stop another prospective operator from gaining approval in the same street he put in plans to the council for approval for a legal brothel. This also was approved. Having two brothels in the same street would have caused a war had there been two different owners.

The approval for 17 Morton Street went through very quickly as it was only for interior renovations and alterations to the existing car park with security fencing separating the building from the street. The approval for 19 Morton Street was more involved and there were several months before Victor could start.

I believe now that Victor may have had ulterior motives for a separate operation of his own later down the track if 17 Morton Street was a success financially. These thoughts that went through my head later was to become a reality, much to the detriment of Daniel Scott.

SANDY was in charge of renovations to the existing building and for the next month, it was all hands, on deck. As I lived a short drive away in Kingscliff, 10 minutes away from Morton Street, I was there every day to make sure the building was being built how I wanted. Safety and security for staff and me was my driving force, and every detail had to be correct.

Work dragged into months and it seemed nothing was getting done. I felt like I was being taken for a fool. I just did not know or understand why he was behaving like he was. Then again, the building was looking great and I thought maybe he had run out of money. I had to get these people off their backsides as I needed to close my Queensland escort service very soon.

Dealing with Sandy and his moods was like trying to nail jelly onto a tree trunk. Bloody near impossible. He said he always had a headache. Something had to be sorted and soon. Even the tradespeople were getting restless. They were sick of his nasty demeanour. He was a foul-mouthed, pig-headed sorry excuse of a man. I was also unhappy with the way Sandy spoke to his son Daniel and so was everyone on site. I called Victor Elliot and arranged a meeting away from the building; we met at his plush home in Fingal.

After a few hours of discussion, we decided that as he and Sandy had been friends for many years, he would approach Sandy to find out if anything was bothering him. If Sandy needed extra funds, Vic would have put forward any shortfall. We needed to get the doors open or staff I had organised would go and work for other people.

Vic approached Sandy that night and Sandy agreed he would seek medical help for his seemingly worsening anger and medical issues. Vic organised appointments at Tweed Hospital for Sandy. In the next few days doctors really put Sandy through the mill medically.

His results from the tests were not good. Sandy had an inoperable brain tumour. Doctors sent Sandy home to get his affairs in order before the tumour took control and he wouldn't be able to control his bodily functions, let alone think for himself. This was devastating news for everyone connected to our project.

I remember sitting at my dining room table that night with my head in my hands thinking what the fuck next is coming my way. Poor bastard, no wonder he was always angry. His headaches must have been pure torture.

I had put just about all my savings into this project and to have it squashed now would crush me financially. There had to be a workable solution as there was no turning back for me.

Vic had the money to finish the project, but we had plenty to do administratively. I knew from experience that once Sandy had passed away, his bank and business accounts would be frozen. Victor had to organise for Sandy to transfer money to the business account and get his name off the account so we could keep operating later. This was a minefield, however my accountant sorted it out.

Sandy called a meeting with Victor, myself and Daniel in the workers shed and set out what he expected us to comply with after he was gone. He wasn't nice to us and to my shock he reached into a cupboard and pulled out a fully loaded pistol.

Sandy put the gun on the table in front of us and said he had contacted an old associate from Sydney. He said if his son was taken advantage of in anyway by Victor or myself, this gun would be used to take care of us. Guns do not frighten me, never have. It's the idiot holding the gun you have to be careful of.

I said I was a woman of honour and had been in this business too many years to put up with his threats. I told him I knew people of my own I could call on if necessary.

Sandy's paranoia and probable fear of dying was very evident and rightly so. He just didn't understand how the business worked on paper. He was in a heightened emotional state and I understood he knew he was leaving Daniel very vulnerable both emotionally and financially. This was probably the first time in his life that he had an issue he had no control over.

I relied on my accountant and lawyer to protect my interests and I was so glad I did when everything went to shit later. In the beginning I thought what could go wrong? There were legal partnership agreements with a change of ownership from Sandy to his son Daniel being prepared.

Every day we battled to get this project off the ground and it wasn't just the tradies that were working their guts out. There seemed to be a never-ending list of people to get organised. The newspaper ads, phones connected, credit card machines on premises and for outcalls. Staff rosters to be prepared, all the small but very important supplies to be ordered and placed into stock control cupboards. The list seemed to go on forever.

It was difficult trying to deal with a grieving Danny who would soon lose his father. He was near inconsolable, and he wandered around the building site like a lost puppy.

SANDY was re-admitted to hospital as his condition became critical. Two weeks later Sandy passed away. Daniel was devastated and really traumatised. He no longer had his protector, his mentor. He was all Daniel had to guide him through life, now he was gone. I tried to get him to agree to go into grief counselling but that was like talking to a brick wall.

I tried to find out about Danny's mother. She had had a nervous breakdown after the marriage broke down and Sandy got custody of Daniel. The break-up of the marriage was very vicious and Daniel was never permitted any contact with his mother. I felt Danny needed contact with his mother. He knew where she lived so I tried to encourage him to contact her. Finally, after many weeks he took my advice. I told him we have only one mother and there are always two sides to every story.

This young man was hurting deeply and needed some stability and direction in his life. He came to me one day at the worksite and asked me to go have a coffee with him, I stopped what I was doing and took him into the office in the work shed. He asked for my advice, he had contacted his mother. He seemed a little more relaxed but conflicted.

She had no car and was living in a small rented home unit. He said he still had the car his father had taken off her when the marriage broke up. He wanted advice on whether he should give the car back to her. I told him to give her the car back.

I truly believed Daniel was not mentally stable, still wasn't coping with the loss of his father. I was saw an unhealthy dependence happening between Daniel and Victor.

After Sandy's funeral the building project took off. Every day I arrived at 17 Morton Street to find everything running very smoothly.

FOUR weeks later we prepared for opening night. This was going to be a night of celebration on one hand, but sad that Sandy was not going to be there. I walked through the building amazed at what we had as a team achieved, each room was beautiful, opulent and very upmarket.

The place defied the impression of brothels being filthy, dirty, run-down places full of women who were physically abhorrent. They were wrong and this place was a perfect example of how wrong they were.

Each workroom was designed with a different theme. They were the Asian room, Jungle room, the Egyptian room and the Beach room, complete with an old surfboard on the wall.

There were security cameras in all hallways, office reception and in fact all public spaces, the only place there were no cameras was in each the workrooms. Each workroom had an alarm button. There was an alarm in reception that went straight to a security firm. Our car park also had security cameras that recorded everything.

When a client walked into the lounge room, he was greeted by a stunning, opulent design. There were lots of separate, single leather chairs around the room and two small separate little alcoves for a private chat between a client and a chosen lady if needed. There was room for six to eight clients at any one time.

Excitement built as opening time got closer. I knew we were going to be busy all night after the celebration earlier for owners and all the tradespeople who worked so hard to pull this project together. The building became party central once all invited guests arrived. I took the microphone and thanked everyone for all the work they had put in and we gave a salute with speeches for Sandy. I watched the tears roll down Daniel's face as I spoke.

After these celebrations were over and half the male guests had gone home, paying clients started to arrive. This was one night I was glad I was not a drinker. We were full on all night long. I could have had another six ladies on staff. The whole night went off very successful financially and without any issues between clients and staff. The opening night was going to be a huge success and the money was pouring in the doors.

I was exhausted just answering phones, taking money, getting ladies into rooms with clients and in between times loading washing machines and dryers. I was glad I had hired another receptionist to open the business again at 10am the next day because I didn't get home until 6. 30am the next day. I fell into my bed, content and thrilled with the takings for our first night. I knew my other two partners were going to be very happy with this new venture.

After only one week of Chinderah being opened, I knew this business was going to be very successful financially. I hired a very experienced receptionist who had moved to Tweed from Sydney, tall, with long dark hair, somewhere in her 40s. I didn't know why at that time but I do remember thinking I would have to watch this woman as something did not ring true.

After a few weeks, she convinced Victor she was going to stay long term and needed a place closer to the business. She said she would work as many days and hours as needed. Vic put a large mobile home on an acreage block he owned and connected it with water, and electricity for her. Free rent and not that far from work.

On one hand you had a very well-educated man who held down an important job at the local hospital but is not a very good judge of other people's character especially those in the sex industry, On the other hand, an extremely street-smart woman who has worked on the edge of Sydney underworld for more than 20 years. A match made in heaven for her.

She showed her intentions when she mouthed off about going to claim squatters' rights on Vic's block of land. She said this many times, but I did nothing about repeating it to Victor, mainly because I didn't believe she could or would try anything so stupid. Besides that, I knew Victor had no romantic inclinations of any kind towards her, which she often said he did.

With Chinderah up and running and my income in a much more stable position I quietly closed my Brisbane escort agency and bought the two ladies down the Chinderah to work one week on and one week off and I put my Brisbane unit on the market for sale. I was relieved I had gotten away without any police attention and pleased to bring my illegal activity up there to a halt.

A few months went by and the takings at our Chinderah brothel flourished handsomely. I believed both Vic and Danny were more than happy with the income being divided between us after expenses were deducted. I was saving my money as fast as I could because I wanted to know if I fell sick at any time, I would be financially okay.

I also had uneasy feelings on and off over the behaviour of not just the receptionist, but Victor and Danny seemed to be off. Maybe I was just physically and mentally tired, which I was. How stupid was I? Indeed, too stupid and ignorant to realise what was being plotted behind my back.

I had been working very long hours day after day, week after week and was totally committed to our business. Financial records had to be checked and double-checked after every shift. Takings had to be calculated at the end of every day shift, ladies' payments had to be calculated and checked. Once there was an incident when one shift had a shortfall of $100 from the partners' takings. I spent hours going through all paperwork and still I could find nothing amiss. This left me with only one conclusion ... we had a dishonest receptionist. Knowing it and proving it was another issue.

I called Victor and Daniel and arranged for them to come into the premises that night as I was on reception. I believe I knew the answer but knew I would have a problem convincing Victor. I went to work that afternoon and waited for my business partners to arrive. On arrival they came into the office and we went into a very lengthy sometimes-heated discussion over this missing $100. I pointed out that this daily paperwork was designed by myself many years ago and was infallible. The paperwork could not be forged or altered, and everything written on these sheets were written in biro, not pencil which could be rubbed out. I did not outright accuse the shift receptionist of pocketing the missing $100, but my gut feeling was she was bloody guilty as hell.

My suggestion to both partners was to get a security camera in above the desk, this would ensure funds never went missing ever again on anyone's shift. My suggestion was not well received. I did not understand this attitude because the takings were enormous. I felt I must insist on having this camera put in. It was going in even if I had to pay for it out of my own pocket.

I tried to make sense of their reluctance to protect our business funds. I knew this $100 theft was just testing the waters for future embezzlement. My instincts were rarely wrong. I had been around people in this industry for a very long time and had myself been taken for several financial rides of dishonesty over the years.

I went home from work early hours of that morning feeling unsettled and physically not well, I had been putting up with ongoing dizzy little turns on and off for weeks. I felt devoid of energy and mentally worn out. I had told both my partners I was putting the security camera in over the reception desk, and I was going to pay for it myself.

Later that week I passed out on the floor in my kitchen at home and went to hospital. All sorts of tests were done but nothing conclusive. Losing consciousness for no reason was concerning but I chose to ignore it. I was just too busy, so I thought. This was on account of blood test results showing I was anaemic and I needed either top-up injections or an iron transfusion.

I followed my doctor's orders and went on total bed rest. Four days later I was ready to go back to work and rang Vic to tell him I would come into work and sort out my time sheets. Yes, I was still tired, but I was I felt on the mend.

Victor. Told me he and Danny wanted a meeting to discuss a few things. This concerned me on two fronts. Firstly, because nothing had come of the tests in the hospital I still didn't feel well and, secondly, what happened with the $100.

We met for coffee in the local Kingscliff Park the next day at 9am. Danny said nothing and was very quiet, letting Victor do all the talking. I carefully watched their faces and felt shivers of dread.

Victor told me he and Danny had voted me out of the company and that my services were no longer required. I sat there and looked at them astounded. How could they do this legally? I was speechless.

They said they had changed the locks on the building and that if I tried to enter the building I would be arrested. I was so shocked and bewildered I could barely get up from my seat. I remember saying to them as I walked away, "Make sure you both get a good legal mouthpiece because you are going to need one".

I was going to fight these bastards with every breath and dollar I could muster. I called my long-time accountant at Robina on the Gold Coast. He was astounded but assured me what they had done was illegal. He then proceeded to find all our company documents and told me he would call me back. I was also relieved I had been saving all my money from my share of the takings for a rainy day as I was going to need every dollar.

When the company had been set up, Vic and Sandy could not gang up on me and vote me out of the company which meant I had two votes, not one. When Sandy passed away and his son took over as director in his place this meant nothing had changed. But Daniel owned the property where the business was being run from. Therefore, I had no control over the property, I was merely a business partner.

My accountant sent me to a very well-known law firm on the Gold Coast and I supplied the law firm with copies of the original company documents and the altered ones putting Danny in his father's place as a director after Sandy died. All the paperwork was legal and correct and would serve me well once all this got into court.

Victor and Daniel were served with papers to attend court. This bullshit went on for months. My lawyer advised me to take this as far as we could take it, what they had done was against the law. What I did not know was that receptionist had been rewriting the books to give false calculations of the financial figures in the weekly takings. They tried to prove the business had not been making the money weekly that I had claimed it was, so I was not entitled to claim a share of the profits.

Luckily, I still had several pages of takings signed by staff working when they collected their pay after their shifts. I also had a couple of pages of proof of takings after expenses over a couple of weeks. I took these pages home only the day before I passed out and ended up in hospital. The $100 missing from takings made me take these documents home; I was looking for other anomalies of past takings that may have been missed.

At the end of the day, all the rewriting of the books done by that receptionist from Sydney on Vic and Danny's behalf would get them nowhere once my lawyer got it into court. Any handwriting expert would be able to prove all the signatures on the few pages I had were genuine and the books she cooked for those exact same days would probably only bring criminal charges against both of them.

Thankfully I still had some original day sheets to present to the court to prove they had cooked the books and committed fraud. I knew they had no idea I was holding these day sheets and these would end up being my ace card when my lawyers could get a court date.

This was going to be a fight they wish they had never taken on. I had a brilliant lawyer on the Gold Coast. Bring it on, arseholes.

I WAS prepared for a fight but I was so stressed leading up to that court case I had several health-related issues and my relationship was in trouble. This was in fight for my very financial survival. My lawyer and my accountant met me on the steps of the Supreme Court with all the relevant documents they would need to present to the judge. My lawyer also had supplied copies of all the income documents that I had been holding to their lawyer.

I expected to walk into court ready for a huge fight but in the last few moments, they conceded they would go into a settlement negotiation. You must know I came so close to telling them to fuck off. But with my stress levels the way they were I decided to leave the negotiations in the hands of my lawyer.

A judge would have been horrified if I had lost my cool in his courtroom and he probably would have leaned sympathetically towards my ex-partners had I thrown a tantrum.

I just wanted my money back and my personal belongings and a few original paintings I had put into the building plus my legal and accountancy fees.

My lawyer was brilliant, he got me exactly the outcome I wanted nothing more and nothing less. I guess I could have taken them for the loss of my share of income to the tune of something around $50,000 but that would have been eaten up in legal fees. Small fish are sweet and protracted legal action is sometimes not worth the stress or cost.

I went home happy with the outcome and arrangements were made for my funds to be deposited into my bank account, my lawyer and accountant were paid and for me to pick up my personal belongings from their lawyer's his office.

This contented girl needed a glass of vino and another new life. I had plans but with I would be very cautious about whom I trusted in any potential future business venture.

CHAPTER 24

Out with the old in with the new

IN THE next few months I did my homework and bought a huge house on a lake in Ballina, NSW. It was on Racecourse Road in an industrial estate with an upstairs and downstairs sections and was fully secure and fenced. I also found the town potentially was a great spot for a sex business.

A woman in her 30s had a couple of girls working for her from a couple of apartments and motels in and around Ballina. She also worked in the business and her boyfriend was a bodyguard of sorts. This was being operated as a serious business, but I had already decided to start up again on my own after the debacle of Chinderah. I knew I had a better chance of succeeding if I owned the property because an agent or owner couldn't evict me if the nature of my business became public knowledge. Racecourse Road was quiet most of the time and as I would not be advertising the exact address.

I had moved into our new house in Kingscliff and would travel about an hour's drive each way to Racecourse Road. I wanted council approval before starting the business. I intended on submitting a development application for approval the property.

The NSW Government had designated that all brothels must be in and on council-approved industrial land or in commercial premises not close to any housing estates, churches or schools of any kind. The government also said that the town must have more than 10,000 residents for an application to be considered for approval.

The Queensland years and Chinderah sage were over, it was time to put my absolute energy and time into making this new project in Ballina a financial and personal success. The house here in Racecourse Road was set up and I was operating the business with caution on every level. I was working the business myself five days a week and on weekends I was travelling back to my home in Kingscliff to rest and stay connected to my family and Nellie. Every second weekend I went back to Brisbane to spend time with my mother and to give my brother Mick a break from looking after her.

Mum had been diagnosed with a failing heart and emphysema. She had never smoked a cigarette in her life and had never drunk alcohol. She had been a chef, so I guess in those days people smoked indoors and in every restaurant. Passive smoking was discovered as a killer way too late for many people. Mum was one of them. Health authorities organised an oxygen machine for her and she was able to live relatively well hooked up to the machine.

TROUBLE found me pretty quickly in Ballina. I had made it my business to stay away from the darkness of being involved in the criminal world of standover merchants, drug dealers and any other illegal activity in the sex industry.

What I didn't realise when I bought the Racecourse Road property was that just the street was a local bikers group clubhouse. They had chapters all over NSW. I had seen bikes coming and going out of the estate but took no notice. They weren't my concern. I had too much else on my plate to even notice.

One weekend I was away in Brisbane at Mum's house when my receptionist Ammie called late one night. She said three men in full club colours had come into the business demanding to speak with the owner. She had told them I was away and would not be back until Monday morning. Ammie said they behaved in a threatening manner and were using foul language.

The staff were scared and Ammie felt threatened.

I told her to call the security company and put them on notice in case she needed them.

The bikers did not leave names. My security system recorded all visuals of arrivals, so I was not over duly concerned. Their faces were recorded if any attacks happened.

When I arrived back on Monday, I waited for them to contact me, but they didn't show. So I put the issue aside. I was going to train a part-time receptionist for two shifts a week to relieve myself and Ammie.

The week progressed and I still not had contact with the bikers, so I decided to head home to Kingscliff house until Sunday night. On the Friday night, I was asleep my phone rang. It was Ammie on the phone, The bikers were back. Ammie said they left a message for me … unless I paid them $500 a week, they would put me out of business. Once again, I told Ammie to contact the security company and that I would be back in the morning.

I was concerned for the safety of my staff and receptionist, but I was in no way scared of these bastards. My partner and I discussed the possibility of negotiating with them. I made it very clear I would never allow myself to be put into an uncompromising position ever again. I had played this game in the past and lost my freedom. It was not going to happen again.

I arrived back in Ballina after lunch the next day and I waited for them to call. Again, they did not make contact. Two of the ladies working for me were so terrified they left and the trainee receptionist quit on the spot after the bikers had left my premises the night before. I was so angry I could barely contain myself. There wasn't a remote possibility my business could afford to pay protection money.

I was on the phone with my partner and told her to stop her panic. I would handle this situation. No, I was not going to the cops. She was insistent. It was then that I told her this was my business, not hers and regardless of the property being in both names she needed to shut the fuck up and let me handle this.

I owned the business totally. I would not agree to any police getting involved under any circumstances. She asked what if they carried out their threats of burning the house down and people died inside?

Monday went by with no contact from these so-called tough bikers and I was beginning to think that maybe they just wanted to disrupt my business only on the weekends. Friday and Saturday nights were when my business made the most money.

The next morning the work phone rang. The male voice on the other end asked to speak to the owner of the business. I thought it was a representative from a supplier or even the local newspaper seeking advertising.

No, this was one of the bikers. He asked me if my staff told me of the conditions I would have to comply with if I wanted to stay in business in Ballina. Big tough biker setting down conditions to me over the phone. I just lost my shit. Staff came running up the hallway wondering why I was suddenly screaming at the top of my voice.

"Who the fuck do you think you are? You lowlife, gutter-crawling thug. You threaten to bash my staff and me; you threaten to burn down my house. You demand $500 a week to allow me to keep my doors open? You threaten drive-by shootings at my property. This is the year 2000, not the '50s, '60s or even the '70s, you fucking piece of shit. Do you visit the local butchers, bakers or any other business and demand protection money? No! you don't. You will not be getting a fucking cent, nothing from me, not one fucking dollar and if you come near me or my business ever again, I will blow your fucking head off. I am not frightened of you or any of your fucking lowlife biker friends."

He listened to me lose my temper and was very quiet. He waited until I calmed down and then he said to me, "Suzy, it's going to be more beneficial to you long term if you come to an arrangement with us. How about if I give you my phone number and we talk about this another day?"

I wrote down his phone number and hung up in his ear, I was furious. I walked around the house ranting and raving like a banshee. Who the fuck do these people think they are the mafia? I rang my partner and told her what had happened. I shouldn't have and don't really know why I did really.

It took me hours to calm down. One benefit from losing my cool was it gave my staff confidence to stay working for me. They knew I was not scared of these thugs and would stand my ground, no matter what it took. Word got around to all the staff not on the premises that day. I made myself a coffee and sat quietly thinking about how I was going to handle this situation.

Firstly, I had to make sure I was protected. I called a close friend of mine in Brisbane and asked him to borrow a gun. His nickname was Bent Axle. He is no longer with us. He said he could bring down a .38 and ammunition, but you must be very careful it has a hair trigger.

I called another friend Garry, who worked in the kitchen cabinet-making business. I needed a secret little shelf built into my receptionist desk ASAP.

I then phoned another friend and explained what was happening to me. He had contacts with a well-known biker's group, in Brisbane. He said he would get someone to call me tonight. It was going to be a case of fight fire with fire, or pay the fucking money. There was no way in God's hell was I paying them a cent.

It was around midnight I had a call from the Brisbane bikers club. He listened and said he would come down to Ballina and speak to the president of the local club to negotiate on my behalf. "But for me to do that it will cost you a negotiation fee which you will have to pay to my club," he said. I agreed to pay his fee and he said he would call me back the next afternoon.

Two hours later Bent Axle arrived with my gun and I took it downstairs to hide in my living area The gun was loaded and ready to protect me and the staff if need be.

No one except myself and Bent Axle knew I had the gun. I slept very well that night. The next day we worked as if nothing had happened, I waited for the call from the Brisbane club. The contact rang about 7pm and said he had made many phone calls, on my behalf and arranged a meeting between himself and his own bodyguard to meet with the president of the local club. This meeting was to take place in Byron Bay at midnight on the coming Saturday night.

He asked me if I would keep my business open so they could come to Ballina once the meeting was over. He wanted his negotiation fees available in cash, no problems here.

Saturday night was looming and I was getting nervous. I had called my Mum to tell her I would be up for Sunday and Monday instead of the weekend. I had also changed rosters with Ammie so that she would work on Friday and Sunday and Monday. I did not want her on the premises when the Brisbane people arrived early Sunday morning.

It was a very strange atmosphere that Saturday night, work was flowing well but everyone was on edge. I kept looking at my phone waiting for the call. My phone rang at 2.30am. The meeting was over and they would see me in about 30 minutes.

A small black Mercedes pulled into the driveway. Two men came up the stairs. The shorter of the two guys was the man I had spoken with. The second guy was huge. He sent chills down my spine. These men were not run-of-the-mill biker thugs. They had an air about them that spelled more than trouble.

The man I had spoken with on the phone started the conversation. "Suzy, you did well to stand your ground. This attempt at getting you to pay up has not and will not ever be sanctioned. The three guys are acting on their own. What you decide to do about it is up to you. If you do decide to pay you will be paying well into the future. They will no doubt put pressure on you for more."

I replied, saying, "I believe in negotiations on any issues before action. This is why I contacted you before things got out of hand, I am very grateful to you and your club for representing me and I thank you both." I handed over the envelope with the cash and said if there was anything I could ever do for them all they had to do was call me.

We exchanged business cards and they finished their drinks and they left. Even though the fee I had paid would set me back a couple of weeks, it was the right decision.

Later that morning I left Ballina and headed for Brisbane to visit my Mum. She was lacking female company even though her granddaughters visited her every couple of weeks. It wasn't the same.

I ignored probably 20 calls from my partner over the last few days. I was just too busy. I would call into the Kingscliff house before going back to Ballina. I left Brisbane and headed to Kingscliff. My partner was not there so I just left a note saying I would be at my reception desk in the morning and to call.

On the Tuesday morning my partner rang and asked why I had not been taking her calls. I told her I had been dealing with the threats from the bikers. She floored me when she told me she had contacted the Crime Commission in Sydney and police would be contacting me.

I was horrified I could barely speak. I told her she was an idiot. "The one thing you do not do in this business is involve the police unless it is an emergency."

I told her to call them back and tell them the matter has been sorted. She said, "No, Suzy, I am listed as part owner of that property and I have rights over this matter, I have put this in the hands of the police and they will be coming to see you very soon." I could have reached down the phone and shaken the shit out of her. Part owner! It's on paper only. For fuck's sake, it's my earnings that pay the fucking mortgage.

I decided to tell the cops the whole matter had been sorted. But I knew it was far from being sorted because I knew these thugs were going to come at me again. This situation may not have been club-sanctioned but scaring people into complying was their game.

The cops arrived. I was relieved they did not look like cops. They looked like a couple of thugs and were very discrete. The police had a folder with signed statements from my partner as being part owner of the property and a statement saying the local bikers had made some very serious threats.

It didn't matter what I said. They had evidence to back up her statement. I could not divulge my clandestine negotiations. They asked me if the bikers contacted me again. I said no. and my reply was no. They also had security film proving these three thugs of men had been on my property.

The cops' plan was for me to take my staff out for breakfast on Friday morning. We had to be away from the property from 7am until 10am. The police team would enter the house and wire up the reception area with cameras and sound. There was nothing I could do to stop them. Extortion was a very serious offence and so were threats of violence against women. Burning a place down with people inside or trying to was attempted murder.

I did what I was told to do and none of my staff was any the wiser. I left late in the afternoon to go to Kingscliff. Sure enough, around midnight my phone woke me up. It was Ammie on the phone saying the bikers were parked out the front and had called demanding to speak to me.

They wanted an answer to their demands. They were swearing, calling everyone names and demanding a face-to-face meeting with me. They gave Ammie a phone number for me to call. She then said they had all driven off and everything was quiet again. I told her to call security if anything went down. The cops would have known by morning that something had happened at my business as my security company service was being filmed via 24 hr recording.

CHAPTER 25

The police takedown

I WAS AWAKE at 6am next day when the cops phoned. The detective in charge wanted to see me. I arranged to meet them at Lennox Heads as I did not want to be seen with them in Ballina or anywhere else for that matter but Lennox Heads, the least noticeable place.

The rogue bikers wanted me to call to set up a meeting on my premises for Monday morning. I called the number several times but no answer. I told the cops I would let them know as soon as they answered, but it probably be in the afternoon.

The police were insistent that they be present when I called so I could put it on loud speaker for them to hear

About 2pm I rang the number again and said who I was. I also had a go at them for upsetting my staff late at night. My voice raised "So you have demanded a face-to-face meeting with me? Well, I am available on Monday at 9am at my premises. Don't be fucking late. I have a business to run."

I hung up and listened to their plan for Monday morning. I was to engage the leader of these thugs in a conversation about the amount of money I was expected to pay. I was to get them the spell out what protection I could expect in return. Seal the deal and set a time for them to collect their first $500 for protection.

When they left my premises, the police would block their exit and arrest them and take them into police custody to Lismore to book them.

They asked if the thugs were armed. I didn't know as I had never met them and all the threats had been by phone.

I had better get Bent Axle to come to get his gun. I rang him from the post office and told him not to call me on my phone. I explained what was happening. "Please come tonight to pick up your toy. I do not want to be caught with an unlicensed weapon."

He arrived about midnight and I explained everything in detail. Bent Axle said, "Suzy do not stress. What they were doing to you was not club sanctioned and their arrests over their standover protection racket will not go down very well with the club president. They will be bringing shame on the club."

As the week progressed, I was starting to feel very edgy. On the Sunday night I had a very restless night and everything that was going to happen on my premises this morning went absolutely against my grain. The cops reminded me several times that I had better not fuck this up or I would face charges of my own for obstruction of justice.

I had to talk myself into believing that all this was for the best because if the situation got out of hand people could be seriously hurt or even killed. I had several phone calls from the cops to check on their sound levels and was told to speak louder when talking.

I had no idea where they had placed their secret cameras or microphones.

The allotted time came and no bikers, where the fuck were they? At 9.15am the cops rang and told me to call the number they had given me. I dialled the number and a male voice answered. I said, "This is Suzy. Where the fuck are you people? I told you 9am and it's now nearly 9.30. I also told you I had a business to run and for you not to be late." He spluttered and carried on about having things to do but might get here after lunch. I had had a couple of bourbons to steady my nerves earlier. I had enough grog under my belt to let fly. I raised my voice to a point of near screaming and told him if they were not here by 10am they could go fuck themselves and if it was a fucking full-on fight with no holds barred that's what they would get. "If you are not on my doorstep at or before 10am don't bother coming. I will see you on the battlefield."

This outburst sent the cops into a spin. The head detective rang straight away and told me I had stuffed things. "Suzy, you have fucked up." He ranted and raved worse than I could ever have. I listened without speaking until he finished his rant. Then I said, "I beg to disagree. They will show up. These thugs love scaring women. They are not used to a woman speaking to them like I did and there is the matter of a potential extra $500 a week income for them. They will show up."

I think I was on my third bourbon and Coke when I heard a motorbike pull into my driveway, followed by a white delivery van. Two men got out of the van and the other one who was on his Harley spoke to them and they walked up to my front security door and rang the bell. I released the door and walked out from behind my desk and watched them walk up the stairs. I watched the two van guys run their hands up the handrail and look around both sides of the wall. They were looking for listening devices for sure. They were out of luck. The police IT guys who put in the surveillance gear did a brilliant undetectable job.

I went back behind my desk and I looked at them intently. I fired off a barrage of abuse at them ... the usual bullshit about them picking on women. I must have begun to overstep my mark because my phone rang and I answered it as if it were from a client. It was the head cop telling me to shut up and get the evidence they needed.

I hung the phone up and looked the leader square in the face.

I turned to the leader of this little band of three stooges and asked what protection could they give me if I decided to pay them $500 a week. I said $500 was a ridiculous amount of money. He started to rattle off about them being available to drive my staff to outside bookings. They would be available to sit on my premises on busy nights to make sure there was no trouble from clients. If there were issues with bad clients all I would have to do is call and one of them would be here.

I told them I was not aware of their club being in the same street as my business. "You know if you guys had come down here and introduced yourselves and asked for a monthly contribution for your non-profit club when I first opened up in this town, I probably would have been happy to support your club. I more than likely would have even given a couple of your guys with cars a driver's job. Instead, you chose to try to bully and frighten my staff. I lost several very good girls and a receptionist because of your nasty antics. Why did you take this path?"

He sputtered and even apologised for their behaviour. He even stated they would have been very happy with a couple of cartons of beer each month.

"Well, it's now come to this. I either pay you protection money or we have an all-out war on our hands, don't we? We both know what happens in wars, don't we? Innocent people get hurt. Only this would be very, very bad, especially if you guys killed or seriously wounded a woman here or myself. Publicity involving women being harmed for not paying protection money would be a very bad look for your club.

I also knew by now the cops were getting very annoyed with me for dragging this out, being half pie-eyed on alcohol. I really didn't give a shit. I knew it was the cops on the phone because my phone never stopped ringing. I then said to the head honcho, "Okay, I will pay the money you want for my protection but only for two weeks. Then we will then negotiate a fairer deal."

He looked at me and smiled, shaking my hand to clinch the deal. I looked at him and smiled back, knowing the moment they stepped foot into my car park it was all over Red Rover for them. All three guys proceeded down the front stairs to leave.

They stepped into the carpark and went to walk over to their van and bike when all hell broke loose. There was screaming. "Down on the ground, get down on the fucking ground."

Five heavily armed men in uniforms took control. I thought it looked like a raiding team in Iraq. This was like a scene from a movie. This was like nothing I had ever seen before in my life and I had witnessed many strange goings-on over my lifetime, I am glad I was half pie-eyed from my few drinks or I might have been scared shitless.

I had no idea this police operation was so huge. As far as I knew the arrests would be done by the two Sydney cops. These cops did not know if these bikers had guns. I understand why the whole operation was kept secret, including from local police.

I even forgave my partner for getting the police involved. She was a normal person who was worried and scared for not just our property but for the lives of myself and the staff.

The three-biker offenders were arrested and thrown into separate cars. I guess this was to make sure they couldn't get their stories in sync. They were taken over to Lismore and charged with an array of offences. The police also put into place a DVO, so they were forbidden to come near me, my property and staff.

The three bikers made bail. A date was set for a hearing a month later and I was expected to appear, which I did. They were remanded for another date. I just did not care and was glad their harassment had ceased. It had to or they would have been put back behind bars. Again, this saga went on for months, delay after delay.

Over the next six months, all was quiet on my home front, business was flowing but I just did not feel myself inside, I was having a few worrying issues.

The new court case was coming up and I seriously did not want to be involved, a date had been set up and I was informed I had to be in court in Lismore for the three bikers' court cases.

I drove across to Lismore taking one of the girls that had been threatened by these three with me, as she would be needed to give evidence against them in court. I parked my car well away from the courthouse and we walked up to the courts. I couldn't believe my eyes. There were at least eight bikers all in club colours standing outside the court.

The girl that was with me was terrified, I just looked at them. I was waiting for the taunts but they never said a word to us. In fact, the lead instigator smiled at me and said hello. What was this? An attempt to intimidate me? Then I looked at his group of supporters. His wife and two little kiddies were by his side as were other women with the other two guys.

I could feel myself soften up inside. I did not want anyone to go to jail especially someone with a family. After a morning of legal mumbo jumbo, the judge called for a recess. We all walked out of the courthouse and the girl and I stood there as the bikers and supporters filed out.

The instigator spoke to me and I listened. I was no longer angry. I had had six months of peace and quiet from them. I said to him, "Listen, you idiot, if you had approached me in a different way, I would have supported your fucking club in some way. You know that I know and was aware the whole time that what you were doing to me was not club-sanctioned. You also know now that it was my partner who involved the cops, which I was not happy about. It was out of my hands. Pulling in my own negotiator to speak with your president cost me a shit load of money. You and your mates did all this on your own.

"I do not want anyone to go to jail, and all I want is for you all to stay the fuck away from my business and me. The cops have not yet, approached me, or the prosecutor over what is happening here, but I am not stupid. Deals get done, no one knows or understands this more than me. I have been in the exact position your lot is now in. I chose jail rather than open my mouth. You know nothing about my background or me, but you also know I will fight fire with fire and the way this has played out probably has saved lives.

"I will do everything I can to assist you people on one condition! You all stay the fuck away from my business or me. You know there is a DVO against you all and if you break it, I will call it in and if you do not get to jail this time you will face jail for breaking the DVO conditions. I have no idea how this will play out right now.

"Give me your word and assurance of peace and I will try to help you. I see you have a wife and kids and know personally what it feels like to be taken away from your family."

Jesus Christ, here I was on the steps of the courthouse doing a deal with the devil. But I just did not want anyone to go to jail and innocent kids to suffer. I was given his word and I walked away from him.

Just before recess was over the cop in charge and prosecutor called me into to a room to talk to me. They wanted this situation to be taken to trial. I flat-out refused to co-operate and told them that I was ill, which I was. The cops were furious and I knew my partner would not co-operate either because I had called her and discussed what had transpired.

The bikers' lawyers pushed for the matter to be dealt with that day. They received good behaviour bonds and I think one received a suspended sentence because of past criminal history. A suspended sentence means if that person breaks the law again, they will go to jail for this offence on top of a sentence for the crime committed.

We all left the courtroom and the head biker offender came across and thanked me for not sending them to trial. I just looked at him and said, "We have a deal. Keep it or you will end up in jail." We smiled at each other and walked off.

CHAPTER 26

A new day another fight

WITH ALL the dramas in my life, I had been feeling tired and exhausted for several years. I had had several small incidences of losing consciousness and had ended up in hospital when I was at Chinderah. I had never followed up anything. But in the last few months of 2000 I had been making a few mistakes, such as paying my bills but forgetting I had paid them or believing I had paid them, but hadn't.

I was having really bad headaches, so I went to a specialist in Lismore and had all sorts of tests. The results were a terrible shock. A small tumour had shown up at the base of my brain. A scan showed I needed an operation.

I rang my partner but all she could think about was the luxury car I owned. That was it as far as I was concerned, I would deal with her later. A date was set for the operation in Lismore. To top all this off a letter came from Ballina Council saying I was operating an unlicensed brothel and to cease business.

Sure, I was guilty, but the NSW laws pertaining to where a brothel could be situated allowed my business to be there. I went straight to a local lawyer with a good reputation. I kept my business open while my lawyer handled the fight.

I had my operation and ended up with a paralysed right arm and a few days of paralysis of my left hand. I was absolutely devastated but had been assured my right arm would come good with time. My lawyer sued the doctor and anaesthetist.

My brachial plexus was crushed and radial nerve damaged which left my right arm paralised. The brachial plexus is the network of nerves that sends signals from the spinal cord to the shoulder, arm and hand. How the fuck did this happen? These people are professionals. My neurosurgeon told me I had to retrain my brain. He told me to make a list of everything I had to do every day and tick off each chore as I do them.

I taught myself to write with my left hand, which thankfully had come good a couple of days after my operation. I still had to write cheques to pay bills and do my business paperwork. I was also going to a physiotherapist every second day to ensure I was doing the right exercises to keep the muscles in my right arm from losing tone. I exercised non-stop every couple of hours while I was at work. There was no way this was going to beat me. I didn't have time to be sick or to wallow in self-pity. I had to fight. My very future depended on it.

I still went to Brisbane to visit Mum and to Kingscliff. I tried to carry on with life in between juggling two very trying, emotional and financially draining fights.

Some days I just wanted to curl up and cry. The fight with the council was heating up and I was astounded that right in the middle of the fight they changed the Local Environment Plans, the council laws about how and where businesses could operate.

They then knocked back my application for a brothel licence. I decided to take the council to the Lands and Environment Court. The council made my life hell, I had to pay more than $5000 to put a car counter across the road to prove the traffic in the street was not attributed to my clientele coming and going. Certain local residents added deliberately to the count by driving over it many extra times during the day and night.

What if I lost in the Lands and Environment Court? Where would I go from here? I had to come up with a plan to allow me to still operate legally.

My legal team was costing me a fortune, as I now needed a barrister to represent me in court. Go broke I might but I was determined I was not going to walk away. I had fought too hard to be here, not just with the bikers but also with my own health issues.

There was no way in hell I was going to walk away from this fight. If

I was forced to operate illegally I would. I was very experienced at cat-and-mouse games with the police.

MY LAWYER settled my medical case out of court without my authority. I was so fucking angry I could barely speak. I found out only because I had to call a Brisbane specialist to confirm my appointment with him for Monday. The appointment was to help with my case. His receptionist told me she had just received a fax from my lawyer saying the case had been settled.

I hung up the phone and rang my lawyer. I was seething with anger. He told me this was the best settlement. I told him I would have wanted to take this case to the Supreme Court. That same lawyer was later charged with trust account fraud and disbarred from practice.

He told me the deal was done and could not be changed. I grabbed the local phonebook, searched for another lawyer and started dialling numbers. The third one agreed to see me later that day.

I repeated my story to the lawyer. He was astounded that the first lawyer hadn't spoken with me before accepting the insurance company's payout.

He suggested I report him to the Law Society and in the meantime, he would put a garnishee on the monies the insurance company was going to pay into the first lawyer's account. He also sent off an immediate request for full disclosure of the initial lawyer's fees and who was owed money so he could discover what my payout would be.

It was 6pm before I walked out of my new lawyer's office but I felt confident. I fired the first lawyer and he had to be accountable for every dollar and every decision he had made on my behalf. The one thing I was concerned that my first lawyer was representing me in my fight with the council and in the Lands and Environment Court.

The outcome of all this debacle was the new lawyer cost me another $4000, money well worth it. However, to have the first lawyer investigated by the Law Society and get a complete breakdown of his exorbitant fees was not only time-consuming but would have tied up my funds. I just could not afford to lose any more money.

At least my physiotherapist received her money. I was furious that the first solicitor walked away with more than half my medical insurance payout but there was nothing more I could do about it.

CHAPTER 27

The execution of Victor Elliot

THERE WAS more drama heading my way. I was at my desk at work when the work phone rang. It was a woman who had been working for me only a week before and we were on great terms.

She was rambling so much I could barely understand her. It took a few minutes to calm her down. The story she told me just about blew me out of my seat. I was speechless for the second time this year. I could barely breathe. I remember looking at my watch. It was 6pm on May 26, 2000.

She told me that Victor Elliot had been gunned down in the driveway of his half-finished new brothel in Morton Street and had been killed. She had been working there. There were cops everywhere and everyone was terrified.

This was not at my old workhouse at No.17, but in the driveway of No.19. Remember I had helped Victor get a brothel licence to stop any other prospective business from ever opening there.

I remember these moments as if they were yesterday. I remember thinking this was karma payback. I thought, "Victor, was what you have been manipulated to do worth losing your life over. You were once a highly respected head chief radiographer at the local hospital and now you lay dead in the driveway of your unfinished brothel."

He did not deserve to die in a hail of bullets. I warned him that by coming into the sex industry he would be dealing with people with no morals and scruples.

The killing made national news. Not knowing the circumstances made everyone very nervous. So many unsubstantiated stories floated around it was ridiculous.

The following part of this story is only hearsay. These tidbits may be truths, half-truths or just plain gossip. However, some are very close to the bone.

It seems that Victor was being guided by the very same receptionist who worked for us while I was involved in the business at Chinderah. They had decided that after taking control of the family home that belonged to Danny's father Sandy, who had died from a brain tumour, to open 17 Morton Street, leaving Danny with little or no staff and a struggling business.

Compare the personalities of Victor and Danny. Danny was a grieving, young man and had been heavily reliant on his domineering late father Sandy. So, he blindly trusted Victor and probably would have signed anything Victor put in front of him. Victor was his new father figure. Then there was Victor, a highly educated, successful business owner in his own right even without the brothel business. He was earning top wages from the hospital, plus thousands more from selling beef cattle and rents from storage sheds he owned at Billinudgel. Plus, God knows what else.

But he was being guided by a person with little or no morals or scruples. Victor had no street smarts; he was ruled only by the accumulation of assets and money. Once again, I need to point out to you that a lot of this is hearsay. This woman was so obsessed with Victor that she secretly changed her surname name to match the occurring circumstances she had planned from day one.

I believe he had no idea of anything she did and he believed she was his right-hand girl who was loyal to him. After all, she had left Danny's business at No.17 and taken most of Danny's staff and was heavily involved with helping Victor set up his new brothel next door. Victor needed her. They needed each other.

Danny was manipulated out of his family home on the waterfront at Tweed Heads, worth a fortune. He was now being destroyed financially over his business at 17 Morton Street.

There was bad blood in the air; it was inevitable that a very dangerous confrontation was coming. I was grateful I was no longer part of this.

But I still soaked up every bit of news I could get my hands on about the killing. I kept getting phone calls from past staff and staff working at 17 Morton Street. This went on for weeks. It was said police were looking for a four-wheel drive, but no one knew what to believe.

All these calls set off alarm bells in my head. I was convinced my phones were being tapped again. After my experience with Victor, Danny and that receptionist I can understand why I was being named as the driving force behind Victor's killing. During some calls when I feared the phone was tapped, I said, "You got this, Mr Policeman? Make sure you write all this down. Don't trust your recording man."

GOSSIP in this business travelled fast. Girls spread the news about which places or owners to be very wary of. It was no surprise that the gossip was that I had had Victor Elliot murdered. A few weeks later I had my first call from police. I had been waiting patiently for it. I knew I would be a suspect in Victor's killing.

The caller identified himself as a Homicide Squad detective from Sydney who was at Tweed Heads investigating Victor's murder. He wanted to speak to me in person.

Even though I knew this was coming it still sent shivers down my spine. It seems certain people said Victor's death was my payback for what he had done to me.

I agreed to meet him, so we set a time of 9am next day at my Racecourse Road premises. That night went smoothly. Ladies were working happily and there was lots of laughter at the antics of some clients. Seriously I swear some men think sex workers are clueless, when in fact they are very smart. Some of these women have survived some pretty horrendous situations in their lives.

I didn't sleep very soundly and was up early so I could get all the house chores done, staff ready and I had organised my phones to be answered and business taken care of while I was being questioned.

I finished all my cleaning and restocking chores and went downstairs to shower, put on my make-up and looked for something suitable to wear for my police interview. Dressed in jeans, T-shirt and RM Williams boots, I looked more like a farmer's wife than a brothel madam.

JUST BEFORE 9am two tall, well-dressed men came to the door. I let them in and they showed me their police identification and gave me their police business cards.

I ushered them both out onto the front verandah and they sat down on the chairs at the outdoor table setting. I made their coffee and took the cups out to them. I joined them and waited for one of them to speak.

I was not concerned about the business being interrupted by my appointment with these two police officers as I had arranged for a receptionist to work the day shift and with us being behind closed glass doors shielded by heavy inside curtains, over all our space was very private.

For discretionary purposes I will call them Bob and Jim. I estimated Bob was in his 40s, tall, slim and had brown hair with a little greying at the sides. He had a firm but controlled voice and piercing green eyes. I felt he was a no-nonsense type, with many years, experience in the police force. He was dressed like a businessman.

Jim was in his mid or early 30s, also tall but a little heavier than Bob. He also had that look of no nonsense but I felt he had a softer side to his nature. Again, I estimated he also had many years, experience in the police force.

Our conversation went back and forth. They were like a pair of cats, playing with a lone mouse. I was the mouse; only this mouse was not guilty of stealing the cheese. I have been dealing with police and playing their games for bloody years and I was not intimidated by either of them.

I told them straight out that if I had planned to kill Victor Elliot, I would have done the job myself. I wouldn't have hired idiots like the people who fucked up Victor's murder. I also would have taken out his offsider. If I needed an issue dealt with, I did my own dirty work.

The look on both their faces was classic. The facts were my issues with Victor Elliot and company ended on the steps of a courthouse in my favour. I closed that chapter in my life and moved on. Why the fuck would I jeopardise my life and freedom over people who in my opinion were scum of the earth.

I told them they needed to be looking closer to home for answers. I also pointed out I had records proving where I was and who I was with every day, backed up by phone records and paperwork, for the last few weeks.

After two hours of all this pussy-footing I guess these detectives believed or at least half believed I had nothing to do with Victor Elliot's death. I agreed to drive up to Tweed Heads two days later for a formal written statement. I was mentally exhausted.

I know how I felt as somebody innocent of killing or planning the killing of Victor Elliot. I couldn't comprehend going through something like this being guilty.

Two days later I drove to Tweed Heads for my formal, typed interview with the Homicide detectives. I had been hoping I would not be there very long. I sat in my car thinking about everything that had happened and I hoped today would at least put an end to all the accusations.

The attitude of the uniform officer on the desk bordered on rude. I thought it's only 9.30am what is he going to be like at the end of the day? I told him who I was and who I was there to see. He called through and then told me to wait.

Some 10 minutes went by and I was feeling restless. I remember thinking I was either a suspect or the Homicide cops were just being arseholes. I was just about to leave when Detective Bob called my name. He apologised for making me wait which surprised me.

Bob showed me into an office and sitting there was another detective whom I did not know. So here was the deal Bob was going to ask the questions and Peter, I would call him, was going to do all the typing.

After all the formalities about address etc. they asked about who I knew and didn't. They mentioned names I didn't know. They asked if I had any recent contact with either Danny Scott or Victor Elliot and what my history was with them. They asked me the same thing over and over. I was losing my temper. How many times did I have to say I knew nothing about Victor Elliot's death.

I had to give every detail of my past relationships with Sandy, Danny's father, Danny and Victor from the day I first met them at 17 Morton Street. I told them I was sure they had phone recordings of every conversation I had in the past few months.

"You people are so far off the mark it's pathetic. How many times do I have to tell you, Bob, I did not kill Victor Elliot? I had nothing to do with organising the killing of Victor Elliot. Blaming me for murdering Victor Elliot is pure gossip from people I surmise with a lot more to hide other than me."

I opened my bag and produced every document proving my movements over the last six months and they photocopied everything. I was feeling very frustrated and knew I was going to be here for many hours. I was sick to death of these cops trying to muddle with my brain and trip me up with my answers.

I was not responsible for the shooting death or planning of the shooting death of Victor Elliot at 19 Morton Street Chinderah on May 26, 2000 ... end of story. I did not arrive at the Tweet Heads police station with my lawyer by my side because I had nothing to hide. Arriving with a lawyer would have been pouring good, hard-earned money down the drain.

It was 2. 30pm when I walked out the front door of the Tweed Heads Police station. I felt like I had been through a washing machine at full speed. I had a headache, was hungry and certainly did not feel up to driving back to Ballina. I felt like my head was spinning.

One answer I got from Detective Bob made me feel better. I asked if I was still a suspect in the murder. His answer was, "No, you are not a suspect at this stage but you could be a future witness." How could I be called as a witness when I knew nothing about the murder.

Months went by and the investigation dragged on into several years. I believed at that time however the police were getting closer to making arrests.

I was very aware that certain people still were blaming me for his death. I have always believed it was a projection of their own guilt over many hidden, dirty little dealings. The industry is so toxic at times one has to continually question what is truth and what's just gossip.

Then why did I stay involved in the industry? It's not as if I did not try to exit the industry. I spent 12 months re-educating myself, started not one but three legal, legitimate businesses and each time I hit a brick wall.

I have had to support myself nearly all my life and have had to fight for my independence, so giving it up for a life of suppression by a partner was not on my agenda. I chose this industry to support my husband at the time and to support my family. I stayed in it because I believed every woman has the right to choose her path in life and most of all because I believed every sex worker had the right to be able to work without violence or loss of life

I remain disgusted at the attitudes of people who judge us when they know nothing of the background of the women involved in the industry.

CHAPTER 28

Arrests made over Victor's murder

DANNY SCOTT was arrested and charged with being an accessory before the fact of the murder of Victor Elliot. Police charged Mike Grupe, for the murder.

Apparently Grupe and his army buddy Dayal Utz met Danny and planned to kidnap Victor and rob him of $500,000 that was said to be hidden in his home.

The story as told by the media was that Danny had sent these two standover merchants to threaten Victor Elliot over $500,000 supposedly owed to Danny by Victor. Danny paid these men $50,000 to scare Victor, not kill him, so the story went.

The altercation with the pair and Victor got out of hand and they gunned him down in the driveway of 19 Morton Street. This was the heading of one of the Gold Coast newspapers – Victor Elliot was gunned down by two balaclava-clad men with an AK-47s.

This was pretty scary stuff for the ordinary citizen out in the real world.

Sure, there is and has been over many years violent altercations between brothel owners and their rivals within the industry. Or attempts of takeovers by criminal elements of established brothel businesses, however there is and has been many owner operators like me who have stayed away from these crime family elements of darkness.

One Sydney newspaper reported:

"A MAN who allegedly recruited a Sunshine Coast ex-army officer and his friend to intimidate a man who was shot dead appeared in a NSW Supreme Court this week.

"Daniel Clayton Scott pleaded guilty on Wednesday to being an accessory before the fact of the manslaughter of Tweed Heads Hospital senior radiographer Victor Elliot in May 2000.

"Scott, 36, is alleged to have hired Stanley River resident Michael Anthony Grupe, 28, and Dayal Utz, two former Australian Army serviceman. He paid the pair $50,000 to scare Elliot, his former business partner in a brothel at Chinderah called The Stardust Club. The 50-year-old doctor was confronted outside his own unfinished luxury brothel by two men wearing balaclavas on May 26, 2000,

"Grupe would later tell police that Utz shot Dr Elliot at least 14 times with an AK-47 rifle. Utz and Grupe had stolen nine guns from the Army.

"The crime went unsolved until March, 2003, when Grupe shot Utz dead during an argument at his house near Maleny. Utz's friend Troy Pinwill, who was at the house and was shot in the leg in the gunfight, later spilled the entire sordid story to police.

"Grupe was arrested soon after but escaped and became the target of one of the biggest police manhunts in Queensland.

"He handed himself in two days later and led police to his own mini-arsenal deep in the Conondale State Forest.

"Grupe, who was already serving six years in prison for an armed robbery committed with Pinwill, was acquitted in December 2004, of the murder or manslaughter of Utz.

"Three years later Grupe pleaded guilty in the Sydney Supreme Court to the manslaughter of Dr Elliot and was sentenced to at least 14 years in jail. Scott pleaded guilty to being an accessory before the fact to manslaughter and accessory before the fact to assault with the intent to rob while armed."

Another story ran:

"A BROTHEL owner has been jailed for at least nine years for his role in the violent killing of a former 'father figure' who became a rival.

"Daniel Clayton Scott, 37, was jailed on Friday for a total of 12

years for the manslaughter of Victor Elliot, who died on May 26, 2000, at Chinderah in northern NSW after being repeatedly shot by two masked men.

"Sentencing Scott on Friday, NSW Supreme Court Justice Peter Hidden said he had not been one of the shooters but had been involved in arranging the attack on Mr Elliot.

"Scott and Mr Elliot had owned and operated a brothel, the Stardust Club, at Chinderah, with Scott inheriting his share after the death of his father, who was friends with Mr Elliot.

"'After the death of his father, (Scott) looked upon Mr Elliot as a father figure and it seems that they got on well,' Justice Hidden said.

"However, the relationship soured, with Mr Elliot wanting to be bought out of the business, before announcing plans to build another brothel some 300 metres down the road.

"Scott, who was once an Army reservist, enlisted the help of two former Australian Army men – Dayal Utz and Mike Grupe – to 'intimidate' or 'harm' Mr Elliot during a staged robbery.

"The men have since been identified as Mr Elliot's killers.

"Scott provided them with a photograph of Mr Elliot, told them where he could be found, and also supplied a .22 pistol.

"'I have no doubt that (Scott) was emotionally wounded by what he saw as his betrayal by Mr Elliot, a man he had looked up to and who had supported him in difficult times,' Justice Hidden said."

I KNEW I had nothing to do with Victor Elliot's murder, but I was very relieved when these people had been brought to justice. I felt very sad for Danny, as I knew he was being manipulated when Victor and Danny both turned on me.

I knew even back then that Danny would be destroyed both emotionally and financially.

Never in my wildest imagination did I ever think Victor would be killed, with Danny behind the attack. When his father died, Danny relied on Victor's support and guidance. Victor had promised Sandy he would look after Danny and at the end of the day it was Victor who manipulated Danny's financial and business position. The court records showed the altercation happened because Victor owed Danny $500,000.

In my opinion Danny was unable and not mature enough to sit down with a lawyer and allow the correct procedures to get his money back from Victor. His anger and grief at Victor's betrayal were too much. He retaliated in the only manner he was accustomed to ... with violence.

STILL today, more than 23 years later I feel nothing but sadness for Danny. He had no chance of winning against the two very cunning people he was involved with. A little boy played a big boy's game and lost.

I often think about this and am very thankful that these people manipulated my removal from that business at the time. My experience of being betrayed by these two men caused me immense emotional and financial stress, but at the end of the day I walked away unscathed. Unlike them.

I was relieved that Chinderah and its identities were finally behind me and that chapter in my life was over for good.

CHAPTER 29

Another court case, another letdown

URING THE time I had been operating in Racecourse Road I had become friends with a family living and operating their business in the estate. He had driven my staff on a few outcall bookings. He was not working because of a serious health issue and had been selling his equipment off on and off to supplement his income. I am telling you this now because you will understand later why I made some decisions.

The fight with the council was dragging on and was costing me a small fortune, but I just had to ride it out. I had no option. The possibility of beating the council wasn't looking good because they changed the rules to suit them in the middle of the fight. My house and the business now sat in the wrong zone. The NSW Government put laws in place for legal brothels to be able to operate in an industrial estate, which is exactly where I was, but now was in the wrong part of the estate.

The Land and Environment Court decision was looming and I was very concerned. If I lost my fight with the council, my business operations in the house in Racecourse Road would have to cease and I would have to start an outcall service only.

Using local motels to send clients to wasn't a safe alternative. It was dangerous for the single lady working on her own and not of financial benefit to me having to pay a driver to sit outside a motel room for an hour. There were many issues I had to try to work out for my survival in this town. I had come way too far for me to just give up and walk away.

What to wear to court? I did not want to look overdressed then again,

I did not want to look like a bogan. I chose old faithful, a tailored black jacket, long dress pants, a white dress shirt and a black-and-white long chiffon narrow scarf to wrap around my neck. Overall, I think I looked the part, a normal businesswoman attending a function.

The household was preparing for the day's work. Receptionist Ammie had arrived and the ladies were up having breakfast, the air was filled with hope and enthusiasm for my court case this morning.

My case was first up and it dragged on for the whole morning. By lunchtime the judge announced he had made his decision and would advise my legal team in due course.

I left the courthouse with my future still up in the air. I was feeling negative. I have to reorganise because I did not have a good feeling about all this. I was not impressed by the representation on my behalf by my legal team and knew I could kiss goodbye to the near $20,000 I had paid into their trust account.

I didn't go back to work; instead, I drove to the local lookout and parked there staring out at the beautiful ocean. Where were the whales today? I must have been there for more than an hour thinking about my future.

I rang my partner and told her I wanted to sell the property and use the money to buy a block of land in the 'legal' section of the estate and build a purpose-built building. This was the only way I was going to beat this fucking council. The NSW Government decreed all brothels must be in an industrial estate or commercial zone and there were no suitable commercial premises available.

She agreed. I sat in my car for a little longer and tried to calculate the amount of time I had left before the council forced me to close. I also needed to approach a few motels and ask the owners if it was okay to send clients to them. I would get all this organised but not today. Today I would wallow in self-pity because deep down I knew the council was going to beat me. I drove, back to Racecourse Road to my staff. What news? No news? Was that a good or bad sign?

I needed to prepare my staff for an unpredictable, unstable future, but as in previous life-changing situations I was determined to never give up. There is a solution to every problem; you just had to find it. I knew I had to have a serious meeting with my staff and give them the option of leaving for a more stable workplace or staying with me and working under more difficult circumstances.

I looked at these amazing women and was proud of them for deciding to stay with me and not packing their belongings and moving on to better pastures. I had a great team. I think they stuck with me because I was a woman owner and I treated them with respect. I didn't scream and rant and rave at them unlike other owners, male and female, that I have known. No one knows better than me what it takes to do the job that they do or tolerate the physical abuse they have had to live with.

They listened to my plan and agreed to work under any difficult conditions until I was able to get a block of land and build in the other section of the estate. No one was feeling regret more than me that I would have to sell this beautiful house overlooking the lake, a house that had made many of us great money and was the saving grace for many.

I CONTACTED several estate agents and arranged for them to come and appraise the house. They all knew what was going on here. It was town knowledge. I decided on an agent and planned to canvass the motels. The next day around lunchtime, the for-sale sign went up on the lawn outside my house.

Within a day the people I had made friends with in the estate called me. The man who had helped drive my girls to clients contacted me and asked what was happening. He asked if the court ruled against me. I told him no, but I expected bad news. He asked what I was going to do and I told him my plans.

Once the house was sold, I would go rent a house to live in and run an outcall service with ladies working from motels until I could buy the block of land. He offered me storage space in his huge work shed if I needed it.

I had to approach the motel owners to be able to get this show on the road because once the ruling came down. I would have to cease allowing clients to come to this house or the fines would financially cripple me. I figured I would have a maximum of two more weeks and once the house sold I would have only 30 days to vacate.

Over the next two weeks, I organised a house for me to live in through a landlord one of my former workers knew. It was a little cottage in the main street with a back lane entrance. They knew what I was all about. I would not be kicked out had I rented through an agent. This would at least allow me to send a couple of girls that came to stay every week somewhere to sleep at night when they worked. This would allow me to get the Racecourse Road house cleaned up, and all the security implements removed. I was ready to rock'n'roll. All I needed was to sell the house and buy the block of land.

I had been expecting a disappointing decision by the court so when it came down I was ready. I was very annoyed, but I hadn't dropped my bundle. I was prepared for the worse. The news made it into the Northern Star newspaper, but what the hell I was used to publicity, good and bad.

I stopped all operations from Racecourse Road that very day of the court's decision and we all moved to the little house on the main street. While this house wasn't very flash it was comfortable and would serve its purpose until I could get land and build.

A few weeks later I had a contract for the sale of the Racecourse Road house. I was not happy with the price, but I needed it sold. I would not have enough money after the mortgage was paid out to buy land and have enough for the deposit to build.

In the meantime, the male partner of the family I had made friends with asked me to come around to their home/business shed in the industrial estate. I had some of my belongings stored in his shed so off I went to see what he wanted and to pay him some more storage rent.

We sat down and Ron – I will call him Ron only because he still lives in the town – said he had found a block of land in the estate with the correct zoning for $110,000. He asked if I would consider taking him on as a business partner. Would I trust another partner? We chatted about what he expected.

I didn't have enough money to pay cash and legal fees for the block of land plus the deposit of putting a building on the block. The building would cost $350,000-plus, and another $50,000 for fitting it out.

I had to think about this proposal very carefully. I told Ron I wanted to have a look at the land and where it is situated. Ron and I then drove in our separate cars down Piper Drive to look at the block of land.

It was a huge block of land. On one side was a steel engineering factory business, across the road was a concrete supply large supply business and down on the corner was a heavy trucking business. I was very impressed and thought it was perfect. We chatted some more and I told Ron I would give him an answer by the next morning.

I needed to think very carefully about taking on yet another business partner. The last one not only nearly destroyed me financially it near sent me crazy.

Nevertheless, I told Ron I would seriously consider his proposal, but needed to check my finances, so I would call him from Brisbane in the next couple of days as I was going to my Mum's house. Even though Mum had no business sense, I still talked it over with her. She agreed to go ahead.

I rang Ron the next morning and told him I was in and to arrange for us to buy the block of land with the agent who had it up for sale and that I would be back in the morning to sign the contract. I drove back to Ballina. I felt uneasy but contented that at least this was a start towards finely getting my long-awaited legal entity together.

A legal, licensed brothel that no authority could take off me and better still no unwarranted police attention. The very thought of all this made me feel, for the first time in all these years, that stability was just around the corner.

A few days later Ron and I signed and paid for the block of land in Piper Drive in cash plus transfer and legal fees. This was to be an amazingly exhilarating experience.

Ron was put in charge of chasing finance and I gave him my last two years' tax returns to help with any application to any financial institutions.

We had all settled into the little house in the main street and, although the work situation was certainly compromised over any on-property work I was doing okay. The extra dollars being spent on motel bills each week were eating into my profits, but I had my eyes on the prize.

From my understanding and experience getting finance on buying a property or building usually took about three weeks to a month. However, this situation was dragging out week after week after week and it was going into the middle of the second month. I was starting to get nervous. Ron kept saying an answer would come through soon. We had received two approvals, but Ron said the interest rate was very high on both. One was 30 per cent; the other 35 per cent. This was ridiculous. I wanted to know why because the normal interest rate in 2002 was approximately 10 per cent on such questionable projects. I said no, which did not sit well with anyone including Ron.

I am not an idiot and as it was, I had already paid out more than $60,000 on the land. Ron suggested mortgage my house and borrow on the collateral. If I refused to put up my house to fight charges of official corruption, fucked if I was going to put it up to go into partnership on building a brothel. If I had bought the land on my own, I probably would have borrowed against my house.

There was no way I was going to be caught again. This saga dragged on another two weeks. In the end, I rang my accountant and explained what was happening. A couple of hours later he rang back and told me why we couldn't get affordable finance.

The reason we had struggled to get finance was the only income Ron and his family had was social security payments. He nearly owned the property he and his family were living in, but he still had a mortgage.

He had had a life-threatening illness and couldn't work and had to close his business. His financial situation was why no normal finance company would touch us.

Col advised me to either buy his half of the block of land or request a sale and walk away. I couldn't do that. I had already been in contact with a builder and had plans being drawn up. I was feeling defeated and overwhelmed at what to do. I just felt lost and mentally drained ... again. I had to get myself together and think this through very carefully.

One thing I was sure of was I wasn't going to go ahead with any exorbitant, high-interest finance deal.

I felt that no matter who I seemed to connect with were out to take advantage of me financially. I questioned my ability to make correct decisions on a personal level. I was a businesswoman and I considered myself very astute. As a female brothel owner/operator, I had a good name. Tough but very fair, yet I kept being so gullible, and believed everything would work out. Again, I was stuck in a quagmire of total bullshit. I had no idea how I was going to work through it, even if the land was put back on the market it may take months and months to sell.

I had to go out to my landlord and pay my rent on the little house and when I arrived, the wife asked me what was wrong. I sat there for the next hour and a half telling her and her husband what had been going on.

They lived on a beautiful property about 15 minutes' drive from Ballina, tucked away in the bush up north on a back road. Their home was beautiful and peaceful. They were both retired and the little house belonged to her father who was in a local nursing home. He wasn't very well so they visited him nearly every day. My rent helped them pay for all the little extras he needed.

I headed back into town. I pulled over at the side of the road before I arrived in Ballina and broke down in tears. I felt like shit, looked like shit and I needed to vent. I just sat in my car feeling devastated not knowing which way to turn. I always had a plan, but this time I had nothing.

I waited three days and decided I had to bring the situation to a head. I called Ron and asked if there was any progress. He said the high-interest loan was available and we should take it. My reply was no and we needed to talk about where we were going from here. I made an appointment to come around to their house the next day after lunch.

It was the next morning that I received a phone call from my landlords Wendy and Bob (again not their real names). They asked me to come and see them, as it was important, as soon as possible.

My first thought was they needed me to move out of the little house as they wanted to sell it. After all, Wendy's father was in palliative care. If this were the case I would well and truly be in deep trouble in keeping my business alive and running in this town.

I cancelled my appointment with Ron as I had an urgent matter to attend to and rescheduled our meeting for the next day. I drove out to Wendy and Bob's house expecting at any moment that the sky would open up on me.

CHAPTER 30

A lifeline from nowhere

AS I PULLED into their driveway and got out of my car I could barely breathe. They both greeted me and ushered me into their lounge room. Wendy came back from the kitchen with cups of coffee and we all just sat there looking at each other in silence. I waited for the axe to fall.

Bob spoke first, "Suzy, we have spent many hours talking about you and your problem with the person you bought the block of land with and about your intended project. We would like to buy half of the land from him and work with you to build your building.

"Before you say anything, we do want you to know we have given this a lot of consideration and we trust you."

I sat there like a stunned mullet, broadsided by a proposition I just never saw coming. Here I was expecting to be asked to leave the little house and instead these people were throwing me a life jacket. This was the most incredible thing that had happened to me in my life.

I could feel myself getting emotional. I could see that they were genuine and I needed them to know what they would be getting themselves into by doing this with me and for me. We spent many hours talking about every facet of the business. The good and the bad.

I told them everything there was to know about me and my background. I did not hold back and then we devised a plan for me to approach Ron to sell his half of the land to them. This wasn't going to be easy. I knew that once I told Ron that I had found out the reason we had not been able to get reasonable finance he would be furious and I would have yet another fight on my hands.

What the fuck. I had waited this long, another six or 12 months would be a walk in the park now that I could see that light at the end of the tunnel. I needed a night of restful sleep, but I knew my fight was not yet over.

No more hiding in motels and running escorts from the little house. No more staff safety worries. The new building would be fitted out with high-tech security.

I woke up the next morning dreading going around the estate to face Ron and his wife. It had to be done. I quietly confronted him with the information my accountant had acquired. It was his turn to squirm. His face paled white, then he went red. He said his financial situation was none of my fucking business. He was very angry I spoke softly to him. "Ron, you should have told me your situation before we bought the block of land. What you have done to me is just not fair and it's unacceptable, you were not honest with me. We cannot move forward because your financials are not acceptable to any financial institution of any reputable status. Sure, the disreputable companies have said yes but at 30 per cent interest that's just not viable for me and at the end of the day you either."

I told him that I had found a buyer for his half share of the land and he near bit my head off. He jumped up off his chair and started ranting and raving at me, I just sat there and let him vent. He quieted down and stood standing over me. I was not intimidated, not by a long shot. I have had loaded guns, put to my face by bigger and tougher men than him, in my life he was nothing.

I told him to get legal advice, "but at the end of the day neither of us can afford to spend any more money. Our agreement must come to an end." He ranted about all the work he had done chasing finance and that he wanted repayment for it all and that I would be getting an account for it before he signed anything.

He said the price of the blocks in the estate had risen and he expected half of the current market value. I was starting to feel angry but kept my cool.

I got up off my chair and told him to call me when he was ready to sign within two days or get his lawyer to speak to mine if we were going to take this through the courts.

I then left his premises. I drove up the road and called Wendy and Bob and explained what had happened which is close to what I told them would happen anyway. It was now a waiting game. I bought a takeaway coffee and sat in my car and contemplated what had happened in the past 48 hours.

Business went on as usual and I waited and waited some more. On the third day after my meeting with Ron, he rang me. He said he had worked out what he was going to charge me for all the work he had done in trying to arrange finance. I was very cordial, but all I wanted to do was smack his face.

I told him to drop any paperwork off to me in a sealed envelope and I would look it over. He said if I didn't pay his fee's he would not sign a sale contract. The very next day Ron handed me an envelope.

When I later opened the envelope, I was astounded at what he wanted to be paid.

Not only did he want his $55,000 back, plus his entire legal fees and transfer fees, which was fair enough, he demanded extra money covering the increase in the land's value. He also demanded being paid six hours a day, five days a week for over eight weeks for chasing the finance.

Why do I always manage to attract these unethical bastards? I hate unscrupulous people taking advantage of women in dire circumstances. I was determined that one way or another that he was not going to get away with this.

I called Wendy and Bob asking to come visit them with Ron's demands. My concentration on work that evening was non-existent. I was surprised we got any work at all. It was difficult being nice to clients when I felt nothing but anger inside.

The next day I drove to Wendy and Bob's home. When he saw Ron's demands, Bob said, "He has to be fucking joking." Only this was no joke. At least he was willing to sell half of our land, but there was no way I could buy him out on my own.

I left a copy of Ron's demands with Bob and Wendy and drove back into town. Bob later contacted several other real estate agents to get an opinion on the supposed rise in the value of our land. There had been no rise in two months. This was just another scam to extort more money from me.

Ron and I argued back and forth for days on end. This was mentally and physically draining. I cannot begin to even tell you how much money I had lost or been scammed out of over the last six months. I felt I had to either walk away or suck it up or make the best of a very bad situation. While all this was going on Wendy and Bob had set about getting building prices for the plans I had been holding onto from a local architect. They had also been arranging finance for the building to begin once the land had been transferred out of Ron's name. I still had not come to an agreement with Ron on a final amount he would accept and this was pissing me off.

Wendy and Bob did everything they could to make this deal come to an amicable conclusion. After some very forceful words between myself and Ron we agreed on a deal.

I am describing this scenario in this manner to protect myself from any potential future legal comeback. I called Ron to a meeting on our own down into the little house. After this conversation between us, for the very first time, he saw another side of me. We agreed on how much he was going to accept for signing away his interest in the block of land. He went straight his lawyer's office and signed on the dotted line.

CHAPTER 31

Change of tactics

THIS HAD been probably the most overwhelming, extremely difficult decision I have had to make in my entire life. I agonised over this decision and for weeks I cried tears of absolute devastation. Yes, I had a solution to getting Ron to sell his half of the land, but at what cost? I couldn't believe that being pushed into making such a decision would affect the rest of my working life.

I agreed to sell the land to Bob and Wendy. They would own the land and the new building. The total cost of land and building would be approximately $550,000 – a huge amount of money 21 years ago. I had no hope of raising half of this money without putting up my family home as collateral. The only money I had left was $50,000 I had put aside to fit out the building, plus whatever I was making daily.

Wendy and Bob were decent, clean-living people, what we in the industry call straight people. No criminal ties and I believed them to be honest, no-nonsense people. They had borrowed all this money from their own home because they believed in my project. At the end of the day, they would have a very valuable property and they knew it.

I will never forget our meeting with their lawyer when it was time to sign all the documents. I was at one of the lowest ebbs of my life and believe me I had had a few of those.

I had to try to put everything into perspective. I was finally going to achieve what I had been chasing for many years ... a legal, licensed brothel that no government entity could deny its right to exist.

We all walked out of their lawyer's office and straight into the Lennox

Heads hotel for a drink. We chatted for about an hour and agreed as of the next day it was all hands on deck. We had to get the building plans submitted to the Ballina Shire Council. This in itself was going to be a trial of fire. The council just did not want a brothel in their town. There were two other applications for brothels – one from a long-established illegal operator in Alstonville; another from a brothel owner in Coffs Harbour. I had known the owner from my Maroochydore years.

This time the council would have no choice on our application for a licence because the last thing they needed was another expensive fight in the Land and Environment Court.

I don't know how I kept going in the following months waiting for an all-important public meeting over these three brothel license applications. I was tired, stressed and mentally drained. I knew only too well what it was like dealing with this council. Council had called for public objections, and I knew many multiple objections had been sent in.

The bottom line was our application complied with the government rules that permitted brothels in the correct industrial zoning. They had changed the zoning to get rid of me once. They could not do this again.

All three brothel owners fronted up to the meeting. The public gallery was packed and that included the press. This was going to be quite a spectacle. Thank God I had dressed appropriately. The meeting had heated discussion for and against all applicants.

Coming to a resolution and agreement must have been a nightmare for the councillors. Eventually they approved our application and the one from Alstonville. They rejected the Coffs Harbour application. Council knocked back my request for permission for a private worker to work on her own from her residence. At the time I was very annoyed, but later I would use their law to fight them.

Finally, the days of running an illegal brothel were coming to a close. We were off and running and there was excitement in the air. I had so much to do and the project had not even yet begun. We had meetings with the builder and I will give credit to Wendy and Bob as they included me in everything.

The building of the first legal brothel in Ballina was an epic project. The building company Bob and Wendy chose caused quite a few hassles. Some of which I cannot make public because the people concerned are still alive. Needless to say, there were many issues between Bob and Wendy with the builder.

It got so bad that the builder put up huge steel gates and fencing and padlocked the front gates. I could do nothing because I was only the owner of the intended business. I had to play the waiting game and shut my big mouth. What should have taken only 12 weeks seemed to be taking forever.

The delays kept coming. The council made certain demands to the builder. To conform with their requirements added many, many thousands of dollars to the cost of the building. I expected nothing less because they didn't want a legal brothel in Ballina.

Luckily the income from my operation was holding its own. I was thankful the stress of not having to find all the extra dollars was a relief for me.

The building was being built to my exact original plans. I had spent many hours on this when I owned half this block of land.

All the work was being done by local tradespeople, keeping the money in the town. This made me feel so good knowing the dollars were supporting local families. I made a few very useful connections with some of the male workers. One in particular, Garry, was a chippy. He was such a comedian and he was a very talented tradesman. He was an all-rounder who helped me on many future projects.

The first of the two most infuriating demands from council pulled was changing the direction of all locks on the building. This cost me $600. The second was the big one ... contributions to roads fee.

What the fuck was this? Piper Drive was an already established road. It had been in use for many years. It was just a money grab. I ranted and raved for days. Where was I going to get yet another $22,000?

During the past 12 months, I had gained two female councillors on my side. One woman definitely, did not approve of my business, but she believed in adhering to council laws. And in her eyes, I was a legitimate tax-paying, rates-paying member of the Ballina community and I had rights. She guided me through this contribution to road issues and this saved me more than $10,000.

The other was a woman of standing within the community and she also believed I had the right to be able to conduct my business in the same manner as everyone else in the community. Over the years I came to admire and respect her. I voted for her because I knew she was an honest woman and worked for the people, not her self-serving agenda.

The building was just about complete and keys were ready to be handed over to Bob and Wendy and then onto me.

I needed to get in there and furnish the building, set it all up and get my doors open for business. As for staff I had an array of very attractive, well-presented, drug-free female staff ready to start work. I still had Ammie as a receptionist and I needed one more reliable mature-age lady at the front desk. I also had to organise the installation of the security system. I was indeed very excited.

IT WAS IN the middle of 2003 when I finally opened the very first legal brothel in Ballina. Getting this done was one of the most stressful projects I have ever attempted. All I ever wanted was to be able to operate legally without forever playing hide and seek with the police or authorities. I had lost thousands and thousands of dollars and been ripped off by several unscrupulous so-called upstanding members of two communities. Been to hell and back with accusations of murder and stood over by bikers on several occasions.

I had gone through and come out the other side of several serious health issues. It was now my time of legitimacy. I had flooded all the social media and newspapers up and down the highway on my opening date.

We all celebrated with gusto on opening night. Wine, women and song! What more could a man ask for? Several of the tradesmen turned up for food and drink, and then went home. Clients coming and going all night long kept everyone on their toes, plus of course on and off their work beds. We doubled our anticipated income and I fell into bed a happy, exhausted madam at about 5am.

The Northern Star newspaper took some of terrific photos of the rooms. There were shots outside the building of myself and some staff. They ran a two-page story with the pictures, starting on the front page. Making front page news wasn't new for me. The only difference was now I no longer had to hide. News stories highlighted my past fights with Ballina Shire Council to become legal.

Wendy came to work in reception with Ammie. I trained Wendy knowing I would have at least two honest, kind women who would look after the business. I knew they would treat the ladies with respect when I was away in Brisbane looking after Mum.

I had state-of-the-art recording audio/video security and signs up outside the building and on the front fence warning that anybody caught causing problems would be on film. Outside of the building were motion-detecting spotlights. During working hours these lights were left on to light up the whole building.

The reception desk was protected by shatter- and bulletproof, hardened glass. No access could be gained from the client hallway, the car park, hallways and back entrance and the client exit was recorded 24/7. In every workroom and my office, there were duress buttons if pushed would bring security guards and police. This building was very safe.

Under the same roof as the working, and business section of the building was a separate ladies' relaxation centre. This consisted of a five-bed dormitory with its ensuite, lockers for their clothes and a full-length mirror for them to apply their make-up. Their kitchen was fully stocked with a full-size stove to cook their meals. All crockery, pots and pans were supplied, as was a full closed-door pantry. There was an outdoor smoking area. And a gym with exercise bikes, walking machines and weights to keep them happy and fit. I lived in separate quarters in the building five days a week. The clients were well catered for too. There was a secure car park and a client reception lounge. The lounge was beautifully furnished with leather lounges and had a small, private, open-air smoking space. The lounge room also had a cold drinks fridge.

There was also a party room between the client lounge and the corridor to the workrooms. It had a raised stage with a dance pole at the far end of the stage. Clients could sit around the stage, watching girls dance if they had paid for this extra service. The whole room reeked of a classy Moulin Rouge setting for dancing girls.

I had a party spa room separate from the workrooms, which had its shower and held an eight-person spa bath. After the first $1500 electricity bill I soon turned that room into a fully equipped BDSM playroom. There was also the African room with a smaller four-person spa bath. All the workrooms, client lounge, office, girls sleeping section and dance hall were air-conditioned. On the housekeeping side of things there were two commercial-size washing machines and three clothes dryers mounted on the wall to dry clients' linen and towels.

I was so proud. Ballina Exclusive Company was the first legal brothel in the Northern Rivers. The business and building far surpassed expectations.

CHAPTER 32

The trials and tribulations of running a brothel

PEOPLE IN THE real world have no idea of what it takes to run a brothel. They believe only the bad publicity and the perception of owners having money to burn. They also have misconceptions of brothels being filthy little rundown houses tucked away in no man's land. Even in the old days of illegality, this was not the case.

The everyday cost of running this type of business is very high, with excess water rates, high electricity costs and wages. Then there's the cleaning products and the constant linen and towel replacements.

Having the ability to keep ladies happy and stable mentally and physically is an art. They are trying to get the money together to escape their own personal difficulties which bought them into the industry in the first place. This is sometimes very trying and stressful for receptionists and owners.

Showing kindness and treating the women who worked in brothels with respect was very important, and a happy work environment is paramount for achieving a financially successful shift for whoever was in reception on the day. The overall job of a receptionist is not easy.

Some ladies who work in the industry suffer mild to very serious mental health issues. Some of them are medicated; some not. It is important for a receptionist to be able to recognise which ladies need extra patience. Otherwise, all hell would break loose.

Being a good receptionist is a balancing act. One has to be firm but fair in handling the issues that might arise between these ladies.

For example, a lady might have a brilliant shift financially while another might not have made much money at all. The way I handled this situation and taught my receptionists was to ensure that the ladies not making the money in-house were given preference to be sent on out-call bookings. This evened out the takings for all staff on the shift.

Every lady had her own locker and bed to sleep in if staying over nightly or weekly. They were held responsible for keeping their relaxation, sleeping and kitchen-bathroom spaces clean. They also had to keep their workroom spotless at all times between clients and before they finished their shift.

Apart from Ammie, Wendy and me, I hired a Yamba woman called Kate as a receptionist. She had had many years' experience working at Tweed Heads, for a well-known male owner. She was a tiny, beautifully spoken woman of class. She dressed impeccably and was well spoken. I guessed her age to be around 55 or so. Her silver, precision-cut hair was striking and she took no nonsense from anyone. She was just what my business needed.

She had a very sick husband who needed fulltime care so she had worked for that owner and business for many years. I gave her the job because of her experience and appearance.

I was paying $10,000 a month rent on my premises. Add that to all the overheads and quarterly council rates, water rates plus newspaper ads on top of receptionists' pay. My outgoings were eye-watering, but the business was holding its own and doing well in my opinion. I paid my GST monthly to the Tax Office and accountant's fees quarterly. A couple of times in the next year I was away and didn't get back to town a couple of days after my rent was due.

Wendy asked me to pay the rent before I went away. This was getting more regular because my mother was very ill. My brother was looking after her, but he also needed a break as this was emotionally and physically tiring for him.

I was offended by Wendy's comment because I was paying top rent and I was rarely ever late in paying my rent. I didn't say anything and just agreed.

When I came back from Brisbane, I had a routine. First, I would clear my mailbox at the post office then head to the business. One Monday about lunchtime when I returned, I noticed a hole in the wall of the ladies' lounge room.

Kate told me one of the ladies had a tantrum and threw her high heel shoe at another lady. The shoe missed the lady and the heel of her shoe went straight through the plasterboard wall. Violence between staff is not tolerated so the worker was sent home on the spot.

The hole in the wall had to be fixed and I planned to organise its repair over the next week. A week ran into two weeks, then three weeks. I was flat out at work, tired and still going up to relieve my brother and look after my Mum. I simply forgot.

A couple of weeks later a letter arrived from a lawyer. I was stunned and in total shock when I read the letter. It was from Wendy and Bob's lawyer demanding I get the hole in the wall fixed. I know I had been slack, attending to this issue, but a lawyer's letter? Seriously?

Not only did the letter demand the hole be fixed it also demanded that the tradie fixing the hole be a registered person qualified to fix the hole and supply his registration number. I could feel my anger building. What the fuck was going on here?

I tried to work out how to handle this situation without my big mouth causing a more serious problem. Wendy was on reception, so I would handle it carefully or at least try. I just needed to keep calm.

I drove from the post office to the business. I marched through to my office where Wendy was answering the phones. She looked up at me and smiled. I put my things down and threw the lawyer's letter on the desk asking, "What the fuck is this?"

She picked up the letter and as she read it her face went red. "Suzy, I am the people person and Bob takes care of the business side of things," she said. I couldn't believe what I was hearing. I said to her, "Wendy, all you had to do is ask if is it okay for you to chase down a tradie and get that hole fixed. You know me, Wendy, I would have said to you that would be great. Get it done and I will pay for it. You know I have been flat out working up to ten hours a day and driving back and forth up to Brisbane to look after my mother. There are never enough hours in the day for me to get everything done."

She said to me in a nasty tone of voice, "I own half this building and I agree with my husband." That sent my suppressed anger through the ceiling. I didn't raise my voice at her even though I wanted to scream in her face.

I told her, "Wendy, you may own the building, but I have a five-year lease on this building and an option of five with another option of yet another five. I own this business and you are fired. Get your belongings and get the fuck out of my business. Leave your keys on my desk please."

She was shaking and I could see her own anger building, but she never said a word. I calculated her wages, put her money into an envelope and handed it to her as she walked out the door. Tomorrow was going to be a new day.

I REALLY didn't want to fire Wendy because I liked her and Bob very much. They had been good to me for the nearly three years I had known them. We had been good to each other. I couldn't accept the fact that they would use a lawyer over a stupid small hole in a wall caused by a bad-tempered worker. The hole was no bigger than a $2 coin. A lawyer's letter at that time would have cost a hundred bucks. This made no sense to me.

I paid my rent, on time and had no issues, however I read all my legal documents connected to my lease with Wendy and Bob carefully. I rang three different real estate agents around town and asked what the rent would be for a building the size as my business was in. I received three different amounts.

Going by these figures I was being charged approximately $30,000 a year too much. I was gobsmacked and wondered how Wendy and Bob came up with the amount to charge me.

I spoke to my accountant and he confirmed I was being overcharged.

There was nothing I could do about it as I had signed a five-year lease. I just felt down. Betrayed AGAIN really, confirmation of human greed.

I found another part-time receptionist and sorted out her roster. She was a mature lady who had worked in banking. She had kids, was honest and reliable. That's all that mattered to me. I knew she liked a bit of a toke, but I didn't care so long as she didn't come to work stoned or holding.

The rules in my business were set in stone and not negotiable.

No drugs or alcohol were allowed on the premises at any time by anyone. If any staff member came back from an outcall stoned or drunk, they would be sent home on the spot and no one was exempt.

My sentiments were if you can't handle doing this job straight then you had no business being in this line of work.

Ladies mostly came to earn money. It was not a party house. There were set fees for services and any lady who provided any extra service were entitled to charge what they wanted for the extras.

This extra money was hers and a private arrangement between her and the client.

Clients were advised to treat his chosen companion with respect. They got two warnings but after a third warning about disrespect he would be removed from the building with no refund.

If I had a difficult client in reception, I would always say to him pointing up at the camera, "Smile, as you are being recorded. I am sure you would not like your wife or girlfriend to see your picture on the front page of the newspapers if I had to call the police."

CHAPTER 33

Peter becomes my new landlord

ABOUT EIGHT weeks after I fired Wendy that I received a phone call from a man called Peter who asked to come and have a chat with me. He said he was interested in buying the building. I thought Wendy and Bob were freaked out over my reaction over their lawyer's letter.

I had the hole in the wall fixed by a qualified tradie and sent the proof of paying the bill along with the tradie's proof of qualification off to their lawyer. As far as I was concerned the issue was over. The new receptionist Sammy was working Wendy's shifts and the business was powering. All was well at Piper Drive. I organised a meeting with Peter and he came in early one morning before I opened the business.

After some long and serious negotiations, he agreed to think about my situation here and the fact that I had found out I had been paying $30,000 more in rent per year than the current market value. I told him I had paid several thousand dollars for my five-year lease, but wasn't prepared to pay for another lease.

I pointed out to Peter that I really didn't care anymore. I could get a semi-trailer in here and take everything I owned out and he could have it as a vacant possession. I was just sick to death of being financially taken advantage of and wasn't going to tolerate it anymore. I had had enough.

After showing Peter through the building and explaining to him how everything worked, he left and told me he would call me in a couple of days. I told him of my issues with Wendy and Bob and if he decided to buy the building I would not accept dealing with agents. It would have to be a hands-on arrangement between him and myself. He agreed to what I was saying.

A couple of days later he called and told me he had bought the building and would get all the paperwork organised for me to sign at no cost to me. He also agreed to drop my rent to the current market value. This made me very happy, but I was annoyed because I had lost so much money during this whole saga. Wendy and Bob walked away with more than $350,000 profit. Half of that money should have been mine.

Forget this and keep moving forward, were my thoughts, make this business into the best ever gentleman's club. I had a beautiful website up and running, elegant front street signage, quality business cards and daily newspaper ads. Everything about the business, inside and out, was very upmarket. And now I had a new, potentially great, landlord who was willing to work with me if anything needed attending to.

Not a lot changed over the next few years. Peter handled any problems he was responsible for as a landlord with no complaints.

Under the lease I agreed to paint the inside of the building every five years. I called my friendly tradie Garry and told him about the painting. It was going to be difficult as the business still had to be kept open during the work.

I was excited to be giving the building a refreshed look, but not looking forward to all the hours needed to complete the job. I could have employed a paint contractor but after getting quotes for the job, which I suspected was way more than the normal cost another type of business would have had to pay, I decided that Garry and myself could do the job just as well at half the price. Price gouging was par for the course in this industry.

I bought all the paint, brushes and everything else needed to do the job. I also put staff on notice to be able to work extra hours as I intended to help Garry paint. I could not paint and work on reception at the same time.

BEFORE THE painting started, I had to get signs made to make clients and staff aware of what was being done because of health and safety regulations. I didn't need to have anyone injured while Garry and I were painting. We worked like there was no tomorrow, laughter was the order of the day. By the end of each day, we were physically exhausted. I ended up getting a friend's son in to help. Jonathon was young and overwhelmed by the nature of the business, but he worked like a little Trojan.

The job took three weeks to complete and the building looked classy, refreshed and very professional. It was a credit to the boys for sure and I felt very proud. It's amazing what a coat of paint does for any surroundings. It lifts the spirits and inspires progress. It put a breath of fresh air in the business.

Unveiling what happens in sex industry

I AM GOING to take you on a journey into what happens between a sex worker and a paying client. Not every occasion is the same, as there are no two-sex workers alike and no two clients alike. Nevertheless, the financial side of things is the same – money changes hands and a commercial arrangement becomes a done deal.

It starts when the front doorbell rings. The receptionist checks out the client on the security video screen as he waits to be let into the building. She answers the door and shows the prospective client into a lounge room to wait for the ladies to come out and introduce themselves to the client. The client is probably nervous if he hasn't been into a brothel before or he may be a regular. He has to choose a lady he is attracted to, pay his fees to the receptionist and go with the lady to fulfil his sexual needs.

There are many different types of clients and their sexual expectations can be sometimes complex, fantasyland bullshit. Seriously this is a brothel, not a dating service or a service that allows sexual exploitation of the women who work there. The services provided by these women must be agreed to by the lady and the client. No means no and regardless of the woman being a sex worker, it's up to her to decide what she provides.

In another section of the building, there are usually three to five women waiting for clients. Depending on the time of day their moods may vary. They may be stressed over having to face yet another stranger. The public has no idea what these women go through every time that doorbell rings. For some ladies it's sheer torture, but their driving force to continue is very personal.

Once the doorbell rings the ladies rush to touch up their make-up and change into their chosen outfits for the introduction. They grab their high heels and quickly line up in the hallway to try to appeal to the client. The receptionist watches every move on the TV monitor in the office as each lady attempts to convince the client to choose her.

Let me make one thing clear, the only rooms in the building that do not have cameras are the sex work rooms and the ladies' private dressing, shower and toilet rooms. Every other part of the building, car park and public area is on 24/7 recording. This is paramount for the safety of the staff and clients in the event of any safety issues that may arise.

Once they have all introduced themselves the receptionist asks the client who he has chosen and collects his money covering the time he has chosen to spend with the lady. The lady signs a day sheet agreeing to the timeframe the client has chosen. She then collects him from the waiting room takes him to her workroom.

She tells the client, "If you would like to come with me down to my private room I will look after you." The client, let's call him Colin, touches her arse as they walk down the hallway to her room. She pretends to like it, when in fact all she wants to do is smack him in the face.

She reminds herself that this is a job and she needs the money. That's why she has to tolerate these sorts of incidences. In the room she discreetly looks at her wristwatch and notes the time.

She asks Colin to take his clothes off and put them on the chair, as she needs to do a sexual health check on his penis. She assures him this is necessary for their welfare. She closely inspects his penis for any noticeable strange lumps, bumps, scratches or rashes. If his penis has warts on it the booking is ended immediately, money refunded and the client is given a referral to a local free sexual health clinic. Most brothel premises have an illustrated book of pictures of the different diseases. Ladies are recommended to learn what to look for.

She picks up poor Colin's balls and inspects everywhere for warts, adding insult to injury for him. She then squeezes his penis to inspect the colour of his pre-cum on a white tissue.

Let's face facts. This is a job where if a lady gets sick her income drops to nil. Hence the health checks. Red-faced Colin is directed into the shower to remove any body odour. No sex worker wants to service a man that stinks of BO. She stands in the shower room watching him shower and chitchat about why it's so important every client must be health checked.

She must watch him shower, because she must make sure he is washing every part of his body and doesn't masturbate to get rid of the first lot of semen so he can last longer the second time. Sex workers learn the tricks of the trade from each other and most new women to the industry must learn very quickly to be able to survive.

A half-hour booking entitles a client to a sensual rubdown, oral sex on him for a couple of minutes and straight sex with him climaxing only once. If he wants any other service the lady must agree and he must pay the extra cost in cash before that service is provided.

The lady gets Colin to lie on his belly on the bed's drop sheet and spread his legs so she can slide up between them to give him his sensual rubdown. She then proceeds to caress his naked body, deliberately teasing him knowing he is getting an erection as she touches him intimately. Her objective is that when he turns over onto his back he has an erection, which will make her job easier.

She is amused and smiles as she notices the difference between a once-shrivelled little cock that's grown in size to double what it was. A woman should always compliment a man's ego. "Colin, you certainly didn't get left behind the door when dicks were handed out.".

Unseen by Colin she has opened a condom wrapper and rubbed her pussy with lubricant from the bottle on the bedside table. She then gently puts the condom over his erect penis before starting oral sex on him. The taste of a condom is revolting but necessary.

When she feels Colin close to climax so she pulls away, straddles his body and places his condom-covered penis inside her pussy. She rides his cock like a cowgirl. Thankfully Colin can't hold off any longer and grunts and groans like he is in seventh heaven as he loses his load. She stays on top grateful it is all over, thinking, "I can now pay my electricity bill. "

Getting your body off a man who has climaxed into a condom is also an art, you must hold the base of his penis to make sure the condom stays on the penis and not come off inside your vagina.

Once off you must then remove it and put it into a handful of tissues wrapping it carefully to make sure there is no contact with any of his body fluids. Safety first and foremost is the name of the game.

Not all bookings are as easy as Colin's. He is considered a textbook worker's dream.

Other clients are known in the industry as brothel hoppers, some difficult but most controllable. Every lady who enters the sex industry is warned not to ever give her private phone number to a client. It's dangerous and unethical if working for an establishment.

When a woman decides she has no other option but to become a sex worker she also must decide how far she will go to provide this service. The client's demands can be very offensive and intrusive.

Some will ask for a girlfriend experience, this is an expectation from the sex worker to pretend they are the client's girlfriend in that half-hour or one-hour booking. This involves the lady tongue-kissing him, allowing him to perform oral sex on her and fingering her vagina during foreplay. This of course is extra pay for her.

Other sex workers provide anal sex for hundreds of dollars extra.

These types of extra services can expose the sex worker to potential disease. Herpes is forever, as are bowel injuries. Some sex workers charge clients for the non-use of condoms, which is in my opinion incomprehensible. It is illegal in most states to provide sexual service to a client without a condom, and rightly so. Most sex workers do not tongue kiss clients or even kiss them as they are afraid of contracting herpes. A sex worker with cold sores on her lips is not permitted to work in a brothel. She wouldn't get work anyway as clients would be horrified just looking at her.

There is no greater actress than a professional sex worker. It's her job to seduce and convince the client she is a nymphomaniac who loves her job. Her job is to get that client to spend extra money on her by providing him with all his fantasies during the time he has paid for. Some clients spend thousands chasing their dreams. Again, the lady is in control and it's her decision on what she will provide.

Most clients will ask for what he is looking for at the initial introduction and negotiate an extra price before he chooses the lady. Doing this takes away any aggravation between them during their interlude.

Most clients are amicable but some are a pain in the ass. They think that because they have paid $150 for half an hour or $250 for the hour that gives them the right to treat the lady like shit – calling them sluts and physically rough the lady up by pounding away at her body like she was a piece of dead meat.

Some deliberately try to physically hurt the lady by manhandling her. I have never understood why men do this, even though I hold degrees and have learned over many years of being in the industry to recognise instantly that something is off when a client arrives at reception.

Then there are the predator-type clients who prey on vulnerable sex workers. These men jump from one brothel to the next looking for the type of woman they can con or even fall in love with. They constantly pay for bookings with the chosen lady and give her large tips. They sweet-talk her, trying to get her to see him away from the premises for extra money. They tell her he will look after her and her kids and she will not have to be a sex worker ever again.

Sometimes this works but of the many ladies I have known who have taken that road, not one of these relationships has worked. Most have disintegrated into a toxic, violent union, once again sending the lady back out on the run and into hiding.

There is the professional client who comes in because he has no time for cultivating a long-term relationship. He is working hard to make his business a success and is too tired to be worried about going out socially. He feels it's a waste of time wining and dining a woman and maybe getting no sex. Solution, it's off to the brothel or a private worker, pay the dollars, get the dirt off his chest and home to bed to sleep.

Another is the married man who is either nothing at home for one reason or another. He pays for sex because paying for it and keeping a happy household is easier than a divorce where he would lose more than half of everything, he has worked for all his life. Often the married ones come to the premises because the wife is sick of her horny old husband whose imagination doesn't collate with his penis abilities.

Then there is the single ageing male who is just terribly lonely, has no wife, no close relatives if any and most times they can't even get an erection. They just want cuddles and conversation.

On top of these types of clients, there are the disabled who are bought into the brothel by their carer's and or a parent. Disabilities range from being in a wheelchair, blind, mentally challenged to a paraplegic. All legal premises in NSW must have a room for disabled clients, which are fitted out for the client's safety, and can hold a wheelchair. Regardless of the disability, every client must have the right to a service.

Not all ladies can look after a disabled client. It takes a very special lady to be able to work out how to handle a disabled client. Having patience and pathos is definitely a valued specialty for a sex worker.

The mental stability of a woman who, as a last resort, has chosen to enter the sex industry is very fragile. The fear of not being able to find the money to keep her children safe and pay the mounting financial bills is often overwhelming. On top of that she must learn how to shut off her mind to sexual abuse of the worst kind .... having sex with a stranger and allowing him to take control of her body. In her head this is abhorrent, but bills have to be paid. A roof must be kept over the heads of her kids. Her body is all that she has left to bargain with.

She must learn how to disassociate her feelings and learn fast or she will have a breakdown mentally. I have over many years counselled hundreds and hundreds of women entering the sex industry.

My advice has always been for her to think only of the financial situation she is in, what bills she is going to be able to pay and how much better off financially she is going to be. Don't think about what she will do with the client. Just add up the dollars and what bills they will be able to eliminate at the end of the day. I have told them all to save the money they earn, set themselves up and get out of this job. Their kids come first. End of the story.

I always made a point of saying that once she has been chosen, a sex worker must always remember that she is in charge not the client. Just because he has paid the money to spend time with her and for a sexual service, this doesn't make him the boss. It's her body. If he asks or tries to touch her in any way, she doesn't want she has the right to refuse his advances.

She must warn him by telling him no, and advise him that a third warning would cancel the booking on the spot and he would be asked to leave the building. He would also lose his payment.

My rules for clients who must inject themselves to get an erection is to take your needles with you or do not come back. My premises do not have needle disposable bins. Not all ladies could accept seeing such a client. Rules are rules. Safety of my staff come first and foremost.

Whatever happens in the workroom is the lady's choice and I respected this choice. The bottom line is the erect penis has no conscious. Men's brains cease to function and common sense walks out the door when they are excited. It was a daily exercise teaching clients they must treat the ladies with respect.

The brothel owner from hell

URING THE MANY years I was involved in the industry I encountered and worked for a few owners who should never have been allowed to take charge of other people's lives. They were the epitome of what the general population believed a brothel owner was.

One in particular comes to mind. I will not reveal the state or district or even the legality of these premises because to do so would put too many decent people at risk of being attacked in one way or another. This person is a textbook sociopath, a narcissist of the worst kind. I have more than 45 years' experience in the sex industry and have legitimate qualifications to back up my assessment of this person.

This is a true account of my short association with this person. I guess it took only a week or so to realise that underneath that top layer of icing was a rotting persona of pure evil. Linda (not her real name) was the resident, long-time, suffering receptionist. I listened to the owner's verbal abuse of Linda's ability to do her job.

Not just behind Linda's back but the screaming at her over the phone or in person. I was astounded. No job is worth this kind of verbal and mental abuse. This person played the most obscene mind games with everyone, including with the women who worked there.

I came to realise very quickly that any lady who was stable, smart and in control of her life never worked there for very long. That owner got off on control; thrived on it in fact.

The premises looked quite nice, but the carpets were a filthy mite-infected, infection-spreading cesspit. Ladies were often getting sick with eye infections and marks covering their bodies. Mostly these women stayed on the premises for a week or two at a time. This person watered down the washing disinfectant and the washing-up detergent for the dishes. Even the supplied lubricant staff used in the bookings was watered down.

The toilet rolls were counted and only replaced when things were desperate. The washing machines were on five-minute cycles. Linen and towels were disgusting and I felt so ashamed of having to stock the rooms with unclean, worn-out rubbish.

The pillows looked like they came from the tip. They were dirty, stained messes. It was terrible and embarrassing. Killing germs and stopping potential cross contamination from one client to another takes a washing process of more than five minutes.

The laundry consisted of two worn-out washing machines; one was out of order. There were three clothes dryers, but only one worked.

Linda was sick most of the time from sinus infections and at one stage I started to get sick. I had the office carpet cleaned on several occasions. I paid for this myself, which really upset the owner. Linda and I kept the office clean for each other.

We woke up to the fact that we were being played off against each other. We stopped being part of that game and supported each other. Linda had tolerated years and years of emotional and verbal abuse from this owner because she needed the job to pay her mortgage and survive. Watching all this on a daily basis really upset me.

I witnessed that owner scamming money from staff, overcharging clients thousands of dollars and cheating the Tax Office of thousands. Worst of all was taking advantage of the women who worked there with serious mental health issues.

The owner took half the cash earnings from the ladies' extra services and even keep tip money clients had designated to the ladies. No records were kept.

I saw ladies being thrown out into the car park with their clothes and belongings after being fired. The owner refused to pay money owning to staff that were fired. Staff were told the money was being kept for the inconvenience of the business being left short staffed.

In all my working life I had never come across a person so self-absorbed and one who absolutely had no respect for anyone. The sad part about this situation was the ladies were too scared and/or had issues in their private lives to confront the owner over their treatment or money owed. Emotional, and financial blackmail was the order of the day and I had had enough.

I had several verbal altercations with that owner and after the last time my own pay was short-changed. I was done. I waited for Linda to come on to replace me. I had already packed up my belongings into my car. When Linda arrived, I told her I was quitting.

I left a very short cordial note addressed to the owner, said my good-byes to the staff and Linda, and walked out the door. I ignored many text messages and phone calls begging me not to leave. After six members of staff repeated the threats and lies the owner said behind my back, I could have accepted the abuse or leave this toxic environment.

I chose dignity and self-preservation over the pittance I was being paid. I chose honour and my reputation. Above all was the unacceptable verbal and mental abuse this person dished out daily to every person working in that business. The one lesson, I learned over all the years I was associated in the industry WAS that one must NEVER underestimate the enemy.

Like the Trojan horse of Troy, one must have tucked away! Solders that will decimate and destroy an attack from the not so silent enemy.

I left on my own terms without the aggravation and stress from being verbally abused. A few months later I was told by a staff member that Linda had quit after being hospitalised with a serious, potentially life-threatening infection. While Linda had to take a month off work, the owner reported to the police that she had stolen from the business.

She was so ill she was unable to call or even speak to anyone more than four weeks and she was being accused of theft.

I am sure there are other shocking owners who fit the public idea of what a brothel owner should be like. I assure you there are decent people in the industry who always have had the best interests of the women who worked for them at heart. Do not judge a book by its cover.

Most clients come to brothels to get what they are not getting at home. Reasons vary from having a sick wife to wife who is going through menopause. Then there are the clients who are single or a widower who is just very lonely. It may not be for sex; they are just lonely and need the company of a female. There are also clients who due to a medical condition and a wife who no longer tolerates his high sex drive refuses to comply when he wants to take pills to give him an erection or gives himself an injection to reach the same outcome.

CHAPTER 36

Why the ladies get into this industry

SADLY, THERE are so many vulnerable women in the sex industry who have never known real love. They have lived in a bubble of verbal, emotional and/or physical abuse. Many women in the industry have long-term addiction and mental health issues.

There are several different types of women who work within the sex industry. What people in the general population do not know or perhaps choose to ignore is every single one of these women found themselves in a position of not knowing how to get out of a financial or abusive environment they found themselves in.

It's not until their living conditions become so dangerous or so financially desperate that they try to escape.

On the other hand, there is the professional woman who has chosen to use her ability to financially set herself up for a future of fewer struggles. She pays taxes, invests her hard-earned money in property or whatever, and keeps her profession out of her personal life.

She lives a very secretive double life and has honed the ability to disassociate her real self from her working persona. She protects her identity from prying eyes. For example, her car registration if checked will go back to a post office box many suburbs or even cities away from where she lives. Her priority is to protect herself and her family if she has one.

She keeps impeccable records of funds she has earned and usually has a very savvy accountant to keep her on track. She keeps other workers in an established place at arm's length and makes no friends. Some of these women choose to work privately from premises kept especially for this purpose.

This is a very dangerous way of working. They leave themselves open to rape and robbery. Many ladies have been murdered after being physically bashed. Women who have worked privately and who have been shockingly assaulted by a client have not reported it to the police. This is because they would be outed publicly in the event of the client being caught and charged.

Being exposed as a sex worker in a court case is not what a private worker would want her family to know. Many of these private workers have a security plan in place, such as calling a friend at the start and end of a booking with a client. A rescue plan will come into action if the lady fails to report her safety being okay.

I have given jobs to thousands of women desperate to escape from an abusive partner or a home environment that has put her and her children in danger. A mother who decides the only thing she has left to sell is herself is a mother who will fight to the death for her family no matter what it takes. They have sought help from the authorities. Often over and over. Without any satisfaction.

I have looked after several babies in my own home while the mother worked her arse off to get the money to escape her situation, then helped her plan and execute her run to freedom.

Eighty-five per cent of these women never went back. They used the money they earned to move interstate. They rented a home they could afford and had enough funds to support themselves while they established a better life. Covering your tracks to escape abuse is not easy. It's stressful and dangerous.

Then there have been the university students who have entered into the industry to pay for their tuition and textbooks and to survive the near-poverty of being a student.

I have had staff that used the time while working to educate themselves. I still to this day get calls from ladies who have graduated and achieved getting much deserved brilliant jobs. Nurses, teachers, counsellors. Then there have been the women who have fallen through the cracks, women who battle every day with just staying clean from drugs. Some of these women are so damaged emotionally and physically that they never recover. These are the most vulnerable of the workers in the sex industry.

I have nothing but contempt for the people/owners who take advantage of these women. They cannot get jobs out in the general workforce. They have become too unreliable and unpredictable at even showing up for work. This is why they tend to live on the work premises if they do get a job in the sex industry. They live day-to-day, week-to-week.

Sadly, many of these women have permanent mental health issues. Some are medicated and some aren't. I was always intrigued at which personality I would be dealing with each day when I was in reception. It would only take me about 30 minutes to assess which personality I would have on shift and I would then treat her accordingly.

For example, if the lady was in a heightened emotional state, I would make her a coffee and go sit out in the closed-off area away from other staff and talk her down. If she was depressed then it was a day of encouragement, helping her work out what her next personal chores would be. Helping her with dress choices and make-up would make her feel better.

The most important issue an owner must deal with is keeping the work environment a happy one. No aggravation between staff members is paramount for a successful day's work. A gathering of women competing against each other can be a lion's den.

I had contracts for all staff members and unless they signed them on the day, they started they were not given a job. These contracts made them responsible for paying their taxation and superannuation commitments. They were sole traders, not employed by my company or me. They either agreed to house rules or did not stay to work here.

My daily worksheets on every booking they undertook were to be initialled by each lady on every booking before they entered the workroom. Also signed again at the end of their shift when paid in full for each booking they completed.

I ran a very tight ship but was always firm and fair in my dealings with every lady.

Clients were advised to treat his chosen companion with respect. They got two warnings but after a third warning about disrespect he would be removed from the building with no refund.

If I had a difficult client in reception, I would always say to him pointing up at the camera, "Smile, as you are being recorded. I am sure you would not like your wife or girlfriend to see your picture on the front page of the newspapers if I had to call the police."

I rarely took a client's word on an unhappy dealing with a lady, but I respectfully listened and was usually able to come to a compromise.

Violence of any kind was treated as an assault and the client was given a choice, leave or the police would be called.

No man would want to see their picture on the front page of a newspaper as being involved in an assault against a sex worker at a local brothel especially if he was a married man or in a long-term relationship. Some men who visit brothels think that because they are paying for sex, they can treat the lady in any way they want.

This is not the case and if they step out of line they are asked to leave or they were removed by force by police or security guards.

The death of my son

WRITING ABOUT the soul-destroying death of my son Gregory has been very painful and has dragged up a multitude of self-recriminations. A mother should never have to bury their child. Gregory entered this world under the most stressful and dire circumstances. Born a month late, he had to fight for five days and nights just to breathe. He had tubes forced down his little throat, was hooked up too many life-saving drugs and had blood transfusions.

He was born four pounds and was just 21 inches long with most of his little body shedding all the outer layers of his skin. He was one very sick baby and not expected to survive. He was baptised before he was a day old.

He survived with the help of the latest top-of-the-range humidity crib owned by Dr Patrick Lip, who used this to save his baby only one month before my son was born. Gregory had a very traumatic first few years of his life, having extra toes he was born with removed and being so ill from being unable to keep food in his little tummy.

In saying all this, my little Gregory was very advanced in his progress. He was shuffling around the floor at six months and walking around his cot and the furniture at seven and a half months. As sick as he was, every day he was proving what a little fighter he was.

Those first few years of his life were difficult I know. I had left his violent, drunken father, we had many changes in our living conditions and he had more operations to help him walk properly without constantly falling. And in between all this he gained a stepfather.

He seemed to take all these changes in his stride, but he had a quiet side to him and a fiery temper to match his red hair. Over the years my

Gregory nearly drove me to distraction. When he was 13 when I found condom packets in his bedroom. I spent the first few hours laughing, intrigued at how he could even fit his penis into a condom.

But I realised in a short time this was serious. His girlfriend was 16 and I was too young to be a grandmother. I marched up to the girl's mother's house and told her about finding the condoms. I also said in the eyes of the law my son was a minor and if her daughter fell pregnant, I would press charges against her and her daughter. I told her in no uncertain terms put her daughter on the pill.

When Gregory came home from school, I didn't sound off at him but did tell him there would be serious consequences if he got that girl pregnant. Sure enough, two years later she was pregnant. I was furious, as this girl couldn't look after herself that alone a baby. My son also was only 15 and she was nearly 18 and had given her mother Margaret so much grief.

Gregory was giving me hell. The pregnancy progressed and we arranged that I would adopt the baby. When I drove to the Royal Brisbane Hospital to pick up the baby, the mother told me she had changed her mind. I did get to hold the baby and have a picture of me with him. She named him Cameron. I never saw him again until after the death of his father, my son. I found out that Cameron had been kicked from pillar to post in multiple foster homes and had endured a terrible life.

This broke my heart, as I know I could have given him a better life and he would have been a stabilising influence on my son's life. Gregory was beside himself that he would never get to have his son grow up with him. There was nothing I could have done as she was the baby's mother and my son was too young to claim custody.

I know that losing contact with his son affected Gregory mentally and sent him into a downward spiral of pill-popping and self-destructive behaviour.

He later became involved with a young lady called Raylene when he was nearly 19 and she was approaching 21. They had four children. This relationship also did not last; no fault of Raylene's. My son was a lost soul.

He developed mental health issues from drug abuse. He took pills and smoked dope at every opportunity. I rescued my Greg from financial difficulties many times over the coming years.

Raylene leaving him was the best decision for herself and the children. My grandchildren could not have had a better mother. I am so proud of my grandchildren and love them dearly. My son went missing again and I heard nothing for months. The last time I had heard for him was late October 2006. I was franticly worried. He would always surface within a month or two.

Eighteen months passed and still nothing, then one day in 2009 about 9.30pm Raylene called. She told me that she had just had a visit from two men from the Child Support Agency and they told her that my son was deceased. They had been tracking him down for non-payment of the child support he owed to Raylene.

My mind and body went into shock. I felt like I had hit a brick wall at 100 miles a minute. I could not speak. The tears poured from my eyes were like an unstoppable waterfall. I asked Raylene where he was and she said she had no idea; the men did not tell her.

Nothing, on this earth prepares you for being told your child is dead. The inner shock waves are horrendous. Your whole being is numb; no voice only tears. I put the phone down and I just sat in my office in my Ballina business, trying to pull myself together. I felt shattered, totally shattered. I would never forget this moment in time. I do not remember how long I sat there before I realized I had to call my family and make arrangements for Ammie to come and take over my business so I could find where my son's body was being held.

How I drove home that night is beyond me. Greg was unpredictable, prone to going underground when life became too much for him. In the past he had disappeared but turned up in rehab and again tried to kick his pill habit. I walked the floor all night that first night, bashed myself up emotionally and cried a river of tears.

I was on the doorstep of the local hospital to speak with a social worker at 8.30am. With her help we tracked down that my son was being held at the Melbourne City Morgue. A woman there spoke to me with the utmost kindness. It was the most bizarre conversation I have had with anyone in my entire life.

My son had died from a drug overdose and had been in the morgue since May 23, 2008. It was now October 2009. This was the 18 months he had been missing. He had been lost in their system. My son had his father's name. I had my real husband's name, which is why they were unable to find me. It was like he was waiting for me to find him and bring him home. I knew that when people that pass away end up in any state morgue. If there is no family to claim them, the state takes care of their bodies and buries them in a pauper's grave.

I felt like I was going to lose my mind. I knew I had to pull myself together and get my Greg home to Brisbane for our family to grieve and be able to lay him to rest.

The next lot of news added to my grief. I was told I could not bring him home via public transport as his body had not been embalmed and he had been deceased too long for this procedure to be done. I told the lady at the morgue I would get his return to Queensland organised through a funeral home in Brisbane and they would be contact them. I hung up the phone and called my little sister Aileen. Like me she was in shock and in tears. I had not told my mother yet as I couldn't tell her over the phone.

I packed my suitcase and headed to Brisbane to organise my son's funeral. This was the start of the most devastating journey I had travelled in my entire life. I felt paralysed. How I made that drive without having an accident still amazes me today.

It was late in October 2009 and my Greg's birthday was coming up on November 17. He would have been 37. I would never get to speak to him again, never hear his voice again. Regardless of the stress and worry he caused in his short life he was my son. My only son and I loved him beyond words.

I told my mother and we cried together in each other's arms. My sister arrived and we arranged for us to all go to a large Brisbane funeral home.

My 'Gregory Peck', a nickname that stayed with him all his life, was coming home. Bringing my son home was not easy' his body had to be kept at a certain temperature which meant private refrigerated transport.

AS USUAL THERE was a hiccup. I had organised to take my latest partner Kaye's two sons to Thailand for a 10-day holiday. She had paid for one son's airline ticket and I had paid for the other. What was I to do? It was going to take two weeks to get my son's body home to Brisbane and his funeral was organised for his birthday on November 17. I would lay him to rest on the very date he came into this world.

How could I break the hearts of two boys going on their very first overseas trip? I was trying to cope with my grief, but there was no point punishing the boys so I conceded. I decided to put aside my grief and look after the living.

My mother was furious that I was taking two kids overseas so close to my own son's funeral. I tried to explain to her there was nothing left to do. Getting Greg home to Queensland had been a logistical nightmare. The expense of bringing him home and the funeral was three times the cost of me taking those boys away and their trip had already been paid for.

I took the boys to Thailand and the whole time I was away I do not think there was a day I did not break down in tears. I found solace in the temple with the monks and I bought a tile dedicated to the life of my son. These tiles were to be laid around the base of the Big Buddha's feet. I know my Greg would have loved this dedication to his memory.

Greg was crazy mad over the music of his favourite band Guns N' Roses. I organised for the band's album covers to drape his coffin and his pallbearers to wear the band's T-shirts and bandannas. His favourite music played throughout his service. My Greg would have been dancing in the aisles, I am sure; he probably was in spirit.

This day was one of the saddest days of my life, I am thankful I have photo memories to look back on and console me on my down days. There has never been a day or night that I have not talked to and thought about my Greg. I still cry tears of grief at not being able to see him.

I look through my photos of him and listen to his music. A mother's grief is eternal; her love for her children is with her until she breathes her last breath regardless of what they put us through. I love and miss you, my Greg, my darling son.

My Son

We are connected my child and me, by
An invisible cord not seen by the eye.
It's not like the cord, that connects us 'until birth
This cord can't be seen, by any on Earth.
This cord does its work, right from the start.
It binds us together attached to my heart.
I know that it's there though no one can see
The invisible cord from my child to me.
The strength of this cord is hard to describe.
It can't be destroyed, it can't be denied.
It's stronger than any cord man could create.
It withstands the test of time and can hold any weight.
And though you are gone,
Though you're not here with me,
The cord is still there but no one can see it.
It pulls at my heart I am bruised. ... I am sore,
But this cord is my lifeline as never before.
I am thankful that God connects us this way,
a mother and child, death can't take it away!
I love and miss you, my only son.
My Gregory (Peck)

–Author unknown.

CHAPTER 38

My daughter's birth changed me

MY DAUGHTER Sandra was conceived in August 1977, another shock to my system. After the horrendous ordeal of having my son five years earlier I did not want to go through this again. Back in those days government laws stopped married women from terminating a pregnancy without her husband's consent.

My husband refused to sign the paperwork. I was four months' pregnant when I went into hospital in Brisbane. My baby was lying transverse (crossways) and the doctors couldn't turn her. One issue that had been fixed since Greg was born was the discovery of a serum to correct the antibodies in my rare blood type. I was relieved and I knew my baby would not suffer as my son had during and after his birth. They insisted I stay in hospital because had I gone into labour I would have died and probably my baby with me.

I was very upset that I was being pushed into having another child and insisted that during my planned caesarean operation that the doctor tie my tubes so there would be no further children. This was to be my husband's first child and he was excited but concerned about this birth affecting my health. Knowing I had to stay in hospital for five months was a bone of contention between us.

I patiently sat out these months, being jabbed with needles weekly to combat the antibodies in my blood. I was weighed every second day, prodded and pushed weekly to see if they could turn my baby for a normal birth. All to no success.

The day before my caesarean, I was given an amniocentesis. No one explained to me what this was. But I sure found out very quickly when the doctors put a big needle into my very big stomach to test whether the baby's lungs were mature enough for them to take her from my body next morning.

I had a cardiac arrest on the operating table and a near-death experience that I was unable to talk about for many years later. The bruising on my chest near down to my waist was shocking and I came out of all this very upset. I was angry towards my husband for putting his need to have a child over my mental and physical welfare. I found out my tubes had been tied and I received my permanent birth control at 28.

All this anger dissipated within a few days when I was wheeled down to the hospital's nursery to see my beautiful little girl. Sandy was such a good baby, happy, healthy and full of life. I fell in love with her and spoiled her rotten.

My children's childhoods were not easy with us constantly moving from one place to another. Living up on the Sunshine Coast was probably the most stable years of their lives. They both went to private schools and had lots of friends. My move back to Brisbane caused deep problems for both my kids. My son stayed with my husband and Sandy came with me.

When I decided to leave Queensland Sandy was upset and decided to go back to the Sunshine Coast to live with her father. I think it was mainly because I was too strict with her and she still had friends up on the Sunshine Coast from when we were living there.

Sandy is a gorgeous, intelligent young lady and it pains me to write all this, as it would any mother who misses their children and thinks about them every day. Sandy became involved with a boy much to my despair and they went off to live in north Queensland.

Sandy and Wes had three children, a boy and two girls. This relationship lasted only a few years and again I got in my car and drove 12 hours to pick them all up. Sandy was just not coping with three children and Wes had become involved with another woman. In the next year I organised several places for Sandy and the children to live but she gave into pressure from Wes and the children went back to live with Wes and his new lady, whom he later down the track married.

Jelina became my three grandchildren's stepmother and she had several more children to Wes. I never got to meet, this amazing woman who brought up my grandbabies. She died suddenly from a medical event. She did an amazing job and I am forever grateful. I am very close to Holly-Lee, the eldest girl. She is a beautiful, talented, intelligent young lady and I am very proud of her. I love all my grandchildren from both children.

Sandy is out living the life she has chosen and as difficult as it has been for me to stop enabling her lifestyle, I had to pull the pin. Our children as young adults must learn that parents are not walking cash registers. I made the very same mistakes with her as I did with my son. I drove all around the country pulling them out of the dark holes they got themselves into. I made excuses for their antisocial behaviour and refused to face reality.

There has to be a cut-off point at some time in their lives when a mother says no more. But these words do not take way my ingrained heartfelt love for my children. My love for my lost son and my daughter is branded deep in my very soul and will be there until my last breath.

My daughter and I have become estranged in the past few years. I don't even know where she is. She used to always call me on my birthday, Christmas and Mother's Day. But there has been no contact since Covid hit. I received a text message in mid-2022 and when I called the number no one answered. I have called that number many times to no answer. All I can do is hope and pray she is okay.

One day she may make contact again. I will be waiting.

CHAPTER 39

My parents' lives and deaths

CHILDHOOD MEMORIES of my mother and father are bitter and yet sweet. My mother was born into a family of 16 children; only two were female. She had a very hard life with little mother-child physical displays of love. Once I started a degree in counselling later, I gained valuable insight into understanding why she found it difficult to physically show her children affection.

She never knew how. Why would she when she rarely was shown any during her childhood. My mother was a beautiful, hard-working woman. She worked to feed and clothe us all and was fiercely loyal to our family. I believe the only thing that kept her physically safe from my father's drunken rages was the fact she had older brothers who would have jumped in to protect her.

Dad was terrified of Mum's brothers. They were a very hard-headed, hard-working bunch of no-bullshit men.

Early in her life, she was deeply affected by the accidental death of two of her younger brothers who were killed by an explosion while playing with matches near a drum of petrol.

She spoke about this incident often and cried as she related it to my sister Aileen and me.

My mother worked for 14 years at the local golf club as a chef in their dining room restaurant and loved her job. She was offered a better-paying job when the local RSL opened its restaurant in a beautiful new building. She worked for the RSL for 16 years and gained a reputation of having the best restaurant in our little country town.

If it had not been for her love and hard work, we would have starved as my father drank and gambled his money away every payday. She was a great chef and always made sure we had little treats of cakes and biscuits when we came home from school. She would come home on her break between lunchtime and preparations for the dinner rush in the club.

She cooked our dinner. Dad's dinner was put aside, so he had food if he came in before she got home from work at 9.30pm. She never complained and I never remember hearing her utter a bad word against my father. What she did say often though was that as soon as my younger brother Mick was old enough, she would leave Dad.

I was out living my life when Mum left him. The week before he attempted to drive her car home after borrowing it while she was at work and he smashed it up. He was drunk and the car came out second best.

Mum was devastated. This car was her independence and expensive to repair it. She had had enough and told him to pack his belongings and get out. She said she would be contacting a lawyer to divorce him and the house was going to be sold.

His ranting and raving got him nowhere. He packed up and moved into a local hotel room as a permanent border. Now all he had to do was walk from the public bar to his hotel room bed to pass out. The men in the town felt sorry for him; his kids clapped our hands in relief.

She sold the house and split the money. Mum bought a new, 40- foot mobile home. After a few years of travelling between my and my sister Aileen's homes she decided to move back to Narrabri onto the property owned by my grandmother. She lived there for many years until my grandmother died. She sold her mobile home and I bought a house at Waterford West in Brisbane. Mum and I moved into that house which is still considered our family home.

Mum became too sick to be on her own so my brother Mick moved into the flat under the house to care for her. He was so dedicated to Mum even during his battle with cancer. He put her first and was my hero.

She was the matriarch of our family, the glue that held us all together. When she died we became a very fractured family. I had promised her we would never put her into a nursing home. The effects of dementia started to take hold. My sister Aileen, Michael and I kept that promise. Michael became her full-time live-in caregiver.

The last week of Mum's life was filled with love and sadness as her children tried to fill her days sharing childhood memories. Her little dog Maggie May never left her side. The afternoon before Mum died the medical team came and attached a line into her neck to relieve her pain. That night it failed to work.

Here was a woman who never smoked in her life yet had to be on an oxygen machine 17 hours a day. She never drank alcohol, but six weeks before her passing was diagnosed with liver cancer.

The day she passed, Mum woke happily and ordered crispy bacon with eggs, toast and her favourite coffee. She enjoyed every mouthful. Then gave us chores for the day, including giving Kaye permission to mow her lawn.

Then she closed her eyes and left us very quietly.

The nurse told us Mum had passed. It was still a shock even though we all knew it was coming. We kept Mum in the house for the next 24 hours as none of us was ready to let her go. We cried, laughed, held her, talked to her and comforted each other. White Lady Funerals came the next morning and took her into their care, we were all inconsolable.

The departure of our legend from our lives was life-changing for us all. Goodbye, our mother, forever in our hearts and souls.

AFTER MY mother and father divorced, Dad took up residence with another local town identity. Alma was a hard woman who took no shit from my father. His children didn't like her and she had no time for any of us. However, what I give her credit for is regimenting his life.

They spent 37 years together but never married. He probably should have because it would have saved a lot of stress later. From time to time, we visited him individually and only twice did I stay in her home in all those years.

Alma and my father were champion local lawn bowlers, winning many championships. They had a lot in common. They both drank alcohol; Alma in moderation and she controlled his intake. My father was an alcoholic. He had to have a few drinks every day. She made him do his drinking to their garage where he had a fridge. He also brewed his own beer.

She allowed to go to the club on his own only on Saturdays 10am until 1pm. He had to be outside the club at 1pm for her to pick him up or he would have to walk three miles home. They socialised at the club during bowl events and on Friday nights a couple of times a month.

He rang me one afternoon in tears and extremely distressed. Alma had been put into the hospital after she got an infection from a wound while in their garden and the doctors found she had adult leukaemia. Alma died and Dad was so distressed and was worried that her son would kick him out into the street as it was Alma's house.

I packed up my car with enough clothing for a week and drove the nine hours down to my father. He was a total mess emotionally and physically, as he was much more dependent on her than any of us realised. Dad had been diagnosed with Alzheimer's and was on medication for that. He also had had a heart attack and heart surgery.

The violence we suffered as children would never be forgotten but we needed to forgive him for our own mental health. All my father could say was Alma's son was going to kick him out and he had nowhere to go. I assured Dad he was going nowhere and that her son could not remove him from the house. He couldn't accept Alma was gone. Every day after her death he would go to the funeral home and sit by her body and talk to her.

When Alma's son arrived the second day after she passed, he came with an attitude. I was prepared for him and his wife. He started to talk about his rights as her benefactor. I told him we needed to talk about his rights.

I firmly informed him that my father was her husband in the eyes of the law regardless of not having a marriage certificate. Centrelink was paying them a married couple aged pension and the Family Court would protect my father as her partner. I told her son that my father was going nowhere and that his children didn't care about her money or property. But my father was going to live in this house until the day he died.

When the funeral was over, Alma's son realised he could not put my father out in the street to get his inheritance.

It was heartbreaking for my sister and me to watch Dad drive to the cemetery every day to sit by her grave and talk to her. He even bought the plot next to her grave so he could be buried beside her. He was inconsolable, his grief overwhelming. He had relied on her regimentation of his life and now she was gone.

My sister and I had lives of our own and our eldest brother Jack was the only unattached sibling who could take charge of Dad. Michael, our youngest, hated Dad's guts and had not spoken or acknowledged our father's existence since our parents had separated and divorced. Jack moved in with our father to look after him when Aileen and I headed home the week after Alma's funeral.

Putting Jack and Dad together was a disaster. Dad was a grieving, stubborn, alcoholic, who needing his meds, which Alma had regimented daily. Jack was a hard-line party boy who also enjoyed a drink on a hot day. It was a clash of personalities.

Four weeks later Jack rang me to tell me Dad had driven into a wall at the local shopping centre and he had suffered a stroke. I was in Warwick in Queensland at the time, a seven-hour drive away. I packed up my car and drove to Narrabri after speaking to the local hospital.

I knew he had only four hours to take his drugs to halt the lethal effects of a stroke. I arrived at the hospital, distressed at his condition and angry that they had not transferred him to the huge Tamworth Hospital only two hours' away for drug treatment to halt the effects of his stroke.

For 13 days and nights Jack and I sat-slept by his bed. He tried to pull through but the suffering and catastrophic physical effects of his stroke were horrendous. Medical intervention kept him alive and his suffering was just shocking. There was no dignity in my father's death.

It was torture when he had no hope of survival. It broke my heart.

No human being regardless of their transgressions in life deserves this inhumane treatment. There was nothing I could do to help him.

My father looked into my eyes begging with tears to help him, he could not speak. He was paralysed down his left side and could not even sit up on his own. He just cried.

A doctor attached a morphine machine to him the day before he passed which kept him pain-free and in a coma. He opened his eyes on the morning he died, looked at me and I told him I loved him. He slipped back into a coma.

A nurse took out his feeding tube and they stopped sucking fluid from his lungs. At 10.30am the nurse gave him an extra needle saying she thought he was in pain and needed a top-up. At 11.45am Dad quietly slipped away to join his beloved Alma. I do not doubt for one second, she came to collect him.

We drove back to Alma's house to stay while I organised Dad's funeral. At least my sister and another brother Larry and his partner Rosie got to say goodbye. Dad's funeral was very sad but lovely. All his bowling mates and old family friends made a guard of honour leading up to his grave.

I drove away from my hometown feeling relieved Dad was at peace and that I had done the right thing by supporting him in his last weeks. Jack stayed on in Alma's house for another year, then moved out and allowed her son to collect his inheritance.

My young brother Mick never forgave our father for the way he treated us and never mentally recovered from witnessing the death of our cat at the hands of our father. He hated Dad with every fibre of his being. Mick refused to visit Dad in the hospital and refused to attend his funeral.

CHAPTER 40

My sister and brothers

MY SISTER AILEEN endured so much mental and physical pain in our journey of survival within our family. Just being able to accomplish what she has today is an epic credit to her inner strength. There are no words fine enough or deep enough to describe my love for her.

She suffered so much violence at the hands of our father and male partners. She had broken bones from one of those partners and physical injuries that prohibited her from being a mother. She has survived serious drug addiction to become a valued, 20-plus-year employee of a renowned Queensland winery.

A talented artist, Aileen has supported me 100 per cent throughout our lives. She has Protected me verbally, financially and without hesitation on every level. She now is with Jeff who loves her dearly. We are sisters joined by an unbreakable bond that will last for all eternity. I know our mother would be very proud of us both.

The trauma of witnessing the death of our family pet as kids affected every one of us. But we never gave up. We have all suffered from the nightmare of that night and I believe this event scared each of us.

The first-born male in our family was Steven, the nickname Jack stuck with him all his life and still today we call him Jack. A qualified crane driver, he works in the mines of north Queensland. He has worked all over Australia in the mines and is the naughty boy of our family. He has been in and out of trouble all his life, however he has always landed back on his feet. A very personable man, his relationships came and went. He married and had two daughters and several grandbabies. He lost a son in his first relationship, with Cathy, and this loss affected him terribly. He drank to excess. His relationship with our other two brothers, Larry and Michael, was always strained and they had several major disagreements.

Although at times we all felt like punching him, we love him.

The next born male, Larry, was such a funny little kid. He was born with a speech impediment and used to call Aileen Diddy because he could not say sister. This nickname stuck with Aileen all her life. Larry is a very talented mechanic, but like all the members of our family sufferers from a heart condition, controlled by medication.

Larry was sent to the Royal Far West, Australia's only national charity dedicated to improving the health and wellbeing of country children, to learn how to speak correctly.

Michael the youngest was nicknamed Pie and this stuck throughout his life. He never married but he did have a daughter with his first love and girlfriend. He lost many years of contact with her and was heart-broken. Michael moved into our family home to look after our mother full-time. He was a concreter. He contracted a serious cancer that ate away most of the left side of his skull. He endured many operations, skin grafts, chemotherapy and radiation therapy.

He suffered shocking headaches and was so body conscious he never went out in public without a hat or bandana, which covered up the loss of half his ear, an eyebrow and most of the side of his skull. He dedicated his life to our mother and when she passed away, he never recovered. Ten months after her death, he had a massive heart attack and passed away downstairs in our family home on his bed. Larry tried to revive him desperately until the ambulance arrived. Despite all the efforts by Larry and the paramedics Mick died.

We were all in such a state of shock over his death we all still struggle with our loss. Our youngest brother was gone and none of us had a chance to say goodbye. Our family was fractured and none of us knew how to put these broken pieces back together. I hope and pray one day we will all sit around the table and start mending these broken bonds. I know we all still love each other but being able to put aside egos for a reconciliation of family remains to be seen.

CHAPTER 41

The women in my life

MY FIRST INTIMATE experience with a woman was in that so-called home for wayward girls who had been exposed to moral dangers. She was a mature woman in authority, A full account of this is explained in an earlier chapter. Later in life I realised she was a predator, a paedophile. It was a shocking revelation.

The second was my lucky escape from that vile creature in the Catholic convert in Sydney where I was confined. I often think of all the young girls that woman abused. The girls were terrified but too scared to do anything about it. For little girls with no voice of their own, compliance meant survival.

Then there was Judy who lived on the Sunshine Coast. She had two sons and one-year-old twin girls when I met her. This relationship did not last because when I was diagnosed with my first bout of cancer, I flew her to Sydney to be by my side while I was operated on and had chemotherapy.

I had to get out of my hospital bed and take her back to the airport and fly her back to Queensland. I made up my mind that if I survived all this upheaval we were done. If a person cannot cope with a partner's sickness, they did not deserve to have them.

So committed was I to Judy that my husband had taken second place. I did survive. I fought the disease like a caged animal. What was supposed to take a month took six months because I was so ill from the chemo.

I was staying with two gay friends in Sydney while I was receiving treatment and one of their friends called Dawn volunteered to drive me to my treatment and look after me. I was too ill to drive myself back to the Sunshine Coast and Dawn offered to drive me home. I spent 13 hours on the back seat of my car while she drove me home.

Dawn stayed with me and even ran my illegal business for a while. But only until I discovered she had been putting credit card payments from my business straight into her bank account. My biggest problem all my life has been to trust the wrong people. I must have an invisible tattoo on my forehead which reads sucker. She left in a car I had bought for her.

When I bought my hairdressing salon, I had been having a torrid affair with a woman called Tory who lived with an ex-partner in a home they owned on the outskirts of Brisbane. This woman was the playgirl of the lesbian world and she had me hooked. The only trouble was it took me quite some time to realize she was also a cheater.

I caught her cheating with an ex-lover who was also hooked and couldn't stay away from her. She had a line-up of six other women, including her long-suffering ex-partner who owned a home with her.

Tory eventually got what she sought; she always wanted to die. She was diagnosed with ovarian cancer. She called me and told me she was selling everything she owned and would I come to her garage sale. I went to her home with Mum. I was shocked at her decline in health.

A little later she decided she wasn't ready to give up on life. But her body was in such decline she had lost all her inner energy. She had no hope of continuing her fight. She was put in palliative care and her ex-partner Francine asked me to visit her. I said no.

I went to her funeral, but I had met a woman with whom I had fallen in love. My love Kaye drove me out to the funeral home. My tears were not for Tory but for Francine, the only woman who had supported Tory from the start to the end.

I WILL NOT reveal Miss Ananiyy's first name because in the Middle East being a homosexual means imprisonment for a very long time or even death. I belonged to an online group of women from all around the world. Two Sydney ladies, Monika and Michelle, were a couple and we became quite close friends.

Monika organised a get-together of all the members of the online group. Kat came from South Australia; a couple of others came from other states in Australia and we all stayed at Monika's home. Late in the afternoon of the first day a cab pulled up and a woman arrived all the way from Egypt.

Miss Ananiyy was a striking, stunning, tall, dark-skinned, slim Middle Eastern woman aged about 30. I knew what she looked like from our weekly online music parties, much like Zoom.

She was an entertainer and singer with an amazingly beautiful haunting voice. She was also a closet gay women married to an Australian man living and working in Cairo. A look between us started the ball rolling. I was invited to visit her in Egypt. I said yes, but I would not stay in her home with her and her husband.

I also invited her to stay longer here in Australia on this visit and come home with me to Ballina. I was led to believe that she was in an unhappy marriage. Her visit with me over the next three weeks was lovely.

I probably was infatuated with her, not head over heels in love. I did like her but the cultural and language differences were difficult. I was operating in Ballina still illegally, but I had Ammie and staff to look after my business while I went to Egypt for a holiday.

Miss Ananiyy found me a fully furnished unit in Cairo. I was one happy little Aussie girl I can tell you and I loved Egypt. I loved the people, the daily hustle and bustle of Cairo's 17 million people.

We had a ball and I met so many amazing people. We also got along personally very well. In my crazy, mixed-up head I thought I would live in Australia for six months of the year and in Cairo for the other six months. I started to look for a unit there.

Miss Ananiyy found a unit that was being built in Nasr City. It was a beautiful top-floor unit for $37,000 Australian. All I had to do was furnish it. The property was registered in both our names as she was an Egyptian citizen and I could not own the property outright in my name.

I had the lawyer add a clause that Miss Ananiyy could not sell or dispose of this property and if I decided I needed to sell she could not claim any financial gain from my property. I had lost many thousands of dollars in past dealings and it was not going to happen again. She did not receive this very well.

When I organised my trip back the unit had not been finished, so I stayed in a unit on the same floor as one of Miss Ananiyy's friends. The unit was fully furnished and very upmarket for Cairo. I became very good friends with this girl's parents. The mother was a professor at the university and the father was a businessman of high standing within the community.

Two of Miss Ananiyy's girlfriends arrived for a holiday from Saudi Arabia and they came to my unit as we were all planning to go out on the town. When they arrived, they had personal bodyguards with them. There was a lot of yelling and carry-on. I had no idea what was being said, but I knew the two girls got their way.

They girls – I later found out they were sisters – paid off their bodyguards and told them not to come back until midday the next day. As soon as the bodyguards left the girls removed their hijabs and dressed party girls. One would never believe they were the same two girls. Saudi law forbade females to go out on their own. They had to have a relative or bodyguard with them at all times.

The young girl who lived with her parents next door came out with us, but she had to be home at midnight. I went out with them that night but after only a couple of hours, I came back to the unit because I was unwell.

I was feeling so sick, my right eye had swollen up to a near closing point and I had shocking pain in my back. I took some painkillers and laid down on a mattress on the floor in our lounge room.

My unit door flew open and Miss Ananiyy and the young girl's parents were screaming at each other in their language. It was 2 30am. Miss Ananiyy screamed at me in English to get up as we were going to her father's house.

I told her I was going nowhere because I was too sick. There was a sandstorm coming and I would not go out into it. No one went anywhere in sandstorms as they were just too dangerous.

She screamed abuse at me and stormed out of the unit to drive over to her father's. The next morning, I ended up in the hospital with eye and serious kidney infections. I was hooked up to a bag of antibiotics and given injections that were making me sicker.

I am allergic to the pethidine they had been injecting me with for the kidney pain. I was projectile vomiting and I could barely swallow. I spent three days in the hospital and Miss Ananiyy dropped me back at the unit. She said she would be back later.

She came back later, well after she knew that the parents next door had gone to bed. We had some very heated words and she went down to our bedroom and started packing her things. I told her I was not leaving this unit. She lost her cool and put her fist through the wardrobe. She stormed out of the unit leaving me alone

This display of violence was enough for me to know that it would rear its ugly head in the future and I would have none of it. Fuck the unit I had just bought. I would sell it later when it was finished. I also knew she would have to sign the papers for a sale because it was too dangerous for her not to. For the next few days, I slept on the mattress in the lounge room watching TV. The little girl from next door apologised to me and her parents sent their maid in every mealtime to feed me. I stayed for the rest of my holiday on my own and refused to take any more calls from Miss Ananiyy.

I put my unit on the market and flew back to Australia. My English-speaking lawyer handled everything and I was conversing every couple of days with a guy called Hassan.

Hassan had found me a buyer and I organized to fly back to Cairo to sign the sale papers. Miss Ananiyy was to be present to sign.

My friend Monika told her to sign the papers or be outed by me as being gay. I didn't give a shit one way or the other. I just wanted out.

After we all arrived at the lawyer's office all hell broke loose. They were screaming at each other and I had no idea of what was going on. Next thing Miss Ananiyy stood up and said, "Suzy we are leaving now."

I left and was followed by Hassan and the buyer. We got in a car and the buyer got in beside me. He opened his bag and there were 187,000 Egyptian pounds in bundles in cash.

Miss Ananiyy said we were going around to a government building and once the papers were signed and the buyer had the papers, he would give me the bag of money. I wasn't scared but I was very concerned. Anyone could hit me on the head and run off with the bag.

The transaction went ahead as planned and I sat in the back seat of that car with this bag of money at my feet, taking pictures to prove I had it. I tried to send the money home by American Express, but they refused to take it because I did not have an Egyptian bank account.

I rang Monika in Sydney and she told me to call a friend of hers who lived here. No way was I trusting another person with this money. Hassan suggested I go to the money exchange and buy American dollars and send the money home by Western Union.

I sent small amounts of money home from Egypt to my family members, but judging by the way I was treated, I knew that office wouldn't take another transfer from me. Hassan said his cousin was a policeman and he would come with us the next day to make the transfer. He did and they took the transfer.

Hassan's family was just beautiful people. I bought Hassan the latest Apple iPhone as a gift for helping me and gave him enough money to buy food for his family for a month. We became very close over the years. He got married and had two boys. I have paid for these boys' school fees and some medical bills over the years. They are my family.

I love them dearly and one day I will go back to Egypt to spend some special time with them. There are only two classes of people in Egypt, the wealthy and the poor. We speak every week via social media and I am their Nana Suzy.

CHAPTER 42

Then there was Nancy

NANCY ARRIVED in Australia from America over Christmas unannounced. I had no love or sexual interest in her, but she was obsessed with me for some reason. In front of my family, she picked up my phone to check my text messages. Forty-eight hours later I dropped her at our international airport and sent her packing.

Three months later she called me saying she had bought a house for us and was waiting for me to come to America. I was stunned, what on earth happened with this woman? I told her as kindly as I could, "I am sorry, Nancy, I have met someone else."

Thankfully after many tears and attempts by Nancy to change my mind, she got the message.

I was fooling around on the internet on a program for women who wanted to meet women. I was being stupid by saying I was a 99-year-old lesbian looking for interesting ladies. I received an email saying, not bad for a 99-year-old woman. We laughed and joked for quite some time over the next few months and finely she agreed to meet me.

I had already established my legal brothel in Ballina, but did not tell her what I did for a living. I told very few people really because most could not handle the truth.

The day before I was to meet Kaye, she had cottoned on to what I did for a living. I think she was quite taken off guard. Remember this is a very straight-living, clean-as-a-whistle, mother of two sons. A qualified chef, she had been married to a man a lot older than she was.

She and her sons lived with her sister in Redcliffe, in Brisbane. They bought the home together and with Lucie's (also not her real name to protect her) two children, they all lived together. Both Lucie's kids had moved out after getting jobs on their own. Kaye had left her job as chef in a very large hotel and moved into food services at the Royal Brisbane Hospital.

This job gave her financial stability by being employed by the Queensland Government. Her elder son Jonathon had moved up north to live with his father and Bros stayed with her. She still agreed to meet with me and we were to have lunch.

I had not been intimate, with anyone for a very long time. I knew what she looked like and she told me clothes that she would be wearing. I could not believe how nervous I was; this was ridiculous. I was a woman who was mainly in control of my life. Yet here I was feeling like a cat on a hot tin roof.

I saw her before she saw me. My first thoughts were, "Holy cow, what a hot-looking babe this is. I think this one is out of my league." We walked up to each other and it was like a bolt of lightning for me. I was in lust. I was so nervous I could barely eat. I kept piling her plate up with food.

In between all that I asked her what she had planned over this Easter break.

She had days off and her son had plans of his own, also that her sister would be at home with her son James. I looked at her and thought, "Yes, I will definitely take a walk in this park." She was gorgeous and funny, and we clicked instantly. I found her a very attractive woman, not just physically but mentally. She was emotionally stable although hurting from a recent break-up with another woman who I later discovered was her first interaction. I told her I had taken a unit in West End for two days and she was welcome to stay with me or go back to her home. She chose to come with me after lunch to my unit.

I suggested we buy some food and drink. We jumped into my car and drove to a supermarket. On the way back I had pulled up at the traffic lights. On the other side of the lights was a police car and I saw them looking at me. My car was a top-of-the-range hot sports car. My personalised number plate stood out. I drove through the lights and into the driveway of the units. The cops followed me in. Kaye was freaking out. The main cop asked if I owned the car. I said yes. He said I was driving unlicensed. I showed him my NSW driver's licence.

He asked why was my car registered in Queensland and I held another state's licence. I told him my home was in Queensland at the same address where my car was registered, I worked in NSW and under NSW law after three months I must hold that state's licence.

The cop just about threw my licence at me and they drove out. I hopped back in the car to a very unsettled Kaye and said, "No problems, lovely, this sort of thing happens to me all the time. You either get used to it or walk away." Her words were, "I am going nowhere." We loaded up our food and bags and then proceeded to the unit.

On our first night together, we learned lessons from each other. Passion, lust, gentleness and respect for each other's dignity. Oh, and lots of laughter. For example, she had bought along a shoebox with an assortment of adult toys. I had never used them, as strange as it may sound, but it's the truth. If I wanted a penis inside me, I would be with a man.

My second suitcase consisted of a full outfit of a French lace-up, front bustier, silk stockings, for the lace garter belt, stiletto high heels, a very sexy G-string and an assortment of soft handmade leather whips. Not the punishment kind, the teaser kind. Several tubes of beautiful-smelling massage creams and a bottle of French, massage oil.

We were like two different peas in a pod, but it worked beautifully. We both gave over to the desire to genuinely please each other no matter what it took to do so. The bottom line was sexually we needed each other at that time in both our lives.

Female orgasms relieve pent-up stress, so the stats say and I agree, always have. I participated in a sexual journey I had never been down before in all the years of my experience with both female and male lovers. I also was very aware Kaye was in the same boat. After all, she had only had one female lover before me. It was close to midnight and we were both starving for solid food; love did not suffice any longer.

We decided to shower, dress and go find a place to eat. We settled on a very popular West End coffee shop. I knew the owner John, an ex-hairdresser. As we were drinking our coffee and waiting for our food, I saw a familiar face.

It was my ex-sister-in-law Vicky. Kaye and I were like two kids who had been caught being naughty. We reeked of guilt. Vicky always had been a photo taker and true to form started taking pictures of us. With a promise to keep quiet about catching us out off she went into the night. We gobbled up our beautiful food, had a couple of spiked alcohol coffees and off we went back into our little love nest.

We were both floating on imaginary clouds. For the next 24 hours all we did was make mad passionate love, eat, drink and sleep. I did not want to go home or back to the grind of running my business.

After we loaded our cars to go our separate ways, she sat in my car and I said to her, "Well, I guess I will let you go now."

Her words were. "Are you trying to get rid of me?" I wanted to keep her forever. I said, "No, but I thought you had to go back to your family." She said it was not until the next day. "Well then you had better come with me out to my Mum's house."

When we arrived at Mum's I took her upstairs to meet my mother. My bringing a woman into our home was out of character and I knew by looking at her face she was not impressed.

Mum was pleasant enough towards Kaye, but I knew she was not happy watching what seemed to be a crackling sexual undercurrent between us. I will leave it all up to your imagination over what transpired between us down in the darkness of the garage later that night.

Sending Kaye back to her home the next day was very difficult. It wasn't all about sex; I was drawn to her by something much deeper. We spoke on the phone every day and arranged that I would come up and we would spend from Friday night until Sunday afternoon together every weekend. Two weeks later it was Kaye's 44th birthday and I wanted to make this birthday very special.

I booked a motel with a spa and I told Mum I was going to her birthday party. What I didn't say was there were only two of us at the party. Mum made the most magnificent fruit and cheese platter, enough to feed 10 people. We spent Kaye's birthday eating, drinking champagne and sitting in the spa exploring our amazing blossoming love. I remember getting a little emotional because I felt I was overstepping my boundaries. I was notorious for running from any emotional attachments from casual female hook-ups.

Kaye and I agreed that we would not commit to any long-term arrangements until we had been together for at least a year. We would use that year to get to know each other and have a holiday with her two sons to test the waters. We also agreed that if we parted for any reason there would be no going back. Done is done.

This agreement was the foundation of our relationship. We had been together for a year when Kaye called me very distressed. Her younger son Bros had been suspended from school and she had had enough. We agreed for her to move down to live with me in Ballina and her elder son would be arriving in Brisbane after leaving his father's home up north in a couple of days.

CHAPTER 43

The biggest move in our lives

I WAS LIVING in my little flat on brothel premises in Ballina. The race was on for me to find a suitable house for my suddenly extended family. I found the perfect house in a new estate five minutes' drive out of Ballina. It was signed, sealed and delivered in two days. It took another three days to move my furniture in, stock the pantry and fridge, and pack away kitchen equipment. I was no longer a single person. Gaining three more family members was going to be a learning curve for sure.

When Kaye and her sons Jon and Bros arrived, we were all excited. The next few months were spent getting the boys into school. Kaye got a couple of chef's jobs but she was not happy with the work. She applied for a position with NSW Health. She had worked in Queensland Health's hospital food services system for the past seven years.

We settled into a life that wasn't a bed of roses, but we were happy and very much in love. In the soccer season, Kaye would take Bros to play for his team in Brisbane every weekend. I missed them and often wished I had been able to go along but her sister and niece rejected me because of what I did for a living. I was at her house one afternoon when the sister came home from work and she was so rude to me, reprimanding Kaye for even taking me to her home. The daughter has never spoken to me in the 16 years we have been together.

This rejection by so-called upstanding members of the community is difficult to accept. They judge a person, not knowing them at all. It's social discrimination because of my profession. It's rare to come across people out in the normal world who can put aside their abhorrence of those involved in the sex industry. They just cannot accept the fact that there are women out there who have had no choice.

Nine times out of ten when I met new people and they asked me what I did for a living my answer was I worked in community services. I was telling a part truth because after all my business was providing a service to the community. This service was saving marriages and keeping sexual predators off the streets.

My family loved Kaye, especially my sister Aileen. It took Mum two years to accept Kaye and appreciate that I had a genuine, loving, honourable, lifetime partner by my side. We never took advantage of each other. We each paid half of whatever was needed in our household.

Kaye is the only woman Mum ever allowed in her kitchen. The morning Mum died Kaye cooked her breakfast and asked her permission to go and mow the lawn. Mum told Kaye, "You go, girl, get that lawn done." Mum loved Kaye.

We had 10 very memorable, happy years living in that house in Ballina. We all learned lots of lessons. Learning to co-parent was no walk in the park for me. I loved both the boys. I didn't always agree with them on some issues but accepted they must be able live their own lives.

The passing years have quieted my inner hurt and I have learned that we cannot please the rest of the world. What matters is the peace and happiness in your own private space.

People are unable to accept the truth, so I have spent most of my life skirting the issue, not even trying to explain why I chose that path in my life. I have always considered myself to be an honourable woman of substance. I was a wife and a mother who chose to work in an industry that gave my family a better life than the one I grew up in.

CHAPTER 44

It's mentally exhausting too

I WAS OPERATING my legal business in peace. No more hiding. No more of trying to stay one step ahead of the police. No more living in fear of losing everything I had worked for all my life and no more fighting with authorities that designated where and how I could operate this business. To get there, the financial, emotional and health costs were very high.

I had three great receptionists whom I trusted totally. Ammie had been with me for more than 16 years. Kate had clocked eight years and Sammy five years.

The business had very busy and very quiet times during the year. Winter was usually the quiet time. Who wants to go anywhere in the freezing cold? Although in saying that when men were horny, they would walk to the place in the pouring rain.

To get staff I would advertise in the Sydney daily newspapers. The deal I offered the ladies was that if they committed to my business for 10 days in a row and stayed on my premises, I would pay for their airflight back to wherever they came from. This ensured I had staff at least 90 per cent of the time. I also advertised in many NSW country towns because it gave ladies who needed to get away and earn money, some privacy.

We had a good turnover of different types of ladies. I preferred to keep a happy household. Too many ladies on shift at the same time was a disaster. Every lady needed to make money. I usually had two or three on a day shift and the same on the night shift. Thursday, Friday and Saturday nights I liked to have three or four in-house and one extra for the outcall service.

There were only three keys to my safe in the office which was permanently anchored to the concrete floor. Ammie, Kate and I held a key each. Ladies who were staying in-house usually had their pay put into envelopes with days and dates written on the front. The envelopes stayed in the safe until they left to go back home. Their envelopes were sealed and a signature written over the seal. Sticky tape was put on the envelope to ensure they had not been opened by anyone other than themselves.

There were a couple of issues that made me question the trustworthiness of my staff, but I let it slide because I knew mistakes could be made when people get very tired. The receptionists were behind the reception desk for 12 to 14 hours. They directed in-house and outcall jobs, answered phones on top of taking clients' money. Then there was the paperwork each separate booking. There was washing towels and drop sheets.

It was a full-on, mentally tiring exercise. Even after closing time when the building was closed to the public work was not over. There were ladies to pay, paperwork to be signed off on and a tally of the takings to be done.

Running a brothel was no walk in the park. You had to make sure every lady was kept in a reasonably contented mood. This meant making sure they had made the money they needed for the day.

When staff stayed on the premises, I always ensured the night staff could sleep in after working into the early hours. The day shift ladies were under strict instructions not to enter the girls' dormitory. They had to shower in their work rooms and use the toilets in the main building hallway. These rules were often broken when tired angry ladies were woken up unintentionally by incoming day shift staff. Trying to keep the peace was sometimes very tough for the receptionist on shift.

It was a constant struggle to keep everything afloat in the building, mentally and physically. Every dollar spent had to be accounted for so that my monthly GST summery was correct. You didn't want to on the wrong side of the Tax Office. I had to file keep every account document and petty cash docket.

CHAPTER 45

Taking the show on the road

I HAD SPENT decades playing hide and seek with the police, I hide they seek. But after all this aggravation over the years I had only two convictions and fines against me personally.

Was it luck? Was it a case of never being in the right place at the right time for the police to catch me in the act? I think it was because I had learned from very early observations of just how the police planned their raids. In the early years I had very good teachers. The owners and operators of illegal premises in 1970s were criminally very smart.

My first official charge came out of the Fitzgerald Police Corruption Inquiry – owning and operating a bawdy house, a brothel. My punishment was done and dusted. I paid my dues.

The second charge came in the late 1990s as a result of redirecting an escort service from a phone connected in my unit at West End in Brisbane. I answered phones in NSW and then passed escort bookings to staff in Queensland. A lady had been set up on a booking by police and the police had tracked the calls coming from inside my unit. I received a call from the head detective informing me I had better get to the unit ASAP.

I was living in Kingscliff at the time, a minimum of one hour's drive away. I drove like the wind to get there because I was certain I would get robbed if the cops broke down the door and left the unit unattended.

Two plain-clothed officers met me at my front door. They entered and searched for evidence of the crime I was going to be charged with. After taking a few items they considered was evidence, they put me in their unmarked car and took me to police headquarters for questioning.

I was charged and later appeared before a magistrate. My lawyer questioned the legality of the charges saying I had been charged under a wrong section of the laws. Also, the police had taken some of my property they were not entitled to take. My lawyer also applied for my property to be returned. Eventually I was fined $1500. I was stunned but I knew it should have been much more.

A week later I went to police headquarters to pick up my belongings. The head detective told me he was going to make an application under the confiscation of assets law to take possession of my unit.

I was in total shock but held my composure. I told him that if he proceeded I not only would I see him in court but I would take this story to the media. I told him that I paid my taxes on every dollar I earned and my tax dollars paid his wages.

I told him the media will have a field day. The headlines would be explosive Australia wide. "Go right ahead, sir. I will see you in court, I am used to fighting for my rights and in this case, you have no right."

I never heard another word from the police. Maybe after all the shocking exposure of police corruption he decided to let sleeping dogs lay.

The business in Ballina seemed to have slowed down and I didn't know why. Over about 12 months, I found it more and more difficult to meet my financial commitments. I needed a solution.

I decided that I would take a girl on the road to work the small country towns up and down the highway that did not have a legal or illegal brothel. This was going to give me the extra dollars I needed to continue to hold up my Ballina operation.

Ammie, Kate and Sammy agreed it was a good idea and agreed to work more hours in the building. Next, I had to find the girls who would be suitable to take out on the road. I had to be careful. I couldn't take a lady had children in the district or a lady with mental health issues or recovering addiction issues. I needed a mature, stable lady to join me.

I knew this project was going to take massive effort from both of us. We had to be committed or it would not work.

PLANNING the trip took a massive effort. I had to find suitable premises to work from. If the town was small, I needed to be upfront with a motel owner about why I wanted to rent a room. I also needed to check the local newspaper to see what private ladies were working in that town.

To find out where they were working from, I got my security driver from Ballina to makes these calls for me pretending to be a client. I also needed a schedule so we were not in the town at the same time as a private worker. In part, this was my respect for that private worker. It's hard enough working as a private worker, let alone having to worry about someone else coming into town and taking their clients. I also had to organise the newspaper ads.

I needed a workbook to keep track of the bookings in each town. I also had to bring my own supply of work towels, drop sheets and safe sex supplies. Working like this needed much planning, but I had to keep the wheels turning to keep the doors open on my business. I had worked my guts out to make it legal. I couldn't give up now.

Our first road trip was to a town of 7000 to 10,000 people eight hours' drive away. A local motel operator agreed to allow us to operate.

My work phone was running hot with calls from prospective clients from the town. My job was to answer the calls and act as security. When the client arrived, I was outside the room in my car. Within a few moments Kim bought the money the client had paid and handed it to me. She was going to be busy for 45 minutes. This was a good start to the day ahead. We had a very busy day with a constant stream of clients. I chose Kim because of her professional attitude, she was a patient, kind women, and had no addiction issues.

It's great to have younger women to be working but it's more important for the client to be looked after professionally by a more mature-aged woman. I needed a committed lady with me, not a party girl.

Our first trip away was a financial success for Kim and me. She had picked up nearly as much in extra tips as she earned from bookings. My returns far exceeded my outlay. A bonus was that the clients were asking when we would be back in town.

We would work from 9am but never past 9pm. This ensured we would not be contending with drunks. For a visit earlier than 9am the client had to book the day before. These hours showed respect for the motel owners. We kept these hours even if we were working from a security building.

We travelled up and down all over country NSW and even chanced a venture into smaller Queensland towns. Queensland had new laws that permitted private workers to operate legally from premises they lived in.

These trips to the Queensland outback country towns were successful because the police who controlled the legal and illegal operations were stationed in Brisbane. I also was very careful to ensure all incoming calls were convincing enough for the client to think I was a private lady operating on my own.

If in a motel I sat in my car while the lady entertained the client; if in a house I retreated to the spare bedroom while she looked after the client. We also never stayed in that country town more than four to five days.

We had trouble in only one small country town. The client dicked us around from the very start. He never showed up on time, made a new time and didn't show up. He arrived at 8pm and the booking was supposed to cease at 8.45pm. I knocked on the door and the lady said to him, "I told you I had security."

I burst into the room and ordered the client to get dressed and get out. The lady was very annoyed and the client was being a pain in the ass. I noticed the dongle I used to connect to the internet was missing from my laptop. I told him to hand over the dongle or I would call the police.

He denied having it and attempted to leave the room. I pushed him on to the bed and warned him he had 30 seconds to return my dongle or I would punch him in the face and call the police. I told him, "I will have you charged with theft. This town will laugh at you when they see your name and picture in the local newspaper in this week's edition. If you have a girlfriend or wife, you will be thrown out in the street for bringing shame on them in this little country town."

He looked at me and said he didn't have it and started to scrounge around the floor.

Boom, he found the dongle on the floor near the end of the work bed. I told him I was going to blacklist him to every private worker in existence. His details and phone number would be printed in the sex workers' outreach magazine which was printed bi-monthly in Sydney.

CHAPTER 46

Trouble in the camp

I SEEMED TO be going around in circles. It was a never-ending cycle of one country town after another, week after week, month after month. The trips away were becoming very exhausting physically for me.

One trip was a 12-hour drive to a small city, with the only stops for food and coffee. Although there was a legal entity in the town, I knew we would be okay because I knew the owners of the premises and they mostly employed foreign ladies. I found a three-bedroom house close to the centre of town in a very discrete, tree-lined street. The town reeked money.

We made so much money it was astounding, after my huge expenses outlay. I was still going home with double the dollars I had made on any one trip in the past. We probably would have made thousands more each had we worked past our agreed work times, but a girl can only endure so much physical sexual activity.

I was also becoming very tired and I knew I needed to see a doctor as my bones ached constantly and I was always feeling washed out and drained of energy. I certainly didn't look forward to the long drive back home. But I had to get back to Ballina because staff were complaining about one of my trusted receptionists.

I had been working the highways for more than two years every second week for most months, with an occasional fortnight at home. Some months my business was fine financially and this allowed me an extra week at home, but other months the income only just covered expenses. I couldn't understand why. I had long-term, trusted receptionists. Staff was never an issue and ladies were flying in and out to work there all the time. I just was flummoxed to understand why.

While I was away on trips, Kaye used to collect and do my banking from the business. Her job was to pay staff members from credit card bookings. She also stepped in on emergency reception for a few hours if one of the others was late.

The morning after arriving back in Ballina Kaye told me what had happened. It seemed one of the ladies was caught lying and that Kate had not paid her the correct funds she had earned. I believe that if Kaye hadn't made up a story to get that girl out of the building, Kate's life may have been in danger. This lady and her boyfriend had threatened Kate's safety.

The lady concerned and Kate had a huge screaming, verbal altercation over the supposed missing money and the building was in an uproar. The lady threatened violence against Kate.

The gossip was that the girl was going to get her boyfriend to cut the brakes on Kate's car. Kaye had been so worried that she convinced the girl to leave for a week and that when I arrived back in town. I would speak to everyone involved.

Kate was not due back until the weekend, so I had plenty of time to investigate the issue. I called the girl into work for a chat. She lived a 45-minute drive away. She arrived with her boyfriend. I took one look at him and knew the threats against Kate were real.

The lady told me she believed Kate had not paid her for a booking. I showed her the day sheet for that day. I showed her bookings she had completed and was paid for. But she insisted her claim was correct.

I assured her I would investigate and call her back after the weekend when Kate was on the premises and I had spoken to her. I wanted to believe Kate because when I was on reception and tired as hell after doing a 16-hour shift I had made mistakes myself. I remember one night after calculating the day's takings, I found extra money in the takings. I called the staff member into my office and humbly apologised and gave her the job money she had earned.

This wasn't the first time I had received complaints about Kate's financial bookkeeping. I had also been on the end of a con job by a staff member saying she had done more bookings than she had been paid for. This was difficult because written records were unquestionable.

After checking the day's books, I found there were no funds left over to substantiate the lady's claims. One point to consider was that Kate had never allowed a staff member to sit and watch her do a reconciliation of funds at the end of a shift.

Basically, it was Kate's word against the staff members.

After viewing the girl's own list of bookings for the shift in dispute, I decided to give the girl the benefit of the doubt. We also decided that she was not to work on the shifts that Kate was rostered on. This girl had always been reliable turning up on time for work. She was also a dedicated great worker, kind to clients and respectful of their needs.

I paid the lady the $120 she claimed Kate had not paid her and put in place a new requirement for staff to follow on every shift regardless of who was in charge of reception. Every booking done by every lady had to be double checked and initialled twice before going into her next booking. This procedure would stop any future potential dispute between staff.

The successful financial trip away allowed me to stay at home an extra week and I spent this week catching up on all my paperwork for my accountant and to prepare for my next month's GST payment to the Tax Office. I needed also to check every daysheet. Maybe there would be other indications of something not being correct.

I was physically and mentally exhausted and I knew I was not eating properly. My weight had dropped to about 50kg and I was bordering on anorexia and I was worried. I went to my doctor and had some blood tests done. They found I was anaemic, so I had to go have an iron infusion. This only took just over half an hour. Half a day later I felt on top of the world.

CHAPTER 47

Cracks are appearing

KIM AND I had another trip on the highway to one of our favourite small country towns. Clients had been calling asking when we would return, so I knew roughly what we would earn on our trip to that town. It was only five hours away and I was physically back on track, ready to rock'n'roll.

After each shift after a weekend, I wanted the receptionist to text me the takings after expenses. By close of shift on the Sunday night I knew down the last dollar how much the business had taken on the weekend.

There was enough money in my business account to pay accounts that were due over the next few days. This was not counting what money I was earning on the trip away with Kim. On the Monday morning the amount in the business account did not add up and I called my office and spoke to Sammy on reception.

I knew her reconciliation of the weekend's figures would be correct. Sammy was a former bank jockey and people that work in banks rarely make mistakes with money. Sammy called me and told me that in the income figures. There was an $887 discrepancy in what I had been told and what was in the bank. I told her to check the garbage bins for any dockets and discarded paperwork.

Half hour later she called me she had found scrunched-up credit card machine dockets and several pieces of paper with all sorts of figures written down. There were also outcall bookings that had not tallied up with the weekend paperwork.

We cut our trip away by a day. Losing income on this trip was nothing compared to what I calculated we had been losing in Ballina.

I was so angry, the five-hour trip home took me just four hours. How I didn't get booked for speeding was beyond me. I headed straight back into work. I double-checked all Sammy's figures and studied all the evidence she had pulled out of the garbage bins. I was deeply distressed and very, angry with Kate.

She had worked for me for eight years. I felt devastated, betrayed beyond comprehension. I checked my business account to confirm that there was not a credit of $887 in my account. If it had been a credit card deposit it would have been there and it wasn't.

I called Kate and told her very calmly that I had found all the discarded paperwork and that takings were down $887. I told her if this money was not in my account by the next morning, I was going to take everything I had to the police. I would have her charged with fraud. She spluttered, acted confused and tried to make excuses. I don't know how she did it but by late that afternoon the funds were deposited into my business account.

I felt so betrayed. I was devastated. I spent hours trying to estimate how much money this woman had been defrauding my business. I trusted this woman with my business for more than eight years. I worked out money was missing for the 12 months leading up to my decision to go on the road and the subsequent two years.

The amount of money she had been stealing for those three years was beyond calculation. I needed my accountant to work out when my business's figures started to decline in earnings. This was not going to happen because it was going to cost more money that I had available.

At this time, I was probably at the lowest ebb of my entire life. I had stood up and fought back so many adversities over my lifetime and survived. However, this one had me feeling like a rag doll. On average she worked three double shifts twice a month. According to my reckoning she was defrauding me a minimum of $2000 to $2200 a month. The amount she was stealing was mind blowing.

I was angry at her betrayal and my own stupidity for again placing trust where it wasn't deserved. My biggest problem was I saw the good in everyone. I needed to rest, but I knew I had to get rid of Kate. This meant I had to take over her shifts on the front desk.

A few days later Kate called me and asked to come in so we could discuss what had happened with the paperwork. I told her she no longer had a job and that in the next month or two I would put my business on the market as I was not well and had had enough.

She wasn't happy. I asked her to return the building keys when she came to town. Cheekily I suggested she might like to buy the business, as she more than anyone knew just what the takings were.

I chose not to press charges of fraud against her because I just did not need the extra stress in my life. The path forward was going to be hard enough.

CHAPTER 48

My end game

I HAD FIRED fraudulent Kate. I had had enough of being ripped off, lied to and taken advantage of by unscrupulous people. I had a few weeks of complete rest and organised a new work roster. With Kate gone from my business I hoped the financial situation would improve and greatly improve it did.

I was shocked and relieved by the massive financial turnaround. How much had this woman been stealing from my business?

Having these consistent thoughts running through my mind was not healthy. I couldn't allow these thoughts to consume me as I needed to be in full control. Anger and hurt had no place in my life.

I still faced medical issues, which I kept putting off. I came up with all sorts of excuses for not wanting face these issues. I didn't want to admit I was not well. I had to face the music. Besides having a broken ankle, test results revealed I needed intensive, long-term treatment for another medical matter. I was shocked by the results. How was I supposed to run my business? How was I going to work long hours and financially survive if I was sick? I left the doctor's surgery feeling exhausted and drove to the local lookout.

Looking out across the sea to the vast horizon, I put my head in my hands and sobbed. I had to make serious life-changing decisions ... again. I realised it was impossible for me to be able to cope with running a business as well as getting my health issues sorted. I had trusted too many people over the years and had almost lost everything.

How could I trust someone I did not know to manage the business? Besides I couldn't afford to pay a manager's wages nor take the risk of any more funds going missing.

I reluctantly decided that I needed to sell but this wasn't going to be easy. I immediately advised my landlord Peter. He accepted my decision, but I needed his approval of the new owners. They needed to be scrupulous operators. I willingly agreed because I wanted Ballina free from drug dealers and thugs.

A FEW VERY interesting characters came out of the woodwork to check out my business, including one from the Gold Coast. As I reached out to shake his hand, I instinctively knew Ballina would not be ready for this thug. The very presence of this man instilled fear and intimidation. His exposed neck tattoos might have terrified some but I was not afraid.

He offered to pay me an undisclosed amount on paper and the balance in cash. Over the years in the industry, I had been gullible at times, but not now. I knew if had accepted his offer down the track he would have told me to fuck off and wouldn't pay me the balance.

I decided my business needed to be in the hands of a woman and not criminals who would tear down every decent milestone I had reached.

Everyone wanted to take control of my business, but no one wanted to pay the money I needed to be able to walk away. As the weeks dragged on, I seemed to get sicker and the drugs I was on were taking their toll on my body. At this stage, I just wanted out and did not care if I walked away with nothing.

A mature ex-sex worker called Christine asked me to let her have the business. Of course, she had virtually no money, but I didn't care. I just needed to get away from all this stress. I organised for her to meet Peter to discuss the takeover. She had an education and had accreditation in accountancy.

Peter was not happy with her, but I was too ill to give a damn. All she had to do was work the business as it had been run. The fact she would be living on the premises was a bonus. Finally, the business was in her hands and I believed it would be okay. How wrong I was. Within two months she had run it into the ground and taken the work phone number. She cut off all the utilities I had transferred into her name and did a runner. I was astounded and I felt bad for Peter.

Peter asked me to return to the business, but I was just not well. I had no energy or fight left in me to worry about the business. I had a fight far more important and I was determined not to lose that fight.

He finally found another female operator. As far as I know that person is still operating that business. She had called me before I had transferred everything over to Christine. I guess I could have taken her money and thrown Christine to the wolves.

But I am not that type of person. When I say something or agree to something I stand by my word. Even though a woman who had the finance approached me, I would not go back on my word.

After six months of my intensive treatment, I started to feel better, stronger and was getting bored. I knew I would never re-enter the sex industry, so I needed to plan and prepare for a future.

At 5am on one day in April 2013 I stood on the beachfront at Ballina's Angels Beach and felt enormous waves of relief flood through me knowing I was done with an industry that had been financially good to me, but had almost sapped the very life force from my body several times.

The only way forward now was to get well physically and move in another direction. What to do? I already had accreditation in hair dressing, but needed to update my qualifications to get a job in a field I knew I would be good at.

I did an entry exam into a community services diploma course and passed. I might not have finished my high school education, but I had decades of experience in dealing with people with a range of mental health issues. This was a full-time commitment over 12 months.

I could do my modules online and submit my work to my teacher to mark. I worked very hard, sometimes well into the early hours. It was tough mentally and very tiring physically, but I was determined to succeed. I graduated way ahead of my class even though I was the oldest student.

My teacher encouraged me to study for a counselling degree, which would be accepted nationwide. He told me my diploma would count towards half my degree. This wouldn't be a walk in the park for me, but in another six months I would gain another valued certificate. I had to do placement at ACON in Lismore. ACON is a community-based organisation that aims to create opportunities for local people to live their healthiest lives

I loved doing my hours at ACON. The team at ACON treated me so well and I looked forward to going there every week. I passed my degree with ease, even though I struggled with some of the modules. I also completed a short course with the University of Tasmania on understanding dementia. With this extra certificate I figured I would have no problem getting a job in the real world. I did the extra the dementia course because my mother had been diagnosed with early onset dementia. Watching my mother suffer memory loss was heartbreaking.

I had all my health issues under control and even though I was taking thousands of milligrams of medication every day I could function without any serious problems. I was looking forward to getting a job and hoped it would be local.

CHAPTER 49

I don't regret my time in the sex industry

I MADE THE SHORTLIST for several jobs. When I attended the interviews, it did not take long for me to realise once they discovered my age. Aged 65 I had no hope of getting the job. Employers looked for people they were confident would stay with them for five to 10 years.

In one interview I knew within five minutes the officer had done her homework and realised who I was and my past. I walked away disappointed no one wanted to hire a woman of my age, let alone a woman with a notorious reputation. I could never prove the discrimination, but I knew it to be a fact. In the next few months, I was unsuccessful in applying for hundreds of jobs.

I didn't look, dress or act like an old lady. I just needed someone to give me a go, but this was not to be. However, settling into retirement and learning to survive on minimal financial funds was and still is a juggling act.

I thought that by completing the community services diploma, plus the extra counselling degree would assist me towards guiding women and young girls who needed to learn the skills on how to stand up and fight for themselves and expose their abusers regardless of the consequences.

Someone will listen and stand with you. I promise the fight is worth the effort.

At this point in my life, even knowing that I have no chance of getting a job, I still keep applying. On my next birthday, I will be 71. I often wonder how the hell did I make it this far.

I have faced cancer head on three times and come out the other side.

Not without a couple of lifelong side effects but still smiling. I have had a loaded gun put to my head several times with a threat of death. I had my life and property threatened by bikers demanding protection money.

I have had the brakes on my car tampered with and lived in fear of being the next female brothel operator to go missing only to be found dead.

A long-term, dear friend Chrissie from South Australia recently said to me, "Suzy, you not only survived, you thrived within the chaos you lived." This was a true description of me.

I have always had it in the back of my mind to write a book about my life. This is it.

I attempted it many years ago, but my completed chapters went missing to God only knows where. If you are now reading my book, I am grateful that my life adventures have now gone to print. I thank you for your patience.

I hope you now have a different perspective and understanding of the darker side of life. One must never judge a book by its cover.

I think about my life often, knowing that had I not carried the ingrained anger in my soul over the injustice served up to me when I was 11 years old, I would probably, would have never survived. This saying by C.S. Lewis is so very true:

"I sat with my anger long enough,

Until she told me her real name was grief."

I regret nothing. I have lived an amazing life during my 40-plus years in the sex industry.

I HAVE BECOME involved with the several different First Nations people from around NSW and Queensland through the Bullinah Aboriginal Health Services in the Northern Rivers of NSW. Bullinah also runs cooking classes to teach us all how to eat more healthy food.

I have started to provide hairdressing services to these people and their friends in the indigenous community at no cost to them. One of the ladies tried to pay me but I refused payment and would never take any money from them as they are struggling to survive. It's my honour to be available to look after their hair. After all I am a qualified hairdresser.

I attend bone-building classes there with people who have suffered heart attacks and strokes, some with diabetes issues and broken bones. There is long-term education on how to approach physical chores without causing more issues or bone breaks.

I attend these classes three times a week and love being involved. I have had two broken wrists and two broken ankles due to my own bone issues, so I joined to learn how to slow down ... at my doctor's suggestion ... and approach physical tasks in a manner that will not cause any more broken bones. I cannot afford to break a hip as that would probably take me out.

I have this last month or so spent alternate weekends looking after a beautiful 86-year-old mother of a friend who is suffering from Dementia.

Being able to give respite to them has been very rewarding to me emotionally. Volunteering, to help anyone's loved one who is suffering such a debilitating disease is a task that is difficult but appreciated by the family. It's heartbreaking not just for the patient but more so for the family.

My hat is off to ALL members of the Community Services people and nurses that look after dementia sufferers. THANK YOU.

Pride aside, learning some new lessons is the future of 2023 for me.

I believe I have

PAID THE PRICE OF SIN.

9 780645 724103